LONGMAN
MATHEMATICS

Julie Iwamoto

Longman

Longman Mathematics

Pearson Education, 10 Bank Street, White Plains, NY 10606

Vice president, primary and secondary editorial: Ed Lamprich
Senior development editors: Marilyn Hochman, Janis van Zante
Vice president, director of production and design: Rhea Banker
Senior production editor: Robert Ruvo
Vice president, marketing: Kate McLoughlin
Senior manufacturing buyer: Nancy Flaggman
Cover design: Rhea Banker
Text design and composition: Anthology, a Von Hoffmann Company
Text font: Times New Roman
Illustrations: **Susan Detrich** pp. 8, 13, 19, 20, 22, 63, 64, 83, 84, 106, 108
    (top), 151, 157, 223, 230, 241, 250, 262, 273, 276; **Nancy Didion** pp. 5,
    21, 34, 41, 108 (bottom), 109, 168, 231, 278

Library of Congress Cataloging-in-Publication Data
    Iwamoto, Julie.
        Longman mathematics / Julie Iwamoto.—1st ed.
            p. cm.
        Includes bibliographical references and index.
        ISBN 0-13-193023-0 (alk. paper)
    1. Mathematics—Study and teaching (Secondary) 2. English
        language—Study and teaching—Foreign speakers. I. Title.
        QA11.2.I88 2005
        510'.71'2—dc22   2005007986

LONGMAN ON THE **WEB**

Longman.com offers online resources for
teachers and students. Access our Companion
Websites, our online catalog, and our local
offices around the world.

Visit us at **longman.com**.

ISBN: 0-13-193023-0

Printed in the United States of America
2 3 4 5 6 7 8 9 10-BAH-09 08 07 06 05

For my brother Koki

Contents ··

Preface xi

Unit 1 **Base-Ten Number System** 1

Chapter 1 **Reading and Saying Cardinal Numbers** ... 3

1-1 Cardinal Numbers 3
1-2 Base-Ten Place Names 4
1-3 Comma Placement 5
1-4 How to Say Cardinal Numbers 6
Have I Learned? 11
Chapter Review 12

Chapter 2 **Reading and Saying Ordinal Numbers** ... 13

2-1 Ordinal Numbers 13
2-2 How to Say Dates 18
Have I Learned? 23
Chapter Review 24

Chapter 3 **Rounding Off Numbers** 25

3-1 Round Numbers 25
3-2 Rounding Off Numbers 26
3-3 Rounding Off to the Tens Place 28
3-4 Rounding Off to the Hundreds and Thousands Places 31
3-5 Estimation 32
Have I Learned? 35
Chapter Review 36

Unit 2 **Operations with Whole Numbers** 37

Chapter 4 **Addition** 39

4-1 Language of Addition 39
4-2 Commutative Property of Addition 40
4-3 Associative Property of Addition 41
4-4 Additive Identity Property of Addition 42
Have I Learned? 43
4-5 Addition with Carrying 44
4-6 Solving Addition Word Problems 46
Chapter Review 50

Chapter 5   **Subtraction**   **51**

5-1   Language of Subtraction 51
5-2   Subtraction of Whole Numbers 52
5-3   Subtraction with Borrowing 54
5-4   Subtraction with Borrowing from Zeros 56
5-5   Inverse Operations 58
5-6   Using Inverse Operations to Find Missing Numbers 59
Have I Learned? 61
5-7   Solving Subtraction Word Problems 62
Chapter Review 66

Chapter 6   **Multiplication**   **67**

6-1   Language of Multiplication 67
6-2   Symbols for Multiplication 68
6-3   Commutative Property of Multiplication 69
6-4   Associative Property of Multiplication 69
6-5   Multiplicative Identity Property of Multiplication 70
6-6   Multiplicative Property of Zero .70
6-7   Distributive Property of Multiplication 71
6-8   Multiplying Two-Digit and Three-Digit Numbers
         by a One-Digit Number 72
6-9   Multiplying and Carrying 74
6-10   Multiplying Two Digits by Two Digits 75
6-11   Multiplying Two-Digit Numbers by Two-Digit
         Numbers with Carrying 76
6-12   Multiplying Three-Digit Numbers by Two- and
         Three-Digit Numbers 77
6-13   Multiples of Ten 79
6-14   Solving Word Problems with Unnecessary Information 80
6-15   Solving Multiplication Word Problems 81
Have I Learned? 85
Chapter Review 86

Chapter 7   **Division**   **87**

7-1   Language of Division 87
7-2   Dividing with One-Digit Divisors 89
7-3   One-Digit Divisors with Remainders 92
7-4   Dividing with Two-Digit Divisors 94
7-5   Inverse Operations 96
7-6   Using Inverse Operations to Find Missing Numbers 97
7-7   Multiples of Ten 99
7-8   Order of Operations 100
7-9   More Order of Operations 102
Have I Learned? 105
7-10   Solving Division Word Problems 105
7-11   Problem Solving with Remainders 107
Chapter Review 110

Unit 3   **Number Theory**   **111**

Chapter 8   **Integers**   **113**

8-1   The Number Line 113
8-2   Comparing Integers 115
Have I Learned? 117
Chapter Review 118

Chapter 9   **Prime Numbers, Bases, and Exponents**   **119**

9-1   Prime Numbers 119
9-2   Prime Factors 121
9-3   Bases and Exponents 123
9-4   Using Base Ten 125
9-5   The Zero Exponent 125
9-6   Expanded Notation 127
Have I Learned? 129
Chapter Review 130

Unit 4   **Operations with Decimal Numbers**   **131**

Chapter 10   **Decimals**   **133**

10-1   Tenths 133
10-2   Hundredths 135
10-3   Equivalent Decimals in Tenths and Hundredths 136
10-4   Comparing Decimals in Tenths and Hundredths 137
10-5   Thousandths 138
10-6   Equivalent Decimals in Tenths, Hundredths, and Thousandths . .140
10-7   Comparing Decimals in Tenths, Hundredths, and Thousandths . .142
10-8   More Decimal Places 143
Have I Learned? 146
Chapter Review 148

Chapter 11   **Adding and Subtracting Decimals**   **149**

11-1   Writing Integers as Decimals 149
11-2   Adding Decimals 150
11-3   Money 152
11-4   Subtracting Decimals 155
11-5   Using Inverse Operations to Find Missing Decimals 156
11-6   Rounding Off Decimals 158
Have I Learned? 161
Chapter Review 162

Chapter 12   Multiplying and Dividing Decimals   **163**

12-1   Multiplying Decimals 163
12-2   Multiplying Decimals by Multiples of Ten 169
12-3   Dividing with Decimals .170
12-4   If the Dividend Is a Decimal 171
12-5   If the Divisor Is a Decimal 173
12-6   If the Dividend and Divisor Are Decimals 175
12-7   If the Divisor Is Greater Than the Dividend 176
12-8   Problem Solving with Decimals 179
12-9   Average, or Mean 180
12-10   Dividing Decimals by Multiples of Ten 182
Have I Learned? 183
Chapter Review 184

Unit 5   Operations with Fractions   **185**

Chapter 13   Fractions   **187**

13-1   Naming Fractions 187
13-2   Reading and Saying Fractions 189
13-3   Fractions Less Than, Equal to, and Greater Than a Whole 192
13-4   Whole Numbers as Fractions 194
13-5   Changing Improper Fractions to Mixed Numbers 195
13-6   Changing Mixed Numbers to Improper Fractions 197
13-7   Equivalent Fractions 200
Have I Learned? 205
Chapter Review 206

Chapter 14   More Work with Fractions   **207**

14-1   Comparing Fractions 207
14-2   Simplifying Fractions .212
Have I Learned? 215
Chapter Review 216

Chapter 15   Multiplying and Dividing Fractions   **217**

15-1   Multiplying Fractions .217
15-2   Simplifying by Canceling 221
15-3   Solving Word Problems .222
15-4   Reciprocals 224
15-5   Dividing Fractions 225
15-6   Solving Word Problems .230
Have I Learned? 231
Chapter Review 232

Chapter 16   **Adding and Subtracting Fractions**   **233**

16-1   Adding Fractions with Like Denominators 233
16-2   Lowest Common Denominator 236
16-3   Adding Fractions with Unlike Denominators 238
16-4   Solving Word Problems .241
16-5   Subtracting Fractions with Like Denominators 242
16-6   Writing Whole Numbers as Fractions 244
16-7   Subtracting Fractions from Whole Numbers 246
16-8   Subtracting Unlike Fractions 247
16-9   Solving Word Problems .249
Have I Learned? 251
Chapter Review 252

Unit 6   **Ratios and Percents**   **253**

Chapter 17   **Ratios and Proportions**   **255**

17-1   Ratios 255
17-2   Proportions 258
17-3   Solving Proportions Using Inverse Operations 259
17-4   Using Proportions in Problem Solving 260
Have I Learned? 263
Chapter Review 264

Chapter 18   **Percents**   **265**

18-1   Understanding Percents 265
18-2   Writing Percents as Decimals and Decimals as Percents 266
18-3   Writing Percents as Fractions 267
18-4   Writing Fractions as Decimals and as Percents 268
18-5   Solving Percent Problems 271
18-6   Using Percents with Discounts 280
Have I Learned? 281
Chapter Review 282

Unit 7   **Operations with Integers**   **283**

Chapter 19   **More Work with Integers**   **285**

19-1   Positive and Negative Integers 285
19-2   Adding Positive and Negative Integers on the Number Line . . .286
19-3   Absolute Value 288
19-4   Adding Positive and Negative Integers 289
19-5   Subtracting Positive and Negative Integers 291
19-6   Multiplying Positive and Negative Integers 293
19-7   Multiplying More Than Two Integers 295
19-8   Dividing Positive and Negative Integers 296
Have I Learned? 297
Chapter Review 298

Unit 8	**Introduction to Geometry and Measurement**	**299**

	Chapter 20	**Geometry**	**301**
	20-1	Points, Lines, and Planes	.301
	20-2	Intersecting and Parallel Lines	.303
	20-3	Angles	.304
	20-4	Drawing Angles	.309
	20-5	Perpendicular Lines	.311
	20-6	Triangles	.312
	20-7	Circles	.315
	20-8	Drawing Circles	.317
		Have I Learned?	.319
		Chapter Review	.320

	Chapter 21	**Polygons**	**321**
	21-1	Polygons	.321
	21-2	Congruent Figures	.323
	21-3	Corresponding Parts	.324
	21-4	Regular Polygons	.326
	21-5	Similar Polygons	.327
	21-6	Proportions with Similar Polygons	.328
		Have I Learned?	.331
		Chapter Review	.332

	Chapter 22	**Measurements**	**333**
	22-1	Perimeter	.333
	22-2	Circumference of a Circle	.334
	22-3	Area of a Rectangle and Square	.336
	22-4	Area of a Triangle	.337
	22-5	Area of a Parallelogram	.339
	22-6	Area of a Circle	.340
		Have I Learned?	.341
		Chapter Review	.342

Glossary		**343**
Listening Scripts		**351**

Preface

As a math teacher of English language learners, I realized that there was a need for a math book that not only covered math concepts and skills, but also included language instruction necessary to master the subject. *Longman Mathematics* merges the teaching of math with English language acquisition exercises specific to math terminology. It is my hope that this book will make learning math a little less frustrating for the English language learner as well as for any other student who can benefit from the simplified explanations, extensive use of examples and illustrations, and vocabulary exercises found in the book. Although this book is written with English language learners in mind, it is by no means confined to them. Students reading below grade level will also benefit from this book, as language and vocabulary are carefully structured in each chapter.

Features of the book include . . .

1. listening exercises where students identify words or phrases dictated by the teacher;

2. pronunciation exercises where students practice saying cardinal and ordinal numbers, decimal numbers, and mathematical phrases along with vocabulary words;

3. written exercises where students write into words numbers, decimals, and mathematical phrases and terms;

4. reading passages where students read dialogues or other text that incorporates vocabulary specific to math;

5. a review list of vocabulary words and topics at the end of each chapter;

6. chapter review exercises; and

7. a comprehensive glossary of math terms at the end of the book.

Longman Mathematics covers cardinal and ordinal numbers; the operations of addition, subtraction, multiplication, and division; number theory; decimals; fractions; ratios; percents; operations with positive and negative integers; and an introduction to geometry and measurement.

Acknowledgments

I would like to thank all those who have been very encouraging and patient throughout this endeavor: my children, Filip and Sayuri; my husband, Jim; my mother, Alice; and especially my father, Koya Iwamoto, my first math teacher, for his critical help and guidance throughout the writing of this book and for sharing with me his love for mathematics.

Julie Iwamoto

Base-Ten Number System

In this unit, you will learn . . .

- cardinal numbers

- base-ten place names

- the base-ten number system

- comma placement

- how to say cardinal numbers

- the concepts "smallest" and "largest"

- ordinal numbers

- how to say dates

- how to round off numbers

- estimation

CHAPTER 1 — Reading and Saying Cardinal Numbers

1-1 Cardinal Numbers

We count with **cardinal numbers**. We use cardinal numbers to answer the question, *"How many?"*

0 – zero	7 – seven	14 – fourteen
1 – one	8 – eight	15 – fifteen
2 – two	9 – nine	16 – sixteen
3 – three	10 – ten	17 – seventeen
4 – four	11 – eleven	18 – eighteen
5 – five	12 – twelve	19 – nineteen
6 – six	13 – thirteen	20 – twenty

21 – twenty-one, (twenty-two, twenty-three, twenty-four, twenty-five, twenty-six, twenty-seven, twenty-eight, twenty-nine)

30 – thirty, (thirty-one, thirty-two, . . .)

40 – forty, (fifty, sixty, seventy, eighty, ninety)

100 – one hundred, (one hundred one, one hundred two, . . .)

200 – two hundred, (three hundred, four hundred, . . .)

1,000 – one thousand, (one thousand one, one thousand two, . . .)

2,000 – two thousand, (three thousand, four thousand, . . .)

10,000 – ten thousand, (twenty thousand, thirty thousand, . . .)

100,000 – one hundred thousand, (two hundred thousand, three hundred thousand, . . .)

1,000,000 – one million, (two million, three million, . . .)

1,000,000,000 – one billion, (two billion, three billion, . . .)

A **digit** is any one of the numbers 0, 1, 2, 3, 4, 5, 6, 7, 8, 9.

The numbers 0, 1, 2, 3, 4, 5, 6, 7, 8, 9 have one *digit*.
The numbers 10, 11, 12, 13, . . . , 99 have two *digits*.
The numbers 100, 101, 102, 103, . . . , 999 have three *digits*.
The numbers 1,000, 1,001, 1,002, . . . , 9,999 have four *digits*.

Exercise 1

Answer the questions below. Write the answers on the lines.

1. How many digits does the number 56 have? _____*two*_____
2. How many digits does the number 1,257 have? _____
3. How many digits does the number 34,589 have? _____
4. How many digits does the number 642,962 have? _____
5. How many digits does the number 27,348,135 have? _____

Place value is the value a digit has based on its position in a number.

In a *one-digit* number, we write a digit in the

↑
ones place

$$8$$
↑
$(8 \times 1) = \quad 8$

In a *two-digit* number, we write the two digits in the

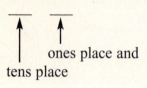

↑ ↑
ones place and
tens place

$$2 \quad 8$$
↑ ↑
$(8 \times 1) = \quad 8$
$(2 \times 10) \quad = \quad 20$
$20 + 8 \quad = \quad 28$

In a *three-digit* number, we write the three digits in the

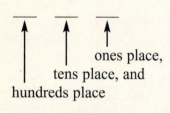

↑ ↑ ↑
ones place,
tens place, and
hundreds place

$$3 \quad 2 \quad 8$$
↑ ↑ ↑
$(8 \times 1) = \quad 8$
$(2 \times 10) \quad = \quad 20$
$(3 \times 100) \quad = \quad 300$
$300 + 20 + 8 \quad = \quad 328$

In a *four-digit* number, we write the four digits in the

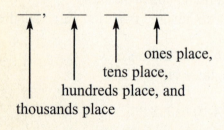

↑ ↑ ↑ ↑
ones place,
tens place,
hundreds place, and
thousands place

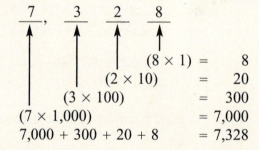

$$7, \quad 3 \quad 2 \quad 8$$
↑ ↑ ↑ ↑
$(8 \times 1) = \quad 8$
$(2 \times 10) \quad = \quad 20$
$(3 \times 100) \quad = \quad 300$
$(7 \times 1,000) \quad = 7,000$
$7,000 + 300 + 20 + 8 \quad = 7,328$

Base-Ten Number System

Here are the **place names** from ones to billions.

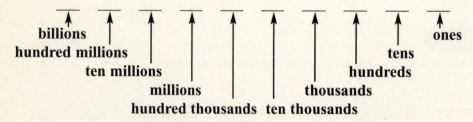

billions
hundred millions
ten millions
millions
hundred thousands **ten thousands**
thousands
hundreds
tens
ones

The digit *0* is a placeholder. In the number below it holds the hundreds place.

875,034

1-3 Comma Placement

In numbers with more than three digits, we write a **comma** "," between certain digits. The comma helps us read the number correctly.

We begin at the ones place and count three digits to the left. ←

Examples:

$$2 , \underbrace{4\ 7\ 5}_{\text{3 digits}}$$

comma

$$3 , \underbrace{2\ 5\ 6}_{\text{3 digits}} , \underbrace{4\ 7\ 5}_{\text{3 digits}}$$

comma   comma

We write a comma before the thousands place, the millions place, and the billions place.

Exercise 2

Rewrite the numbers with *commas*.

1. 34566 _____34,566_____
2. 35879800 _____
3. 1243 _____
4. 1569385 _____
5. 1839984765 _____

6. 12986 _____
7. 3678 _____
8. 4903944 _____
9. 70004301 _____
10. 152946450710 _____

Exercise 3

Write the place name of each <u>underlined</u> digit.

1. 8<u>9</u> ____ones____
2. <u>1</u>94 _____
3. 6,<u>7</u>24 _____
4. 38,2<u>9</u>6 _____
5. 42<u>9</u>,126 _____

6. 7,01<u>2</u> _____
7. 1<u>2</u>5,746,150 _____
8. <u>1</u>1,244 _____
9. 215,<u>4</u>94,199 _____
10. 6<u>4</u>,640 _____

11. 11,<u>1</u>11,211 _____
12. 234,5<u>6</u>7 _____
13. <u>7</u>,345,879 _____
14. 90,08<u>0</u> _____
15. <u>9</u>,824,674,113 _____

Circle *all* the numbers with . . .

1. 6 in the *tens* place.
26   (62)   56   (68)   36

2. 9 in the *ones* place.
89   98   79   95   94

3. 5 in the *hundreds* place.
152   125   345   564

4. 3 in the *thousands* place.
4,356   3,446   5,432   2,345

5. 1 in the *tens* place.
177   712   8,123   13   21

6. 2 in the *ones* place.
28   82   423   9,432   12

7. 4 in the *hundreds* place.
345   564   4,567   3,478   432

8. 3 in the *hundred thousands* place.
366,578   3,467,112
254,533,679   1,348,990

9. 9 in the *ten thousands* place.
19,877   98,399   198,734   195,877

10. 5 in the *millions* place.
45,986,433   4,678,445
153,345,672   65,456,788

1-4 How to Say Cardinal Numbers

For all 3-digit numbers, say *hundred* after the hundreds digit:

2 4 3

two *hundred* forty-three

1 0 6

one *hundred* six

For all 4-, 5-, and 6-digit numbers, say *thousand* after the thousands digit:

1 , 2 1 4

one   two hundred
thousand,   fourteen

3 0 4 , 9 1 7

three hundred   nine hundred
four *thousand,*   seventeen

For all 7-, 8-, and 9-digit numbers, say *million* after the millions digit and *thousand* after the thousands digit:

4 2 1 , 6 0 4 , 0 9 0

four hundred   six hundred   ninety
twenty-one   four
million,   *thousand,*

For all 10-, 11-, and 12-digit numbers, say *billion, million,* and *thousand* after the billions, millions, and thousands digits or at all three commas:

$$2 \quad , \quad \underline{1\ 0\ 3} \quad , \quad \underline{2\ 1\ 6} \quad , \quad \underline{1\ 5\ 6}$$

two *billion,*	one hundred three *million,*	two hundred sixteen *thousand,*	one hundred fifty-six

Exercise 5

Work with a partner. Take turns saying these numbers aloud.

1. 12	**10.** 57	**19.** 101	**28.** 2,001
2. 38	**11.** 93	**20.** 234	**29.** 10,113
3. 55	**12.** 19	**21.** 769	**30.** 85,200
4. 14	**13.** 55	**22.** 500	**31.** 96,002
5. 11	**14.** 20	**23.** 927	**32.** 75,414
6. 0	**15.** 42	**24.** 812	**33.** 125,308
7. 40	**16.** 88	**25.** 1,324	**34.** 2,670,008
8. 79	**17.** 90	**26.** 6,719	**35.** 6,500,013
9. 13	**18.** 19	**27.** 3,010	

LISTENING

Your teacher will read numbers aloud. Listen. Then circle the letter next to the correct number.

1. a. 29 **b.** 290 *(circled)* **c.** 129	**6. a.** 426,030 **b.** 426,300 **c.** 426,013
2. a. 40 **b.** 14 **c.** 43	**7. a.** 6,190,260 **b.** 6,190,260,000 **c.** 6,119,260
3. a. 315 **b.** 350 **c.** 3,500	**8. a.** 5,315,000 **b.** 5,300,000 **c.** 5,250,000
4. a. 999 **b.** 919 **c.** 990	**9. a.** 8,600,095 **b.** 8,695,000 **c.** 8,006,095
5. a. 3,150 **b.** 3,150,000 **c.** 3,115	**10. a.** 600,009 **b.** 609,000 **c.** 600,900

A. Look at the illustrations. Then read the dialogue below.

A Moving Sale

Yori: How much is the computer table?

Marco: It's one hundred fifty dollars. *150*

Yori: How old is it?

Marco: It's two years old.

Yori: How much is the chair?

Marco: It's eighty-nine dollars. *89*

Yori: And the TV set?

Marco: It's seventy dollars. *70*

Yori: Hmm. How about the rug?

Marco: Oh, it's very old. It's three hundred fifteen years old,
and it's seven hundred seventy dollars. *770*

Yori: I'll buy the computer table, the chair, and the TV set.

Marco: It's a sale!

B. Now complete the sentences. Circle the letter next to the correct answer.

1. The computer table costs _____.

   a. $150   **b.** $115   **c.** $105   **d.** $501

2. The computer table is _____.

   a. 1 year old   **b.** 2 years old   **c.** 20 years old   **d.** 22 years old

3. The chair costs _____.

   a. $18   **b.** $98   **c.** $89   **d.** $809

4. The TV set costs _____.

   a. $17   **b.** $700   **c.** $70   **d.** $7

5. The rug is _____.

   a. 350 years old   **b.** 305 years old   **c.** 355 years old   **d.** 315 years old

On a separate sheet of paper, write the words for the numbers.

1. 10 _ten_	**6.** 40	**11.** 77	**16.** 1,980
2. 13	**7.** 0	**12.** 88	**17.** 2,012
3. 12	**8.** 11	**13.** 102	**18.** 12,945
4. 19	**9.** 33	**14.** 158	**19.** 1,345,009
5. 90	**10.** 87	**15.** 207	**20.** 13,405,090

Exercise 8

On a separate sheet of paper, write the numbers for the words.

1. fifty _50_

2. sixty-four

3. eleven thousand

4. one thousand, six

5. six hundred ten

6. forty-five hundred

7. nine thousand, eleven

8. three thousand, thirty-seven

9. eighty-seven

10. fifty-four

11. four hundred five thousand, nine hundred nineteen

12. one million, six hundred thousand

13. two hundred fifty thousand, three

14. sixteen million, nine hundred fifty thousand, four hundred fourteen

15. three hundred eleven thousand, nine hundred fourteen

16. twenty-three thousand, two hundred two

17. seventeen thousand, sixty

18. three million, eight hundred ninety thousand, five hundred twenty-nine

19. eight billion, seventy-seven thousand, sixteen

20. seventy-five hundred

Exercise 9

Find fifteen (15) numbers below that are spelled correctly. Write these numbers on a separate sheet of paper.

1. nineteen	**8.** twenty-one	**15.** six hundred	**22.** sisteen
2. one	**9.** eighty	**16.** eigth	**23.** fiveteen
3. eleven	**10.** one hundrad	**17.** twelve	**24.** thurty
4. foure	**11.** fifteen	**18.** three	**25.** two tausend
5. twenty	**12.** too	**19.** fourty	
6. nine	**13.** cero	**20.** seventy-five	
7. seventeen	**14.** forty	**21.** fifty-eight	

Match the words with the numbers. Write the correct letters.

1. 960   _f_   **a.** nine hundred forty-one

2. 7,432   _____   **b.** seven hundred forty-three

3. 967   _____   **c.** seven thousand, four hundred thirty-two

4. 9,670   _____   **d.** nine hundred sixty-seven

5. 743   _____   **e.** nine thousand, six hundred seventy

6. 94,603   _____   **f.** nine hundred sixty

7. 941   _____   **g.** nine thousand, four hundred one

8. 44,267   _____   **h.** nine thousand, four hundred ten

9. 9,410   _____   **i.** ninety-four thousand, six hundred three

10. 9,401   _____   **j.** forty-four thousand, two hundred sixty-seven

Vocabulary: Numbers from Smallest to Largest

Look at the following group of numbers: 20, 6, 12, 3, 14, 15, 8, 22.

3 is the **smallest** or **least** number.
22 is the **largest** or **greatest** number.
8 is the largest one-digit number.
12 is the smallest two-digit number.

    Look at this group of numbers: 9, 6, 4, 2, 11, 7.

We can write the numbers, in order, from smallest to largest: 2, 4, 6, 7, 9, 11.

Answer each question with numbers.

1. Write 4 one-digit numbers.   **a.** _____   **b.** _____   **c.** _____   **d.** _____

2. Write 4 two-digit numbers.   **a.** _____   **b.** _____   **c.** _____   **d.** _____

3. Write 4 three-digit numbers.   **a.** _____   **b.** _____   **c.** _____   **d.** _____

4. Look at this group of numbers: 8, 24, 11, 3, 12, 16, 2, 6, 13.

   a. Which number is the largest? _____

   b. Which number is the smallest? _____

   c. What is the smallest two-digit number? _____

   d. What is the largest one-digit number? _____

5. On a separate sheet of paper, write the following numbers in order from smallest to largest.

2,342	2,433	2,044	2,244
2,304	2,004	2,343	2,400
2,240	2,440	2,330	2,432
2,043	2,204	2,040	

Have I Learned? (✓)

Work with a partner. Check what you have learned. Review what you need help with.

1. cardinal number ☐
2. digit ☐
3. place value ☐
4. place name ☐
5. ones place ☐
6. tens place ☐
7. hundreds place ☐
8. thousands place ☐
9. ten thousands place ☐
10. hundred thousands place ☐

11. millions place ☐
12. ten millions place ☐
13. hundred millions place ☐
14. billions place ☐
15. comma ☐
16. smallest ☐
17. least ☐
18. largest ☐
19. greatest ☐

Exercise 1

On a separate sheet of paper, write the words for the numbers.

1. 11 _eleven_   3. 15   5. 8   7. 130   9. 3,607
2. 0   4. 12   6. 40   8. 289   10. 57,289

Exercise 2

Write the numbers for the words.

1. three hundred sixteen _____316_____
2. four thousand, two _____4002_____
3. five hundred ten thousand, six hundred eleven _____
4. two million, three hundred seventy thousand, nine hundred fifteen _____
5. thirteen million, four hundred eight thousand, seven hundred forty-one _____

Exercise 3

A. Look at the following numbers.

127,938	427,146,783	129	7,612,483,905
394,398	6,258	11,404	
2,278,500	637,146,783	181,328,934	

B. Write the number with . . .

1. 9 in the ones place. _____129_____
2. 4 in the hundreds place. _____
3. 2 in the hundred thousands place. _____
4. 5 in the tens place. _____
5. 7 in the thousands place. _____
6. 9 in the ten thousands place. _____
7. 1 in the millions place. _____
8. 3 in the ten millions place. _____
9. 4 in the hundred millions place. _____
10. 7 in the billions place. _____

CHAPTER 2

Reading and Saying Ordinal Numbers

2-1 Ordinal Numbers

When we talk about **order**, we use **ordinal numbers**.

1st	2nd	3rd	4th
first	second	third	fourth

1st	first	11th	eleventh	21st	twenty-first
2nd	second	12th	twelfth	22nd	twenty-second
3rd	third	13th	thirteenth	23rd	twenty-third
4th	fourth	14th	fourteenth	30th	thirtieth
5th	fifth	15th	fifteenth	40th	fortieth
6th	sixth	16th	sixteenth	50th	fiftieth
7th	seventh	17th	seventeenth	60th	sixtieth
8th	eighth	18th	eighteenth	70th	seventieth
9th	ninth	19th	nineteenth	80th	eightieth
10th	tenth	20th	twentieth	90th	ninetieth

100th	one hundredth, (one hundred first, one hundred second, . . .)
1,000th	one thousandth, (two thousandth, three thousandth, . . .)
1,000,000th	one millionth, (two millionth, three millionth, . . .)

Write an ordinal number for each cardinal number.

1. 4 _4th_
2. 9 _____
3. 2 _____
4. 7 _____
5. 11 _____
6. 5 _____
7. 33 _____
8. 45 _____
9. 90 _____

10. 1 _____
11. 3 _____
12. 102 _____
13. 70 _____
14. 61 _____
15. 53 _____
16. 99 _____
17. 16 _____

18. 22 _____
19. 31 _____
20. 19 _____
21. 60 _____
22. 42 _____
23. 75 _____
24. 203 _____
25. 3,000 _____

Work with a partner. Take turns saying these numbers aloud.

1. 10th
2. 1st
3. 32nd
4. 25th
5. 50th

6. 13th
7. 43rd
8. 19th
9. 40th
10. 77th

11. 80th
12. 8th
13. 17th
14. 32nd
15. 100th

16. 15th
17. 70th
18. 91st
19. 83rd
20. 93rd

Write the words for the ordinal numbers.

1. 6th _____sixth_____
2. 19th _____
3. 1st _____
4. 5th _____
5. 90th _____
6. 12th _____
7. 42nd _____
8. 3rd _____
9. 40th _____

10. 8th _____
11. 29th _____
12. 75th _____
13. 50th _____
14. 4th _____
15. 20th _____
16. 100th _____
17. 2,000th _____

18. 81st _____
19. 104th _____
20. 203rd _____
21. 77th _____
22. 88th _____
23. 1,001st _____
24. 24th _____
25. 402nd _____

Read the following words. Then answer the questions. Write your responses on the lines.

Oh, no! Math class starts at eleven.

1. What is the third word of the line? _____ *Math* _____

2. What is the last word of the line? _____

3. What is the first word of the line? _____

4. What are the first three words of the line? _____

5. What is the fourth word of the line? _____

Read the following poem. Then answer the questions. Write your responses on the lines.

Lost at School

Oh, no! Math class starts at eleven.
I have only three minutes to find room two sixty-seven.
Is it on this floor?
Is the number on the door?
Time is running out; I really have to race.
Will the bell ring before I can find the right place?
How much farther can it be?
Will the teacher be angry with me? . . .
Whew! I had to move fast, but I found the room at last.
Tomorrow will be my second day at this school.
I know where to go now, so I can be cool.

1. What is the fifth word of the first line? _____ *starts* _____

2. What is the second word of the second line? _____

3. What is the third word of the fourth line? _____

4. What is the fourth word of the fifth line? _____

5. What are the last three words of the seventh line? _____

6. What are the last four words of the sixth line? _____

7. What are the third and fourth words of the eighth line? _____

8. What is the second word of the eleventh line? _____

9. What is the tenth word of the ninth line? _____

10. What is the last word of the poem? _____

Listening and Speaking

Complete this activity as a class. Look at the program card below. Your teacher will ask you questions about the card.

López	Raúl	10	10-18-75	9-21-92
Last Name	**First**	**Grade**	**Birthdate**	**Date**

Period	Room	Class Title	Teacher
1	104	English 10	Ms. Bryant
2	323	Algebra 1	Ms. Rivera
3	121	U.S. History	Mr. Carter
4	205	Biology	Mr. Jackson
5	gym	Physical Education	Mr. Ramos
6	313	Art	Ms. Williams

Exercise 6

A. Look at Susan Chong's calendar for the month of May.

May _____

Sunday	Monday	Tuesday	Wednesday	Thursday	Friday	Saturday
	1	**2**	**3**	**4**	**5**	**6** Study for math and English exams
7	**8** Take math and English exams- Periods 2 and 4	**9**	**10** Take first violin lesson- 4 P.M.	**11**	**12** Go to the movies with Anita	**13**
14 Go to first soccer practice- 2 P.M.	**15**	**16** Go to dentist- 3 P.M.	**17**	**18**	**19**	**20** Buy gift for Mom's birthday
21	**22**	**23**	**24** Take second violin lesson- 4 P.M.	**25**	**26**	**27** Study for history and science exams
28 Go to second soccer practice- 2 P.M.	**29** Take history and science exams- Periods 1 and 3	**30**	**31**			

B. Answer the questions. Write complete sentences.

1. What is Susan going to do on the sixth day of the month?

   She is going to study for her math and English exams.

2. What is she going to do on the tenth day of the month?

   _____

3. What is she going to do on the fourteenth day of the month?

   _____

4. What is she going to do on the sixteenth day of the month?

   _____

5. What is she going to do on the twenty-ninth day of the month?

   _____

C. Complete the sentences, using words for the cardinal numbers.

1. There are _____seven_____ days in a week.

2. There are _____ days in this month.

3. There are _____ Wednesdays in this month.

4. There are _____ Fridays in this month.

5. Susan is going to go to soccer practice _____ times this month.

D. Complete the sentences, using words for the ordinal numbers.

1. Look at the first week in the month. The month begins on Monday,
   the _____first_____ .

2. On the _____ day of the month, Susan is going to study for her math
   and English exams.

3. On Wednesday, the _____, Susan is going to take her first violin lesson.

4. Susan is going to go to the movies on Friday, the _____ day of the
   month.

5. Susan is going to go to her first soccer practice on the _____ of the
   month.

6. On Saturday, the _____, Susan is going to buy a gift for her mom.

7. On Wednesday, the _____, Susan is going to take her second violin
   lesson.

8. Susan is going to study for her history and science exams on Saturday,
   the _____ .

9. Susan is going to go to her second soccer practice on Sunday, the
   _____ .

10. On Monday, the _____, Susan is going to take her history and
    science exams.

We write dates in this order: <u>month, day, year</u>.

Examples:

1. April 22, 1957
4/22/57
4-22-57

2. September 20, 2004
9/20/04
9-20-04

To read or say the dates, we use both cardinal and ordinal numbers.

Examples:

1. We see: April 22, 1957.

We say: "April twenty-second, nineteen fifty-seven."

2. We see: 4/22/57.

We say: "four, twenty-two, fifty-seven."

3. We see: September 20, 2004.

We say: "September twentieth, two thousand four."

4. We see: 9/20/04.

We say: "nine, twenty, oh-four."

Exercise 7

Work with a partner. Practice saying these dates aloud.

1. June 2, 1988

2. February 11, 1975

3. December 25, 1991

4. 1/7/87

5. June 8, 1847

6. January 1, 1984

7. 7/11/66

8. March 17, 1981

9. May 3, 1909

10. November 21, 1888

11. July 4, 1776

12. 8/29/71

13. 2/15/03

14. October 12, 2004

15. 8/31/04

Look at the pictures below and on page 20 from Sofia's album. They are *not* in order. Put them in order by writing the numbers 1–10 in the correct spaces. Use the dates at the bottom of the pictures to help you.

At the Theater
December 24, 2001

My First Day at High School
9/6/04

Mario and Chris Surf Boarding
July 18, 2000

Playing Volleyball
at Camp
8/6/99

My First Day at Camp
July 8, 1999

19

Mario's First Day at College
September 1, 2004

Mario and Chris Playing Basketball
May 7, 2000

Swimming
at Camp
7/20/99

The Statue of Liberty
12/27/01

Leaving for
New York City
12/23/01

Vocabulary

Look at the illustrations and read the expressions.

1.

a dozen eggs

2.

a half-dozen eggs (**half a dozen** eggs)

3.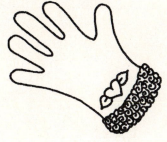

a single glove

4.

a pair of gloves

5.

twin brothers (**twins**)

6.

a couple of chairs

7.

a double scoop

21

A. Look at the illustrations. Then read the dialogue below.

The Flower Shop

Richard: Jason, here's an order for a dozen roses for Mr. and Mrs. Hunt. Mrs. Hunt just had twin girls!

Jason: That's great!

Richard: Here's another order for a couple of green plants for Mrs. Myers. She has a bad back again and is in the hospital.

Jason: I'm sorry to hear that . . . I'll fill the orders right away. By the way, how much is a dozen roses?

Richard: A dozen roses is $24.00. The price doubled in just four years!

Jason: Is a half-dozen roses $12.00?

Richard: Yes, and a single rose is $2.00.

Jason: Thanks, Richard.

Richard: You're welcome . . . Hey, Jason, I have an extra pair of tickets to the county fair this weekend. Would you like them?

Jason: Yes! My girlfriend and I would really like to go to the fair.

Richard: Great! They're yours!

Jason: Thanks, Richard. Oh, . . . and don't forget to call your wife back.

Richard: Right. Today's her birthday. I'll call her back and then I'll send her two dozen roses.

B. Now answer the questions.

1. How many roses will Jason send Mr. and Mrs. Hunt? _____*twelve*_____

2. How many baby girls did Mrs. Hunt have? _____

3. How many green plants will Jason send Mrs. Meyers? _____

4. How much is a dozen roses today? _____

5. How much was a dozen roses four years ago? _____

6. How much are six roses today? _____

7. How much was six roses four years ago? _____

8. How much is one rose today? _____

9. How many tickets did Richard give Jason? _____

10. How many roses will Richard send his wife? _____

 Have I Learned? (✓)

Work with a partner. Check what you have learned. Review what you need help with.

1. order ☐

2. ordinal numbers ☐

3. date ☐

4. month ☐

5. day ☐

6. year ☐

7. a dozen . . . ☐

8. a half-dozen . . . (half a dozen . . .) ☐

9. a single . . . ☐

10. a pair of . . . ☐

11. twin . . . (twins) ☐

12. a couple of . . . ☐

13. a double . . . ☐

Exercise 1

Write the words for the ordinal numbers.

1. 5th _____ *fifth* _____
2. 9th _____
3. 8th _____
4. 12th _____
5. 21st _____

6. 33rd _____
7. 11th _____
8. 200th _____
9. 15th _____
10. 92nd _____

Exercise 2

Write the ordinal numbers for the words.

1. first _____ *1st* _____
2. second _____
3. third _____
4. tenth _____
5. forty-third _____

6. three hundred sixty-second _____
7. one thousandth _____
8. sixtieth _____
9. nineteenth _____
10. seventy-fifth _____

Exercise 3

Follow the directions below.

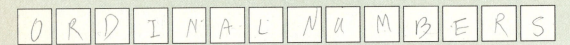

| O | R | D | I | N | A | L | N | U | M | B | E | R | S |

1. Write an "N" in the fifth box.
2. Write a "U" in the ninth box.
3. Write an "E" in the twelfth box.
4. Write an "I" in the fourth box.
5. Write an "A" in the sixth box.
6. Write an "S" in the fourteenth box.
7. Write an "R" in the second box.
8. Write an "L" in the seventh box.

9. Write an "R" in the thirteenth box.
10. Write an "M" in the tenth box.
11. Write a "D" in the third box.
12. Write a "B" in the eleventh box.
13. Write an "N" in the eighth box.
14. Write an "O" in the first box.
15. What expression did you write? Write it on the line.

_____

CHAPTER 3 Rounding Off Numbers

3-1 Round Numbers

What is a round number? Look at the following examples.

40			43
10			15
350			345
5,000	These numbers are round numbers.	These numbers are *not* round numbers.	5,467
70			78
220			228
7,500			7,598
870			871

A **round number** is a number that is written with *zero* as the last digit.

Examples:

20
310

A round number may have more than one zero.

Examples:

200
31,000

Why do you think we call these numbers *round* numbers?

Exercise 1

Which numbers below are *round* numbers? Circle them.

1. (450)
2. 678
3. 324
4. 540
5. 2,400

6. 325
7. 567
8. 45,900
9. 1,000
10. 500

11. 4,909
12. 13
13. 60,001
14. 30
15. 56,677

To **round off** a number means to change a number to a round number. We can round off a number to the tens place, hundreds place, thousands place, and so on.

Examples:

5,231 rounds off to . . .
5,230 (*tens* place)
5,200 (*hundreds* place)
5,000 (*thousands* place)

Examples:

We round off the number 23 to the *tens* place ⟶ 20.

We round off the number 276 to the *hundreds* place ⟶ 300.

We round off the number 6,437 to the *thousands* place ⟶ 6,000.

Look at the **number line** below.

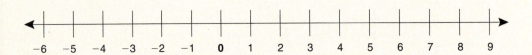

The number line continues to the right ⟶ and it continues to the left ←. There is no end. It is **infinite**. The numbers on the left are **less than** the numbers on the right. The numbers on the right are **greater than** the numbers on the left.

Examples:

5 is less than 6.
8 is greater than 7.

3-2 Rounding Off Numbers

Look at the number line below.

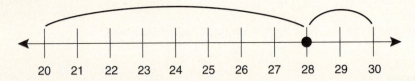

This part of the number line has numbers from 20 to 30. The number 28 is between the round numbers 20 and 30. 28 is closer to 30, so we can round off 28 to 30.

28 ⟶ 30

Look again at the number line above. Is the number 23 closer to 20 or 30? 23 is **closer to** 20, so we can round off 23 to 20.

23 ⟶ 20

Exercise 2

Look at the numbers below. Round them off to the closer round number (10 or 20).

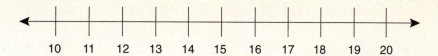

1. 18 → ___20___

3. 13 → ___10___

5. 11 → ___10___

2. 12 → ___10___

4. 16 → ___20___

What about the number 15? It is exactly in the middle, between the round numbers 10 and 20. Do we round to 10 or 20?

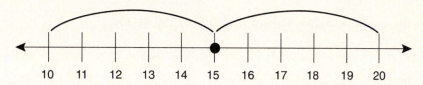

Follow this rule: When the number is exactly in the middle of two round numbers, always round off to the greater round number.

> 15 rounds off to 20.
> 15 → 20

Exercise 3

A. Look at the numbers below. Round them off to 30 or 40.

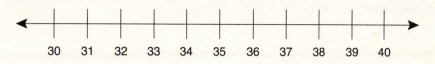

1. 33 → ___30___

4. 39 → ___40___

2. 36 → ___40___

5. 31 → ___30___

3. 35 → ___40___

B. Look at the numbers below. Round them off to 80 or 90.

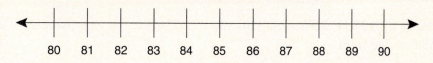

1. 84 → ___80___

4. 85 → ___90___

2. 88 → ___90___

5. 82 → ___80___

3. 87 → ___90___

C. Look at the numbers below. Round them off to 100 or 200.

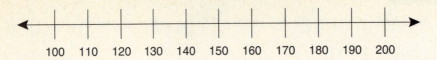

1. 180 → _200_
2. 110 → _____
3. 175 → _____
4. 105 → _____
5. 150 → _____

6. 151 → _____
7. 149 → _____
8. 124 → _____
9. 195 → _____
10. 167 → _____

11. 130 → _____
12. 199 → _____
13. 140 → _____
14. 177 → _____
15. 112 → _____

D. Look at the numbers below. Round them off to 200 or 300.

1. 286 → _300_
2. 225 → _____
3. 205 → _____
4. 269 → _____
5. 250 → _____

6. 244 → _____
7. 278 → _____
8. 249 → _____
9. 233 → _____
10. 261 → _____

11. 283 → _____
12. 210 → _____
13. 291 → _____
14. 213 → _____
15. 280 → _____

3-3 Rounding Off to the Tens Place

We can round off a number to the tens place. For example, we can round off the number 123 to the **nearest** tens place.

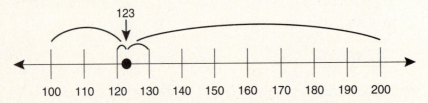

123 is between the round numbers 120 and 130. 123 is also between the round numbers 100 and 200. We can round off 123 to the nearest tens place (120), or we can round off 123 to the nearest hundreds place (100).

To round off 123 to the nearest tens place, underline the tens place digit and look at the number to the right.

1   2   3

This is the tens digit of the **smaller** round number (120).

If this number is less than 5, the number is closer to the smaller round number 120. Keep the underlined number and change the number to the right to 0.

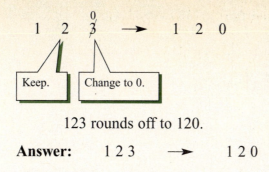

123 rounds off to 120.

Answer: 1 2 3   ⟶   1 2 0

We can round off 156 to the nearest tens place.

To round off 156 to the nearest tens place, underline the tens place digit and look at the number to the right.

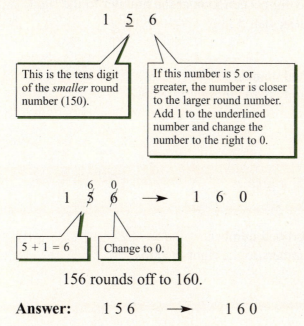

This is the tens digit of the *smaller* round number (150).

If this number is 5 or greater, the number is closer to the larger round number. Add 1 to the underlined number and change the number to the right to 0.

5 + 1 = 6

Change to 0.

156 rounds off to 160.

Answer: 1 5 6   ⟶   1 6 0

We can round off 196 to the nearest tens place.

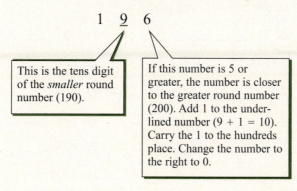

This is the tens digit of the *smaller* round number (190).

If this number is 5 or greater, the number is closer to the greater round number (200). Add 1 to the underlined number (9 + 1 = 10). Carry the 1 to the hundreds place. Change the number to the right to 0.

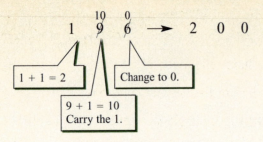

196 rounds off to 200.

Answer: 1 9 6   ⟶   2 0 0

Follow the rule below for rounding off to the tens place.

First, underline the tens place digit. Then look at the number to the right.
If the number to the right is less than 5 . . .

0
1
2   Keep the underlined number.
3   Change all the numbers to the right to zeros.
4

If the number to the right is 5 or greater . . .

5
6
7   Add 1 to the underlined number.
8   Change all the numbers to the right to zeros.
9

Exercise 4

Round off each number below to the nearest tens place.

1. 24 _____ *20* _____   11. 21 _____   21. 957 _____

2. 59 _____   12. 33 _____   22. 806 _____

3. 73 _____   13. 85 _____   23. 4,235 _____

4. 89 _____   14. 39 _____   24. 1,455 _____

5. 15 _____   15. 11 _____   25. 824 _____

6. 65 _____   16. 132 _____   26. 23,493 _____

7. 91 _____   17. 249 _____   27. 711 _____

8. 78 _____   18. 895 _____   28. 6,201 _____

9. 99 _____   19. 451 _____   29. 15,394 _____

10. 18 _____   20. 1,321 _____   30. 2,035 _____

We can round off a number to the hundreds place.

We can round off the number 357 to the nearest hundreds place.

To round off 357 to the nearest hundreds place, underline the hundreds place digit and look at the number to the right.

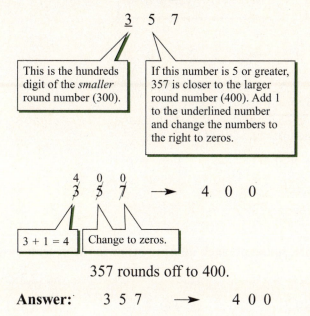

357 rounds off to 400.

Answer: 3 5 7 → 4 0 0

We can round off the number 983 to the nearest hundreds place.

To round off 983 to the nearest hundreds place, underline the hundreds place digit and look at the digit to the right.

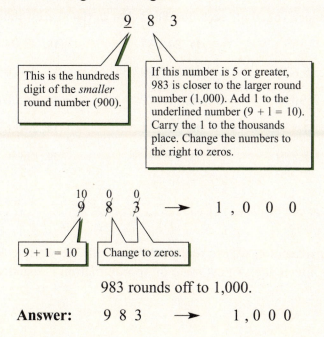

983 rounds off to 1,000.

Answer: 9 8 3 → 1,0 0 0

We can round off a number to the thousands place.

We can round off 32,489 to the nearest thousands place.

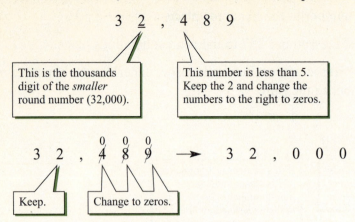

3 2 , 4 8 9 → 3 2 , 0 0 0

Keep.   Change to zeros.

32,489 rounds off to 32,000.

Answer: 3 2 , 4 8 9   →   3 2 , 0 0 0

Exercise 5

A. On a separate sheet of paper, round off each number below to the nearest hundreds place.

1. 124 _100_	**6.** 156	**11.** 913	**16.** 2,395
2. 387	**7.** 989	**12.** 999	**17.** 8,941
3. 506	**8.** 321	**13.** 315	**18.** 7,056
4. 450	**9.** 651	**14.** 849	**19.** 21,994
5. 872	**10.** 721	**15.** 1,429	**20.** 3,651

B. On a separate sheet of paper, round off each number below to the nearest thousands place.

1. 3,455 _3,000_	**6.** 4,355	**11.** 24,937	**16.** 32,941
2. 6,899	**7.** 25,678	**12.** 127,095	**17.** 254,953
3. 1,237	**8.** 2,905	**13.** 11,277	**18.** 365,019
4. 6,987	**9.** 34,439	**14.** 29,821	**19.** 240,677
5. 7,500	**10.** 67,539	**15.** 956,499	**20.** 2,346,771

3-5 Estimation

When we **estimate** or **approximate**, we are really rounding off. We want to know *about how much* or *about how many*. An estimate or approximation is usually not an exact amount.

Example:

Isabel paid $53 for a new dress. She told her mother that she paid about $50. She rounded off $53 to the nearest tens (or nearest ten dollars).

$53 rounds off to $50.
$53 ⟶ $50

The symbol ≈ means *is approximately*.

$53 ≈ $50

Example:

The Tigers basketball team scored 78 points in their first game, 51 points in their second game, and 66 points in their third game. Approximate the total points to the nearest tens place.

$$
\begin{array}{r}
78 \approx 80 \\
51 \approx 50 \\
66 \approx +70 \\
\hline
200
\end{array}
$$

They scored approximately 200 points in 3 games.

Exercise 6

Read each story problem below. Then estimate or approximate each answer.

1. *(to the tens place)* Yoko drove 32 miles on Monday, 47 miles on Tuesday, 56 miles on Wednesday, 39 miles on Thursday, and 61 miles on Friday. About how many miles did she drive altogether that week? _____*240*_____

2. *(to the hundreds place)* At Trent High School, there are 824 students from Latin America, 367 students from Asia, 89 students from Europe, and 1,390 students from the United States. Estimate . . .

   a. how many students are from Latin America. _____

   b. how many students are from Asia. _____

   c. how many students are from the United States. _____

   d. the total student population. _____

3. *(to the ten thousands place)* Steven's salary for the first year was $26,529, for the second year it was $28,986, for the third year it was $34,112, and for the fourth year it was $39,821. Approximate his salary for . . .

   a. the first year. _____

   b. the second year. _____

   c. the third year. _____

   d. the fourth year. _____

   e. all four years. _____

4. *(to the thousands place)* Luisa bought a car last year for $16,927. She sold it this year for $12,291. Estimate what she . . .

a. paid for the car last year. _____

b. sold the car for this year. _____

Exercise 7

Look at the illustrations of the three high schools. Then answer the questions below.

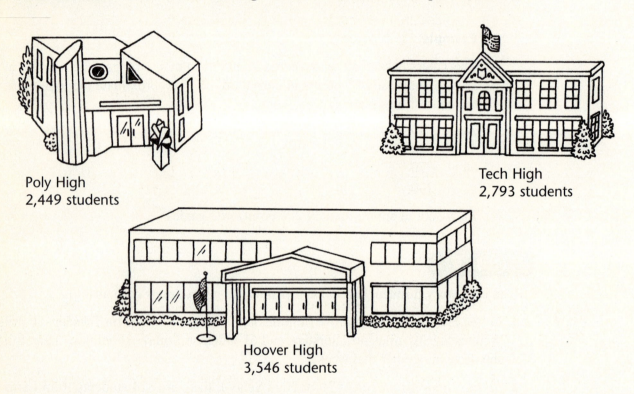

Poly High
2,449 students

Tech High
2,793 students

Hoover High
3,546 students

1. How many students attend Tech High? ____2,793____

2. What is the population of Hoover High? _____

3. What is the population of Poly High and Hoover High together? _____

4. What is the population of all three high schools together? _____

5. Round answer 1 to the nearest hundreds place. _____

6. Round answer 2 to the nearest hundreds place. _____

7. Round answer 3 to the nearest thousands place. _____

8. Round answer 4 to the nearest ten thousands place. _____

9. Which school has the greatest number of students? _____

10. Which school has the least number of students? _____

Your teacher will ask you questions. Listen. Then circle the letter next to the correct answer.

1. **a.** an infinite number
   b. a billion
   c. a million

2. **a.** about how much
   b. exactly how much
   c. the equal amount

3. **a.** numbers
   b. zeros
   c. digits

4. **a.** two
   b. three
   c. four

5. **a.** greatest
   b. smallest
   c. equal

6. **a.** ones
   b. tens
   c. hundreds

7. **a.** approximately
   b. exactly
   c. less than

8. **a.** zero
   b. end
   c. round numbers

9. **a.** equal
   b. ordinal number
   c. lower number

10. **a.** how big
    b. what kind
    c. what order

 # Have I Learned? (✓)

Work with a partner. Check what you have learned. Review what you need help with.

1. round off a number ☐
2. round number ☐
3. number line ☐
4. infinite ☐
5. less than ☐
6. greater than ☐
7. closer to ☐
8. in the middle ☐

9. nearest ☐
10. smaller ☐
11. estimate ☐
12. approximate ☐
13. about how much ☐
14. about how many ☐
15. ≈ (is approximately) ☐

Exercise 1

Round off each number below to the nearest tens place.

1. 54 _____50_____

2. 25 _____

3. 241 _____

4. 375 _____

5. 950 _____

6. 216 _____

7. 1,582 _____

8. 649 _____

9. 906 _____

10. 95 _____

Exercise 2

Round off each number below to the nearest hundreds place.

1. 425 _____400_____

2. 850 _____

3. 668 _____

4. 2,711 _____

5. 1,074 _____

6. 5,802 _____

7. 975 _____

8. 55,251 _____

9. 357 _____

10. 1,508 _____

Exercise 3

Round off each number below to the nearest thousands place.

1. 6,421 _____6,000_____

2. 2,911 _____

3. 8,909 _____

4. 5,500 _____

5. 14,327 _____

6. 26,821 _____

7. 352,911 _____

8. 20,450 _____

9. 75,700 _____

10. 729,700 _____

Operations with Whole Numbers

In this unit, you will learn . . .

- the language of addition
- the properties of addition
- addition with carrying
- the language of subtraction
- subtraction of whole numbers
- subtraction with borrowing
- the language of multiplication
- the symbols for multiplication
- the properties of multiplication
- how to multiply
- multiplying and carrying
- the language of division
- how to divide
- how to use the order of operations
- how to solve addition, subtraction, multiplication, and division word problems

CHAPTER 4 Addition

4-1 Language of Addition

Look at the following **addition** problem.

6 + 2 = 8

We say, "Six **plus** two **equals** eight."

The **sum** is eight. The **addends** are 6 and 2.

What is the sum of 3 and 4? The sum of 3 and 4 is 7.

Exercise 1

Complete each sentence. Write the correct word or words.

1. The _____sum_____ of nine and four is thirteen.

2. Five _____plus_____ six equals eleven.

3. Seven plus three _____equals_____ ten.

4. The sum of three and eight is _____11_____.

5. Ten _____plus_____ ten _____equals_____ twenty.

6. The sum of _____4_____ and six is ten.

7. Three _____plus_____ four _____equals_____ seven.

8. The _____plus_____ of thirteen and three _____equals_____ sixteen.

9. Nine _____plus_____ six _____equals_____ fifteen.

10. _____Twenty_____ plus eight _____equals_____ twenty-eight.

Exercise 2

Answer each question. Write the correct number word.

1. What is the sum of six and five? _____eleven_____

2. What is the sum of fourteen and nine? _____twenty-eight_____

3. What is the sum of eleven and eight? _____nineetin_____

4. What is the sum of seven and seven? _____fourteen_____

5. What is the sum of fifteen and three? _____eighteen_____

6. What is the sum of four and sixteen? _____twenty_____

7. What is the sum of nine and zero? _____ nine _____

8. What is the sum of seven and eight? _____ fifteen _____

9. What is the sum of sixteen and six? _____ twenty-two _____

10. What is the sum of twelve and twelve? _____ twenty-four _____

Exercise 3

On a separate sheet of paper, write the following addition problems using words.

1. 2 + 3 = 5 _____ Two plus three equals five. _____ **5.** 17 + 9 = 26

_____ OR The sum of two and _____ **6.** 24 + 6 = 30

_____ three is five. _____ **7.** 55 + 6 = 61

2. 7 + 5 = 12 **8.** 18 + 9 = 27

3. 0 + 10 = 10 **9.** 42 + 3 = 45

4. 13 + 8 = 21 **10.** 94 + 10 = 104

Exercise 4

For each addition problem, write the addends and the sum.

1. 13 + 2 = 15   addends: _13_ and _2_   sum: _15_

2. 12 + 5 = 17   addends: _12_ and _5_   sum: _17_

3. 0 + 11 = 11   addends: _0_ and _11_   sum: _11_

4. 16 + 4 = 20   addends: _16_ and _4_   sum: _20_

5. 20 + 10 = 30   addends: _20_ and _10_   sum: _30_

4-2 Commutative Property of Addition

Look at the following problems.

> 5 + 6 = 11   6 + 5 = 11
> If we add 5 + 6, the sum is 11.
> If we add 6 + 5, the sum is 11.
>
> 5 + 6 = 6 + 5
> The sums are equal.

The order of adding numbers does not change the sum.

RULE:

We can add numbers in any order. For all numbers a and b: $a + b = b + a$.

Parentheses, ( ), group numbers together. We add together the numbers that are inside the parentheses first. Then we solve the problem.

$(2 + 3) + 6 =$

$5 \quad + 6 = 11$

Exercise 5

Add the numbers inside the parentheses first. Then find the sum.

1. $(3 + 4) + 6 = \underline{\quad 7 \quad} + \underline{\quad 6 \quad} = \underline{\quad 13 \quad}$
2. $6 + (4 + 7) = \underline{\quad 6 \quad} + \underline{\quad 11 \quad} = \underline{\quad 17 \quad}$
3. $2 + (9 + 8) = \underline{\quad 2 \quad} + \underline{\quad 17 \quad} = \underline{\quad 19 \quad}$
4. $(1 + 7) + 3 = \underline{\quad 8 \quad} + \underline{\quad 3 \quad} = \underline{\quad 11 \quad}$
5. $3 + (4 + 8) + 2 = \underline{\quad 3 \quad} + \underline{\quad 12 \quad} + \underline{\quad 2 \quad} = \underline{\quad 17 \quad}$
6. $(4 + 5) + (3 + 7) = \underline{\quad 9 \quad} + \underline{\quad 10 \quad} = \underline{\quad 19 \quad}$
7. $(2 + 6) + 9 + (8 + 1) = \underline{\quad 8 \quad} + \underline{\quad 9 \quad} + \underline{\quad 9 \quad} = \underline{\quad 26 \quad}$
8. $6 + (1 + 5 + 3) + 4 = \underline{\quad 6 \quad} + \underline{\quad 9 \quad} + \underline{\quad 4 \quad} = \underline{\quad 19 \quad}$
9. $(2 + 6) + 9 + (3 + 4) = \underline{\quad 8 \quad} + \underline{\quad 9 \quad} + \underline{\quad 7 \quad} = \underline{\quad 24 \quad}$
10. $8 + (7 + 5 + 1) + 6 = \underline{\quad 8 \quad} + \underline{\quad 13 \quad} + \underline{\quad 6 \quad} = \underline{\quad 27 \quad}$

4-3 Associative Property of Addition

We can group $2 + 3 + 1$ in the following ways.

$(2 + 3) \quad + \quad 1 = \qquad\qquad 2 \quad + \quad (3 + 1) =$

$5 \qquad + \quad 1 = 6 \qquad\qquad 2 \quad + \qquad 4 \quad = 6$

The sums are equal.

RULE:

If we group three or more numbers in different ways and add them together, the sum does not change. For all numbers a, b, and c: $(a + b) + c = a + (b + c)$.

41

Look at the following problems.

$$3 + 0 = 3$$
$$0 + 5 = 5$$
$$6 = 6 + 0$$

RULE:

Adding zero to any number does not change the value of the number.
For all numbers a: $a + 0 = a$.

Exercise 6

First, write the missing number. Then write the property shown—commutative, associative, or additive identity.

1. $7 + \underline{\quad 6 \quad} = 6 + 7$ *commutative*

2. $(4 + 3) + 6 = 4 + (\underline{\quad\quad} + 6)$ *associative*

3. $0 + 4 = \underline{\quad\quad}$ *additive Identity*

4. $7 + (9 + 3) = (7 + \underline{\quad\quad}) + 3$ *associative*

5. $(6 + 4) + 5 = 5 + (\underline{\quad\quad} + 4)$ *"*

6. $19 + \underline{\quad 0 \quad} = 19$ *additive identity*

7. $17 + 11 = \underline{\quad 11 \quad} + 17$ *commutative*

8. $(x + 6) + y = x + (6 + \underline{\quad\quad})$ *associative*

9. $39 + 14 = \underline{\quad\quad} + 39$ *commutative*

10. $(r + s) + t = t + (\underline{\quad\quad} + r)$ *associative*

11. $11 + 0 = \underline{\quad\quad}$ *additive identity*

12. $6 + (9 + 4) = (9 + \underline{\quad\quad}) + 6$ *associative*

13. $(2 + x) + p = \underline{\quad\quad} + (2 + x)$ *"*

14. $0 + 8 = 8 + \underline{\quad\quad}$ *commutative*

15. $p + m + (r + q) = p + (m + \underline{\quad\quad}) + q$ *associative*

16. $10 + 6 + 7 = 7 + 6 + \underline{\quad\quad}$ *"*

17. $\underline{\quad\quad} + 21 = 21$ *additive identy*

18. $(a + c + d) + e = e + (a + \underline{\quad\quad} + d)$ *ass*

19. $3 + 0 = 0 + \underline{\quad\quad}$ *com*

20. $2 + (x + y) + 4 = 2 + \underline{\quad\quad} + (y + 4)$ *ass*

Work with a partner. Check what you have learned. Review what you need help with.

1. addition ☐
2. plus ☐
3. equals ☐
4. sum ☐
5. addends ☐

6. Commutative Property of Addition ☐
7. parentheses, ( ) ☐
8. Associative Property of Addition ☐
9. Additive Identity Property of Addition ☐

Exercise 7

On a separate sheet of paper, add the following numbers.

1. $7 + 3 + 2 =$ _12_
2. $9 + 6 + 4 =$
3. $1 + 6 + 3 =$
4. $2 + 8 + 7 =$
5. $6 + 5 + 2 =$
6. $4 + 3 + 2 + 5 =$
7. $3 + 6 + 7 + 2 =$
8. $1 + 9 + 5 + 4 =$

9. $6 + 3 + 7 + 2 =$
10. $8 + 5 + 2 + 6 =$
11. $4 + 7 + 8 + 9 =$
12. $8 + 2 + 7 + 2 =$
13. $3 + 6 + 6 + 3 =$
14. $9 + 2 + 1 + 5 =$
15. $2 + 7 + 8 + 4 =$
16. $6 + 7 + 8 + 5 =$

17. 23
   + 15

18. 45
   + 23

19. 16
   + 31

20. 32
   + 67

21. 16
   + 3

22. 87
   + 12

23. 21
   + 43

24. 46
   + 32

25. 73
   + 15

26. 82
   + 23

27. 233
   + 142

28. 426
   + 132

29. 127
   + 542

30. 567
   + 121

31. 343
   + 211

32. 361
   + 215

33. 123
   210
   + 734

34. 303
   124
   + 432

35. 625
   231
   + 113

36. 326
   431
   + 131

37.	110	41.	531	45.	1,233	49.	30,133
	454		120		2,412		2,425
	+ 135		+ 243		+ 3,211		+ 1,211

38.	306	42.	422	46.	2,534	50.	23,334
	210		511		1,233		+ 1,422
	+ 153		+ 222		+ 5,122		

39.	524	43.	743	47.	22,655
	231		102		24,211
	+ 242		+ 133		+ 13,122

40.	364	44.	320	48.	12,423
	122		335		2,422
	+ 410		+ 214		+ 1,131

4-5 Addition with Carrying

Some addition problems require **carrying**.

Example:

```
   43
+ 29
```

Add the numbers in the ones place: 3 + 9 = 12.
Write the 2 in the ones place and **carry** the 1 to the tens place.

```
  1
  43
+ 29
   2
```

Add the numbers in the tens place: 1 + 4 + 2 = 7.
Write the 7 in the tens place.

```
  1
  43
+ 29
  72
```

Example:

```
   345
+ 798
```

Add the numbers in the ones place: 5 + 8 = 13.
Write the 3 in the ones place and carry the 1 to the tens place.

```
   1
   345
+ 798
     3
```

Add the numbers in the tens place: 1 + 4 + 9 = 14.
Write the 4 in the tens place and carry the 1 to the
hundreds place.

```
  11
   345
+ 798
    43
```

Add the numbers in the hundreds place: 1 + 3 + 7 = 11.
Write the digits in the hundreds and thousands places.

```
  11
   345
+ 798
 1,143
```

44

Exercise 8

On a separate sheet of paper, add the following numbers.

1. $\begin{array}{r} 54 \\ + 95 \\ \hline 149 \end{array}$

2. $\begin{array}{r} 67 \\ + 45 \\ \hline \end{array}$

3. $\begin{array}{r} 99 \\ + 99 \\ \hline \end{array}$

4. $\begin{array}{r} 38 \\ + 92 \\ \hline \end{array}$

5. $\begin{array}{r} 89 \\ + 98 \\ \hline \end{array}$

6. $\begin{array}{r} 18 \\ + 36 \\ \hline \end{array}$

7. $\begin{array}{r} 34 \\ + 78 \\ \hline \end{array}$

8. $\begin{array}{r} 75 \\ + 75 \\ \hline \end{array}$

9. $\begin{array}{r} 27 \\ + 66 \\ \hline \end{array}$

10. $\begin{array}{r} 456 \\ + 568 \\ \hline \end{array}$

11. $\begin{array}{r} 678 \\ + 877 \\ \hline \end{array}$

12. $\begin{array}{r} 943 \\ + 795 \\ \hline \end{array}$

13. $\begin{array}{r} 590 \\ + 888 \\ \hline \end{array}$

14. $\begin{array}{r} 357 \\ + 927 \\ \hline \end{array}$

15. $\begin{array}{r} 544 \\ + 878 \\ \hline \end{array}$

16. $\begin{array}{r} 909 \\ + 909 \\ \hline \end{array}$

17. $\begin{array}{r} 543 \\ 122 \\ + 822 \\ \hline \end{array}$

18. $\begin{array}{r} 465 \\ 134 \\ + 989 \\ \hline \end{array}$

19. $\begin{array}{r} 672 \\ 195 \\ + 458 \\ \hline \end{array}$

20. $\begin{array}{r} 930 \\ 155 \\ + 988 \\ \hline \end{array}$

21. $\begin{array}{r} 432 \\ 176 \\ + 903 \\ \hline \end{array}$

22. $\begin{array}{r} 767 \\ 388 \\ + 955 \\ \hline \end{array}$

23. $\begin{array}{r} 4,768 \\ 1,499 \\ + 4,576 \\ \hline \end{array}$

24. $\begin{array}{r} 5,722 \\ 1,877 \\ + 7,633 \\ \hline \end{array}$

25. $\begin{array}{r} 7,251 \\ 4,900 \\ + 8,123 \\ \hline \end{array}$

Exercise 9

On a separate sheet of paper, add the following numbers.

1. $64 + 159 + 307 + 14 = \underline{\quad 544 \quad}$

2. $195 + 36 + 2,496 =$

3. $849 + 1,566 + 82 =$

4. $1,927 + 349 + 211 =$

5. $607 + 94 + 8,422 =$

6. $7,431 + 3,206 + 11 + 419 =$

7. $644 + 72 + 1,899 =$

8. $14 + 267 + 396 =$

9. $611 + 924 + 3,264 =$

10. $98 + 88 + 329 + 11 =$

11. $521 + 2,314 + 101 =$

12. $7,327 + 2,433 + 95 =$

13. $693 + 4,207 + 143 =$

14. $27 + 869 + 39 + 492 =$

15. $9,366 + 321 + 4,070 =$

16. $10,322 + 8,011 + 694 =$

17. $175 + 13,012 + 96 =$

18. $429 + 7,863 + 345 =$

19. $16,500 + 399 + 4,631 =$

20. $7,053 + 29 + 398 =$

21. $587 + 3,779 + 348 =$

22. $19,011 + 5,468 + 13 =$

23. $6,344 + 19,993 + 27 =$

24. $782 + 9,399 + 4,711 =$

25. $624 + 20,316 + 1,047 =$

The words *altogether*, *total*, and *combined* in word problems tell us to use addition to solve the problems.

Example:

Yesterday, Rebecca worked 8 hours. Today, she worked 10 hours. How many hours did she work altogether?

The word *altogether* tells us that this is an addition problem. Therefore, we add the hours together.

$$\begin{array}{r} 8 \\ +10 \\ \hline 18 \end{array}$$

Rebecca worked 18 hours altogether.

Example:

Tyler's basketball team scored 34 points in the first game, 62 points in the second game, and 54 points in the third game. What was the total number of points the team scored? [OR What was the total score of the three games?]

The word *total* tells us that this is an addition problem. Therefore, we add the scores together.

$$\begin{array}{r} 34 \\ 62 \\ + 54 \\ \hline 150 \end{array}$$

Tyler's basketball team scored 150 points total.

Example:

Carmen needs school supplies. Books cost $35; pencils cost $4; pens cost $11; and notebook paper costs $15. What is the combined cost of the supplies?

The word *combined* tells us to add. Therefore, we add the costs of the supplies together.

$$\begin{array}{r} \$35 \\ 4 \\ 11 \\ + \ 15 \\ \hline \$65 \end{array}$$

The combined cost of the school supplies is $65.

A. Raymond Lopez is an eleventh-grade student at North Hills High School. There are students from Latin America, Europe, Asia, and the United States in his math class. Look at the chart below. Then answer the questions. Write your answers on the lines. Show all your work on a separate sheet of paper.

Raymond's Math Class				
	Latin America	**Asia**	**Europe**	**the United States**
Girls	8	3	2	5
Boys	6	5	1	7

1. Altogether, how many girls are there in Raymond's class? _____18_____

2. How many boys are there from Asia, Europe, and the United States? _____

3. Are there more students (boys and girls) from the United States or from Latin America? _____

4. How many students are there in the class altogether? _____

5. What is the total number of boys in the class? _____

B. In November, Raymond took four math tests. Look at the chart below. Then answer the questions. Write your answers on the lines. Show your work on a separate sheet of paper.

	Test 1	**Test 2**	**Test 3**	**Test 4**
Raymond's Scores	37	32	30	38
Total Possible Score	40	40	40	40

1. What is the total possible score for the first three tests combined? _____120_____

2. What is Raymond's combined test score for the first three tests? _____

3. Did Raymond do better on Test 2 or on Test 3? _____

4. Which test shows Raymond's highest score? _____

5. Which test shows Raymond's lowest score? _____

C. North Hills High School is a four-year high school. Look at the chart below on the student population. Then answer the questions. Write your answers on the lines. Show your work on a separate sheet of paper.

	Ninth Grade	**Tenth Grade**	**Eleventh Grade**	**Twelfth Grade**
Girls	340	336	249	235
Boys	377	322	325	268

1. How many boys and girls are there altogether in the . . .

a. ninth grade? _____717_____   **c.** eleventh grade? _____

b. tenth grade? _____   **d.** twelfth grade? _____

2. How many boys are there altogether in grades 9 through 12 (9, 10, 11, and 12)? _____

3. How many girls are there altogether in grades 9 through 12 (9, 10, 11, and 12)? _____

4. What is the total school population? _____

5. Which grade level has the . . .

   a. greatest number of students? _____

   b. least number of students? _____

Exercise 11

The seniors at North Hills High School take a class trip to Blackburn each year. North Hills High is located in Redmond City. Look at the map. Then answer the questions below. Write your answers on the lines. Show your work on a separate sheet of paper.

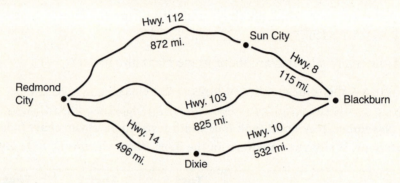

Hwy. = Highway
mi. = miles

1. There are three ways to travel from Redmond City to Blackburn:

Highway ____112____ and Highway ____8____

Highway _____

Highway _____ and Highway _____

2. How many miles do the students travel if they take . . .

   a. Highway 112 and Highway 8? _____

   b. Highway 103? _____

   c. Highway 14 and Highway 10? _____

3. Some of the students will travel from Redmond City to Sun City, and then to Blackburn. From Blackburn, they will go to Dixie. How many miles will they travel altogether from Redmond City? _____

4. How many miles is a round trip from Redmond City to Blackburn (on Highway 112 and Highway 8) and then back from Blackburn to Redmond City (on Highway 8 and Highway 112)? _____

5. How many miles is a round trip from Redmond City to Blackburn (on Highway 112 and Highway 8) and then back from Blackburn to Redmond City (on Highway 10 and Highway 14)? _____

Answer the questions for A., B., and C. below. Write your answers on the lines. Show your work on a separate sheet of paper.

A. Raymond's Math Club has 27 girls. There are 13 more boys than girls in the club.

1. How many boys are there in the Math Club? _____40_____

2. How many students are there altogether in the Math Club? _____

B. The Math Club has $67 to spend on items. Math books cost $13, math games cost $18, computer paper costs $24, and a calculator costs $23.

1. How much will the math books, math games, computer paper, and calculator cost altogether? _____

2. Do they have enough money to buy everything? _____

3. The students spent $55. What items did they buy? _____

_____

C. Each week, the students in Raymond's Math Club compete in computer math games. There are six teams of students. Look at the following total scores for each team.

	Team 1	Team 2	Team 3	Team 4	Team 5	Team 6
Week 1	13,246	12,499	5,294	10,324	8,020	10,244
Week 2	11,597	13,006	13,107	9,261	14,768	11,724
Week 3	12,698	5,772	13,624	14,920	6,492	12,324
Week 4	7,339	11,977	9,021	6,792	12,931	6,549

1. How many points did Team 2 score altogether in Weeks 1, 2, 3, and 4? _____

2. Look at Week 2. Which team scored the most points? _____

3. How many points did Team 4 score for the first two weeks? _____

4. Which team scored more points altogether—Team 4 or Team 5? _____

5. Which team scored more points in Weeks 2 and 3 combined—Team 1 or Team 4? _____

Exercise 1

On a separate sheet of paper, write the following addition problems using words.

1. $7 + 3 = 10$ **3.** $14 + 8 = 22$ **5.** $11 + 23 = 34$

2. $13 + 7 = 20$ **4.** $12 + 13 = 25$

Exercise 2

On a separate sheet of paper, add the following numbers.

1. $13 + 4 =$ **6.** $435 + 283 =$ **11.** $8,534 + 3,455 =$

2. $25 + 9 =$ **7.** $295 + 234 + 34 =$ **12.** $24,544 + 5,643 =$

3. $46 + 12 =$ **8.** $803 + 67 + 21 =$ **13.** $34,551 + 3,500 =$

4. $57 + 11 =$ **9.** $1,256 + 382 =$ **14.** $867,773 + 243,775 =$

5. $96 + 47 =$ **10.** $7,355 + 466 + 89 =$ **15.** $35,488 + 2,344 + 144 =$

Exercise 3

On a separate sheet of paper, write the name of the property shown—commutative, associative, or additive identity.

1. $4 + 3 = 3 + 4$ **4.** $m + (r + q) = (m + r) + q$

2. $0 + 19 = 19$ **5.** $(s + t + x) + w = w + (s + t + x)$

3. $8 + (3 + 2) = (8 + 3) + 2$

Exercise 4

Erica works in a bookstore. She sells both books and magazines. Look at her sales for one week below. Then answer the questions.

	Monday	**Tuesday**	**Wednesday**	**Thursday**	**Friday**
Books	29	16	33	14	68
Magazines	23	45	17	33	58

1. How many books did she sell in the first three days? (Monday, Tuesday, and Wednesday)

2. How many magazines did she sell altogether? _____

3. Did she sell more books or magazines on Tuesday? _____

4. How many books did she sell altogether? _____

5. What is the total number of books and magazines Erica sold for the week? _____

CHAPTER 5 Subtraction

5-1 Language of Subtraction

Look at the following **subtraction** problem.

$7 - 2 = 5$

We say: "Seven **minus** two **equals** five."

The **difference** is 5. The **minuend** is 7. The **subtrahend** is 2.

What is the difference of 8 and 5? The difference of 8 and 5 is 3.

Exercise 1

Complete each sentence. Write the correct word or words.

1. The _____ difference _____ of nine and three is six. *minuend - subtrahend*

2. Six _____ minus _____ four equals two.

3. Ten minus five _____ equals _____ five.

4. The difference of eleven and seven is _____.

5. Fifteen _____ minus _____ five _____ equals _____ ten.

6. The _____ difference _____ of twelve and six _____ is _____ six. *minuend - subtrahend*

7. Eighteen _____ nine _____ nine.

8. _____ minus six equals two.

9. The difference of thirteen and six is _____.

10. Twenty-four _____ twenty _____ four.

Exercise 2

Answer each question. Write the correct number word.

1. What is the difference of eight and two? _____ six _____

2. What is the difference of seven and six? _____

3. What is the difference of nineteen and ten? _____

4. What is the difference of fifteen and nine? _____

5. What is the difference of eleven and eleven? _____

6. What is the difference of eighteen and zero? _____

7. What is the difference of thirty-one and five? _____

8. What is the difference of sixty-four and twenty? _____

9. What is the difference of thirty-three and eight? _____

10. What is the difference of ninety and eighty? _____

Exercise 3

On a separate sheet of paper, write the following subtraction problems using words.

1. $7 - 4 = 3$ _Seven minus four equals three._

   OR _The difference of seven and four is three._

2. $15 - 5 = 10$

3. $11 - 3 = 8$

4. $27 - 4 = 23$

5. $47 - 7 = 40$

6. $15 - 15 = 0$

7. $95 - 10 = 85$

8. $73 - 6 = 67$

9. $52 - 12 = 40$

10. $12 - 0 = 12$

Exercise 4

For each subtraction problem, write the minuend, subtrahend, and difference.

1. $12 - 8 = 4$ minuend: _12_   subtrahend: _8_   difference: _4_

2. $18 - 3 = 15$ minuend: ____   subtrahend: ____   difference: ____

3. $19 - 9 = 10$ minuend: ____   subtrahend: ____   difference: ____

4. $13 - 0 = 13$ minuend: ____   subtrahend: ____   difference: ____

5. $14 - 4 = 10$ minuend: ____   subtrahend: ____   difference: ____

5-2 Subtraction of Whole Numbers

How do we subtract **whole numbers**? Look at the following problem.

$$
\begin{array}{r}
7\,4 \\
-3\,2 \\
\hline
\end{array}
$$

We subtract the numbers in the ones place: $4 - 2 = 2$.
We write the 2 in the ones place.

$$
\begin{array}{r}
7\,4 \\
-3\,2 \\
\hline
2
\end{array}
$$

We subtract the numbers in the tens place: $7 - 3 = 4$.
We write the 4 in the tens place.

$$
\begin{array}{r}
7\,4 \\
-3\,2 \\
\hline
4\,2
\end{array}
$$

To check our answer, we add the difference (42) to the subtrahend (32). The sum should equal the minuend (74).

$$
\begin{array}{r}
7\,4 \\
-\;3\,2 \\
\hline
4\,2 \\
+\;3\,2 \\
\hline
7\,4
\end{array}
$$

Exercise 5

On a separate sheet of paper, subtract the following numbers. Check your answers by adding.

1. $13 - 7 = \underline{\quad 6 \quad}$

2. $11 - 4 =$

3. $18 - 6 =$

4. $14 - 7 =$

5. $12 - 6 =$

6. $11 - 7 =$

7. $15 - 8 =$

8. $18 - 9 =$

9. $12 - 4 =$

10. $11 - 9 =$

11. $10 - 6 =$

12. $15 - 6 =$

13. $13 - 8 =$

14. $16 - 9 =$

15. $17 - 8 =$

16. $15 - 7 =$

17. $\begin{array}{r}13\\-\;2\\\hline\end{array}$	23. $\begin{array}{r}75\\-\;24\\\hline\end{array}$	29. $\begin{array}{r}467\\-\;302\\\hline\end{array}$	35. $\begin{array}{r}459\\-\;354\\\hline\end{array}$	41. $\begin{array}{r}977\\-\;153\\\hline\end{array}$	47. $\begin{array}{r}967\\-\;825\\\hline\end{array}$
18. $\begin{array}{r}34\\-\;3\\\hline\end{array}$	24. $\begin{array}{r}87\\-\;64\\\hline\end{array}$	30. $\begin{array}{r}948\\-\;732\\\hline\end{array}$	36. $\begin{array}{r}966\\-\;833\\\hline\end{array}$	42. $\begin{array}{r}757\\-\;245\\\hline\end{array}$	48. $\begin{array}{r}753\\-\;520\\\hline\end{array}$
19. $\begin{array}{r}95\\-\;4\\\hline\end{array}$	25. $\begin{array}{r}36\\-\;21\\\hline\end{array}$	31. $\begin{array}{r}549\\-\;338\\\hline\end{array}$	37. $\begin{array}{r}784\\-\;320\\\hline\end{array}$	43. $\begin{array}{r}820\\-\;310\\\hline\end{array}$	49. $\begin{array}{r}223\\-\;111\\\hline\end{array}$
20. $\begin{array}{r}85\\-\;3\\\hline\end{array}$	26. $\begin{array}{r}54\\-\;44\\\hline\end{array}$	32. $\begin{array}{r}677\\-\;321\\\hline\end{array}$	38. $\begin{array}{r}741\\-\;620\\\hline\end{array}$	44. $\begin{array}{r}563\\-\;111\\\hline\end{array}$	50. $\begin{array}{r}587\\-\;124\\\hline\end{array}$
21. $\begin{array}{r}98\\-\;2\\\hline\end{array}$	27. $\begin{array}{r}465\\-\;322\\\hline\end{array}$	33. $\begin{array}{r}784\\-\;643\\\hline\end{array}$	39. $\begin{array}{r}688\\-\;521\\\hline\end{array}$	45. $\begin{array}{r}888\\-\;666\\\hline\end{array}$	
22. $\begin{array}{r}56\\-\;22\\\hline\end{array}$	28. $\begin{array}{r}957\\-\;244\\\hline\end{array}$	34. $\begin{array}{r}653\\-\;253\\\hline\end{array}$	40. $\begin{array}{r}762\\-\;632\\\hline\end{array}$	46. $\begin{array}{r}743\\-\;312\\\hline\end{array}$	

Some subtraction problems require **borrowing**.

Example:

$$43$$
$$-18$$

Look at the numbers in the ones place. We cannot subtract 8 from 3. We must borrow from the tens place. The 4 in the tens place tells us that there are 4 tens. We borrow 1 ten, or 10, leaving 3 in the tens place.

$$\begin{array}{r} \overset{3}{\cancel{4}}\,3 \\ -1\,8 \end{array}$$

We add 10 + 3 (10 that we borrowed plus 3 in the ones place). 10 + 3 = 13.

$$\begin{array}{r} \overset{3}{\cancel{4}}\,\overset{13}{\cancel{3}} \\ -1\,8 \end{array}$$

Now we can subtract. 13 − 8 = 5. We write the 5 in the ones place. 3 − 1 = 2. We write the 2 in the tens place. The answer is 25.

$$\begin{array}{r} \overset{3}{\cancel{4}}\,\overset{13}{\cancel{3}} \\ -1\,8 \\ \hline 2\,5 \end{array}$$

We check our answer by adding the difference (25) to the subtrahend (18). The sum should equal the minuend (43).

$$\begin{array}{r} 43 \\ -1\,8 \\ \hline 2\,5 \\ +1\,8 \\ \hline 4\,3 \end{array}$$

Example:

$$326$$
$$-168$$

Look at the numbers in the ones place. We cannot subtract 8 from 6. We must borrow 1 ten, or 10, from the tens place, leaving 1 ten.
We add the 10 to 6 in the ones place. 10 + 6 = 16
We subtract 8 from 16. 16 − 8 = 8

$$\begin{array}{r} \overset{1}{3}\,\overset{16}{\cancel{2}}\,\cancel{6} \\ -1\,6\,8 \\ \hline 8 \end{array}$$

Look at the numbers in the tens place. We cannot subtract 6 tens from 1 ten. We must borrow 1 hundred (or 10 tens) from the hundreds place, leaving 2 hundreds. We add 10 + 1 (10 that we borrowed plus 1 in the tens place). 10 + 1 = 11.

$$\begin{array}{r} \overset{2}{\cancel{3}}\,\overset{11}{\cancel{2}}\,\overset{16}{\cancel{6}} \\ -1\,6\,8 \\ \hline 8 \end{array}$$

We subtract 6 from 11. We write the 5 in the tens place. 2 − 1 = 1. We write the 1 in the hundreds place. The answer is 158.

$$\begin{array}{r} \overset{2}{\cancel{3}}\,\overset{11}{\cancel{2}}\,\overset{16}{\cancel{6}} \\ -1\,6\,8 \\ \hline 1\,5\,8 \end{array}$$

We then check our answer:

$$
\begin{array}{r}
3\,2\,6 \\
-\,1\,6\,8 \\
\hline
1\,5\,8 \\
+\,1\,6\,8 \\
\hline
3\,2\,6
\end{array}
$$

Exercise 6

On a separate sheet of paper, subtract the following numbers. Check your answers by adding.

1. $\overset{4\;14}{\cancel{54}}$
    $-\ \ 8$
    $\overline{\ 46\ }$

2. 73
    $-\ \ 7$

3. 62
    $-\ \ 9$

4. 91
    $-\ 77$

5. 53
    $-\ \ 8$

6. 83
    $-\ 49$

7. 94
    $-\ 78$

8. 71
    $-\ 59$

9. 35
    $-\ 16$

10. 82
    $-\ 36$

11. 96
    $-\ 79$

12. 54
    $-\ 39$

13. 544
    $-\ 288$

14. 621
    $-\ 307$

15. 534
    $-\ 329$

16. 922
    $-\ 688$

17. 617
    $-\ 499$

18. 411
    $-\ 377$

19. 525
    $-\ 489$

20. 541
    $-\ 337$

Exercise 7

On a separate sheet of paper, subtract the following numbers. Check your answers by adding.

1. $921 - 699 = \underline{\ 222\ }$

2. $523 - 376 =$

3. $471 - 188 =$

4. $233 - 127 =$

5. $412 - 289 =$

6. $311 - 278 =$

7. $345 - 67 =$

8. $287 - 109 =$

9. $714 - 575 =$

10. $342 - 77 =$

11. $511 - 78 =$

12. $476 - 183 =$

13. $245 - 67 =$

14. $123 - 56 =$

15. $2,541 - 866 =$

On a separate sheet of paper, subtract the following numbers. Check your answers by adding.

1.
$$
\begin{array}{r}
^{12}\!\!\!\!\!\!\!\!\!\!\!\! \\
^{3\,2\,13}\!\!\!\!\!\!\!\! \\
4\cancel{3}\cancel{3} \\
-\ 2\,6\,4 \\
\hline
1\,6\,9
\end{array}
$$

6.
$$
\begin{array}{r}
4,343 \\
-\ 1,879 \\
\hline
\end{array}
$$

11.
$$
\begin{array}{r}
32,471 \\
-\ 20,488 \\
\hline
\end{array}
$$

16.
$$
\begin{array}{r}
961,833 \\
-\ 171,566 \\
\hline
\end{array}
$$

2.
$$
\begin{array}{r}
321 \\
-\ 199 \\
\hline
\end{array}
$$

7.
$$
\begin{array}{r}
6,433 \\
-\ 2,799 \\
\hline
\end{array}
$$

12.
$$
\begin{array}{r}
45,381 \\
-\ 13,866 \\
\hline
\end{array}
$$

17.
$$
\begin{array}{r}
129,863 \\
-\ 49,127 \\
\hline
\end{array}
$$

3.
$$
\begin{array}{r}
743 \\
-\ 298 \\
\hline
\end{array}
$$

8.
$$
\begin{array}{r}
8,111 \\
-\ 7,277 \\
\hline
\end{array}
$$

13.
$$
\begin{array}{r}
67,122 \\
-\ 34,784 \\
\hline
\end{array}
$$

18.
$$
\begin{array}{r}
457,218 \\
-\ 70,651 \\
\hline
\end{array}
$$

4.
$$
\begin{array}{r}
6,822 \\
-\ 2,767 \\
\hline
\end{array}
$$

9.
$$
\begin{array}{r}
23,451 \\
-\ 19,376 \\
\hline
\end{array}
$$

14.
$$
\begin{array}{r}
37,811 \\
-\ 28,733 \\
\hline
\end{array}
$$

19.
$$
\begin{array}{r}
864,218 \\
-\ 438,628 \\
\hline
\end{array}
$$

5.
$$
\begin{array}{r}
3,512 \\
-\ 1,287 \\
\hline
\end{array}
$$

10.
$$
\begin{array}{r}
75,624 \\
-\ 56,766 \\
\hline
\end{array}
$$

15.
$$
\begin{array}{r}
125,677 \\
-\ 45,877 \\
\hline
\end{array}
$$

20.
$$
\begin{array}{r}
499,321 \\
-\ 89,555 \\
\hline
\end{array}
$$

On a separate sheet of paper, subtract the following numbers. Check your answers by adding.

1. $6,379 - 265 = \underline{6,114}$

2. $55,862 - 4,741 =$

3. $987,695 - 5,384 =$

4. $579,456 - 7,222 =$

5. $682,975 - 31,231 =$

6. $356,742 - 45,320 =$

7. $3,122 - 373 =$

8. $45,677 - 2,338 =$

9. $12,339 - 2,778 =$

10. $3,544 - 1,879 =$

11. $456,921 - 3,876 =$

12. $12,512 - 9,455 =$

13. $17,433 - 9,877 =$

14. $143,566,112 - 45,677 =$

15. $1,243,123 - 997,987 =$

5-4 Subtraction with Borrowing from Zeros

Some subtraction problems require borrowing from zeros.

Example:

$$
\begin{array}{r}
3\ 0\ 2 \\
-\ 1\ 8\ 5 \\
\hline
\end{array}
$$

Look at the numbers in the ones place. We cannot subtract 5 from 2. We cannot borrow from the tens place (0), so we must borrow 1 hundred from the hundreds place (10 tens) first and add it to the tens place.

$$
\begin{array}{r}
^{2}\ ^{10} \\
\cancel{3}\ \cancel{0}\ 2 \\
-\ 1\ 8\ 5 \\
\hline
\end{array}
$$

Now we can borrow 1 ten (10 ones) from the tens place, leaving 9 tens. We add 10 + 2 (10 that we borrowed plus 2 in the ones place). 10 + 2 = 12.

$$\begin{array}{r} \overset{\scriptscriptstyle 9}{\cancel{3}}\,\overset{\scriptscriptstyle 10}{\cancel{0}}\,\overset{\scriptscriptstyle 12}{\cancel{2}} \\ -1\,8\,5 \\ \hline \end{array}$$

We subtract 5 from 12 in the ones place. 12 − 5 = 7
We subtract 8 from 9 in the tens place. 9 − 8 = 1
We subtract 1 from 2 in the hundreds place. 2 − 1 = 1
The answer is 117.

$$\begin{array}{r} \overset{\scriptscriptstyle 9}{\cancel{3}}\,\overset{\scriptscriptstyle 10}{\cancel{0}}\,\overset{\scriptscriptstyle 12}{\cancel{2}} \\ -1\,8\,5 \\ \hline 1\,1\,7 \end{array}$$

We then check our answer.

$$\begin{array}{r} 3\,0\,2 \\ -1\,8\,5 \\ \hline 1\,1\,7 \\ +1\,8\,5 \\ \hline 3\,0\,2 \end{array}$$

Example:

$$\begin{array}{r} 6\,,0\,0\,0 \\ -\quad 3\,5\,8 \\ \hline \end{array}$$

We cannot subtract 8 from 0 in the ones place. We cannot borrow from the tens or hundreds places. We must borrow 1 thousand (10 hundreds) from the thousands place and add it to the hundreds place.

$$\begin{array}{r} \overset{\scriptscriptstyle 5}{\cancel{6}}\,,\overset{\scriptscriptstyle 10}{\cancel{0}}\,0\,0 \\ -\quad 3\,5\,8 \\ \hline \end{array}$$

Now we borrow 1 hundred (10 tens) from the hundreds place, leaving 9 hundreds, and add it to the tens place.

$$\begin{array}{r} \overset{\scriptscriptstyle 5}{\cancel{6}}\,,\overset{\scriptscriptstyle 9}{\cancel{0}}\,\overset{\scriptscriptstyle 10}{\cancel{0}}\,0 \\ -\quad 3\,5\,8 \\ \hline \end{array}$$

Then we borrow 1 ten (10 ones) from the tens place, leaving 9 tens, and add it to the ones place. We subtract the numbers, and the answer is 5,642.

$$\begin{array}{r} \overset{\scriptscriptstyle 5}{\cancel{6}}\,,\overset{\scriptscriptstyle 9}{\cancel{0}}\,\overset{\scriptscriptstyle 9}{\cancel{0}}\,\overset{\scriptscriptstyle 10}{\cancel{0}} \\ -\quad 3\,5\,8 \\ \hline 5\,,6\,4\,2 \end{array}$$

We then check our answer.

$$\begin{array}{r} 6\,,0\,0\,0 \\ -\quad 3\,5\,8 \\ \hline 5\,,6\,4\,2 \\ +\quad 3\,5\,8 \\ \hline 6\,,0\,0\,0 \end{array}$$

On a separate sheet of paper, subtract the following numbers. Check your answers by adding.

1.
$$\begin{array}{r} {}^{3\,10} \\ 4\!\!\!/0 \\ -\,19 \\ \hline 21 \end{array}$$

8.
$$\begin{array}{r} 800 \\ -\,356 \\ \hline \end{array}$$

14.
$$\begin{array}{r} 5{,}000 \\ -\,2{,}896 \\ \hline \end{array}$$

20.
$$\begin{array}{r} 2{,}006 \\ -\,1{,}888 \\ \hline \end{array}$$

2.
$$\begin{array}{r} 30 \\ -\,13 \\ \hline \end{array}$$

9.
$$\begin{array}{r} 200 \\ -\,138 \\ \hline \end{array}$$

15.
$$\begin{array}{r} 4{,}002 \\ -\,3{,}827 \\ \hline \end{array}$$

21.
$$\begin{array}{r} 3{,}070 \\ -\,1{,}664 \\ \hline \end{array}$$

3.
$$\begin{array}{r} 700 \\ -\,212 \\ \hline \end{array}$$

10.
$$\begin{array}{r} 301 \\ -\,187 \\ \hline \end{array}$$

16.
$$\begin{array}{r} 2{,}000 \\ -\,1{,}987 \\ \hline \end{array}$$

22.
$$\begin{array}{r} 51{,}007 \\ -\,7{,}668 \\ \hline \end{array}$$

4.
$$\begin{array}{r} 90 \\ -\,48 \\ \hline \end{array}$$

11.
$$\begin{array}{r} 502 \\ -\,284 \\ \hline \end{array}$$

17.
$$\begin{array}{r} 6{,}001 \\ -\,5{,}992 \\ \hline \end{array}$$

23.
$$\begin{array}{r} 27{,}103 \\ -\,17{,}195 \\ \hline \end{array}$$

5.
$$\begin{array}{r} 906 \\ -\,537 \\ \hline \end{array}$$

12.
$$\begin{array}{r} 700 \\ -\,484 \\ \hline \end{array}$$

18.
$$\begin{array}{r} 5{,}020 \\ -\,3{,}887 \\ \hline \end{array}$$

24.
$$\begin{array}{r} 623{,}400 \\ -\,551{,}982 \\ \hline \end{array}$$

6.
$$\begin{array}{r} 600 \\ -\,156 \\ \hline \end{array}$$

13.
$$\begin{array}{r} 4{,}704 \\ -\,2{,}439 \\ \hline \end{array}$$

19.
$$\begin{array}{r} 8{,}000 \\ -\,2{,}799 \\ \hline \end{array}$$

25.
$$\begin{array}{r} 700{,}000 \\ -\,643{,}797 \\ \hline \end{array}$$

7.
$$\begin{array}{r} 505 \\ -\,499 \\ \hline \end{array}$$

On a separate sheet of paper, subtract the following numbers. Check your answers by adding.

1. $300 - 176 = \underline{124}$

2. $400 - 287 =$

3. $5{,}400 - 2{,}367 =$

4. $340{,}800 - 2{,}367 =$

5. $4{,}000 - 3{,}892 =$

6. $5{,}090 - 765 =$

7. $1{,}900{,}000 - 8{,}211 =$

8. $700{,}090 - 3{,}716 =$

9. $30{,}000 - 4{,}728 =$

10. $5{,}300{,}000 - 654{,}677 =$

5-5 Inverse Operations

Addition and subtraction are **inverse operations (opposite operations).**

Subtraction	Inverse Operation of Addition
$5 - 3 = 2$	$2 + 3 = 5$
$12 - 9 = 3$	$3 + 9 = 12$

In Exercises 5 through 11, we used the **inverse operation of subtraction** to check our answers.

Example:

$$\begin{array}{r} 12 \\ -\ 8 \\ \hline 4 \end{array}$$ We check by inverse operation. $$\begin{array}{r} 8 \\ +\ 4 \\ \hline 12 \end{array}$$

Exercise 12

Check each problem below by writing the inverse operation.

1. $6 - 5 = 1$ ___ *1 + 5 = 6* ___   **6.** $24 - 18 = 6$ _____

2. $8 - 3 = 5$ _____   **7.** $13 - 13 = 0$ _____

3. $11 - 6 = 5$ _____   **8.** $23 - 1 = 22$ _____

4. $12 - 6 = 6$ _____   **9.** $14 - 8 = 6$ _____

5. $8 - 0 = 8$ _____   **10.** $16 - 10 = 6$ _____

5-6 Using Inverse Operations to Find Missing Numbers

We can use inverse operations to find missing numbers.

Example:

_____ $-\ 4 = 7$

We use the inverse operation:

$7 + 4 = 11$

Answer: ___ *11* ___ $-\ 4 = 7$

Exercise 13

On a separate sheet of paper, use the inverse operation to find the missing numbers.

1. ___ *17* ___ $-\ 4 = 13$ **8.** _____ $-\ 35 = 198$ **15.** _____ $-\ 122 = 768$

2. _____ $-\ 6 = 22$ **9.** _____ $-\ 22 = 104$ **16.** _____ $-\ 521 = 673$

3. _____ $-\ 9 = 29$ **10.** _____ $-\ 54 = 94$ **17.** _____ $-\ 744 = 0$

4. _____ $-\ 5 = 33$ **11.** _____ $-\ 67 = 345$ **18.** _____ $-\ 291 = 291$

5. _____ $-\ 13 = 44$ **12.** _____ $-\ 76 = 399$ **19.** _____ $-\ 10 = 99$

6. _____ $-\ 10 = 57$ **13.** _____ $-\ 25 = 450$ **20.** _____ $-\ 0 = 500$

7. _____ $-\ 26 = 68$ **14.** _____ $-\ 0 = 399$

Example:

We can use the inverse operation to find the missing number.

12 + _____ = 15

We use the inverse operation.

15 − 12 = 3

Answer: 12 + __3__ = 15

Exercise 14

On a separate sheet of paper, use the inverse operation to find the missing numbers.

1. 5 + __9__ = 14
2. 11 + _____ = 34
3. 9 + _____ = 22
4. 13 + _____ = 36
5. 24 + _____ = 44
6. _____ + 12 = 55
7. _____ + 67 = 87

8. 45 + _____ = 45
9. _____ + 66 = 156
10. _____ + 35 = 129
11. 89 + _____ = 213
12. 76 + _____ = 166
13. _____ + 188 = 412
14. _____ + 106 = 339

15. 88 + _____ = 631
16. 377 + _____ = 599
17. _____ + 433 = 967
18. 562 + _____ = 1,584
19. _____ + 371 = 2,492
20. 899 + _____ = 3,565

Exercise 15

On a separate sheet of paper, use the inverse operation to find the missing numbers.

1. 34 + __14__ = 48
2. _____ − 15 = 39
3. _____ + 56 = 78
4. 67 + _____ = 125
5. _____ − 56 = 27
6. 78 + _____ = 78
7. _____ − 124 = 0
8. _____ + 92 = 381
9. _____ − 67 = 53

10. 377 + _____ = 935
11. _____ + 271 = 271
12. _____ − 655 = 1,298
13. _____ + 874 = 2,366
14. _____ − 377 = 872
15. 982 + _____ = 5,499
16. 873 + _____ = 984
17. _____ − 659 = 0

18. _____ − 3,455 = 365
19. 721 + _____ = 1,344
20. 988 + _____ = 988
21. _____ − 734 = 21
22. _____ + 1,569 = 4,578
23. _____ − 312 = 312
24. _____ − 937 = 0
25. _____ − 0 = 1,042

60

Complete the sentences below. Use the words in the box.

minuend	subtrahend	addends
plus	inverse	sum
associative	commutative	subtraction
minus	additive identity	

1. The _____ *sum* _____ is the answer to an addition problem.

2. We read "+" as _____.

3. 6 + 2 = 2 + 6 is an example of the _____ property.

4. In a _____ problem, the answer is called the difference.

5. Twelve _____ ten equals two.

6. The numbers that we add together are called _____.

7. In 8 − 5 = 3, the number 8 is the _____ and the

   number 5 is the _____.

8. (7 + 3) + 1 = 7 + (3 + 1) is an example of the _____ property.

9. The _____ operation of 5 − 3 = 2 is 3 + 2 = 5.

10. 7 + 0 = 7 is an example of the _____ property.

Have I Learned? (✓)

Work with a partner. Check what you have learned. Review what you need help with.

1. subtraction ☐
2. minus ☐
3. equals ☐
4. difference ☐
5. minuend ☐
6. subtrahend ☐

7. whole numbers ☐
8. borrowing ☐
9. borrowing from zeros ☐
10. inverse operations ☐
11. inverse operation of addition ☐
12. inverse operation of subtraction ☐

The words *how many more, difference,* and *left* in word problems tell us to use subtraction to solve the problems.

Example:

Jason got 23 words correct on Thursday's spelling test. He got 32 words correct on Friday's spelling test. How many more words did he get correct on Friday?

The words *how many more* tell us that this is a subtraction problem. Therefore, we subtract to solve the problem.

$$\begin{array}{r} 3\,2 \\ -\,2\,3 \\ \hline 9 \end{array}$$

Jason got 9 more words correct on Friday.

Example:

Mr. Lee drove 1,245 miles last year. He drove 1,987 miles this year. What is the difference in miles between this year and last year.

The word *difference* tells us to subtract.

$$\begin{array}{r} 1\,,9\,8\,7 \\ -\,1\,,2\,4\,5 \\ \hline 7\,4\,2 \end{array}$$

The difference in miles between this year and last year is 742.

Example:

Janell had $53 to spend on new clothes. She spent $34. How much money did she have left?

The word *left* tells us to subtract.

$$\begin{array}{r} \$\,5\,3 \\ -\,\quad 3\,4 \\ \hline \$\,1\,9 \end{array}$$

Janell had $19 left.

Exercise 17

First, read each problem. Then underline the word or words that tell you to subtract. Last, solve the problem on a separate sheet of paper. Write the answer on the line.

1. Emmi is 18 years old. Her grandfather is 78 years old. How much younger is Emmi than her grandfather? ___*60 years*___

2. Trevor's horse weighs 1,456 pounds. His dog weighs 47 pounds. What is the difference in their weights? _____

3. Paula's used car cost $8,500. Tami's used car cost $6,800. How much more did Paula pay than Tami? _____

4. Hiroshi had $25 to spend. He bought a model car for $6, a football for $8, and a baseball bat for $9. How much money did he have left? _____

5. The Turners want to buy a television set. Television set A costs $175. Television set B costs $245. If they buy television set A, how much less will they pay? _____

Exercise 18

Isabel and her class attended their school's book fair last week. Look at the illustration and the chart about the fair below. Then answer the questions on the next page. Write your answers on the lines. Show your work on a separate sheet of paper.

South Shore High School Book Fair	
Types of Books	**Number Sold**
Novels	12
Mysteries	10
Biographies	16
Autobiographies	14
History	7
Poetry	3
Children's	6
Science	4
Reference	2
Science fiction	15
Sports	20
Short-story	5

1. Compare the biographies with the novels. How many more biographies than novels were sold? _____4_____

2. Compare the sports books with the biographies. How many more sports books than biographies were sold? _____

3. What kind of books sold the most? _____

4. The school started out with 37 sports books. How many were sold? How many were left? _____

5. The school started out with 18 short-story books. How many were sold? How many were left? _____

6. How many autobiographies, biographies, and history books were sold altogether? _____

7. The school started out with 25 science books. How many were sold? How many were left? _____

8. How many novels and short-story books were sold altogether? _____

9. How many more sports books than science fiction books were sold? _____

10. How many more novels than poetry books were sold? _____

Exercise 19

The James Madison High School basketball team played eight games last year. Look at the chart with their scores on the next page. Then answer the questions. Write your answers on the lines. Show your work on a separate sheet of paper.

Game	James Madison High School's Scores	Opponents' Scores
1	57	48
2	65	73
3	42	48
4	75	60
5	39	64
6	52	45
7	60	51
8	58	32

1. Which games did James Madison High School win? _____ *Games 1, 4, 6, 7, 8* _____

2. Which games did James Madison High School lose? _____

3. In which game was James Madison High's score the highest? _____

4. In which game was James Madison High's score the lowest? _____

5. Look at Game 2. What is the point difference between James Madison High and the opponent? _____

6. Look at Game 3. What is the point difference between James Madison High and the opponent? _____

7. Look at Game 5. What is the point difference between James Madison High and the opponent? _____

8. In which game (Game 2, 3, or 5) is the point difference between James Madison High and the opponent the greatest? _____

9. In which game (Game 2, 3, or 5) is the point difference between James Madison High and the opponent the least? _____

10. Look at the scores for the five games that James Madison High won. What is the sum of those scores? _____

11. Look at the opponents' scores for the same five games. What is the sum of their scores? _____

12. How many more points did James Madison High make for those five games? _____

13. Compare Games 5 and 8. In which game (5 or 8) is the point difference greater? _____

14. Compare Games 4 and 6. In which game (4 or 6) is the point difference less? _____

15. Look at all the games. Which two games have equal point differences?
_____

CHAPTER REVIEW

Exercise 1

On a separate sheet of paper, write the following subtraction problems using words.

1. 6 − 2 = 4 <u>*Six minus two equals four.* OR</u>
<u>*The difference of six and two is four.*</u>

2. 15 − 5 = 10

3. 18 − 9 = 9

4. 28 − 7 = 21

5. 46 − 14 = 32

Exercise 2

On a separate sheet of paper, use the inverse operation to find the missing numbers.

1. 17 + _____ = 123

2. _____ + 201 = 342

3. _____ − 344 = 536

4. _____ − 23 = 79

5. 58 + _____ = 246

Exercise 3

On a separate sheet of paper, subtract the following numbers. Check your answers by adding.

1. 76 − 15 = <u>61</u>

2. 55 − 32 =

3. 278 − 132 =

4. 788 − 254 =

5. 34 − 27 =

6. 243 − 189 =

7. 543 − 289 =

8. 2,133 − 1,967 =

9. 123,834 − 2,875 =

10. 301 − 167 =

11. 200 − 175 =

12. 350 − 286 =

13. 1,200 − 388 =

14. 6,002 − 5,988 =

15. 354,000 − 276,988 =

Exercise 4

On a separate sheet of paper, solve the following problems. Write your answers on the lines.

1. Sarah bought three dozen eggs. While she was driving home, 17 eggs broke. How many eggs did she have left? <u>19</u>

2. Kim got 95 on her math test. Terry got 87. How many more points did Kim get than Terry? _____

3. Pauline jogged 48 miles last week. Her friend Megan jogged 39 miles. How many more miles did Pauline jog than Megan? _____

4. On Friday, 342 people attended the school concert. On Saturday, 415 people attended. How many more people attended the concert on Saturday than on Friday? _____

5. Anita has $72. If she buys a backpack for $30 and a wallet for $15, how much money will she have left? _____

CHAPTER 6 Multiplication

6-1 Language of Multiplication

Look at the following **multiplication** problem.

$4 \times 3 = 12$

We say: "Four **times** three **equals** twelve."

The **product** is 12. The **factors** are 4 and 3.

What is the product of 5 and 2? The product of 5 and 2 is 10.

Exercise 1

Complete each sentence. Write the correct word or words.

1. The _____product_____ of six and two is twelve.

2. Eight _____times_____ two equals sixteen.

3. The product of four and four is _____16_____.

4. Nine times two _____equals_____ eighteen.

5. Six _____times_____ six _____equals_____ thirty-six.

6. The _____product_____ of eight and three _____is_____ twenty-four.

7. _____3_____ times seven _____equals_____ twenty-one.

8. The product of _____3_____ and five is fifteen.

9. Five _____ nine _____ forty-five.

10. Four times _____ equals thirty-six.

Exercise 2

Answer each question. Write the correct number word.

1. What is the product of four and five? _____twenty_____

2. What is the product of nine and nine? _____

3. What is the product of eight and six? _____

4. What is the product of seven and nine? _____

5. What is the product of five and zero? _____

6. What is the product of three and nine? _____

7. What is the product of six and seven? _____

8. What is the product of seven and seven? _____

9. What is the product of two and four? _____

10. What is the product of eight and one? _____

Exercise 3

Write the following multiplication problems using words.

1. 4 × 3 = 12 _Four times three equals twelve._ OR
   The product of four and three is twelve.

2. 9 × 2 = 18 _____

3. 8 × 4 = 32 _____

4. 2 × 6 = 12 _____

5. 1 × 10 = 10 _____

6. 7 × 5 = 35 _____

7. 9 × 4 = 36 _____

8. 8 × 5 = 40 _____

9. 6 × 7 = 42 _____

10. 5 × 4 = 20 _____

Exercise 4

For each multiplication problem, write the factors and the product.

1. 6 × 8 = 48   factors: _6_ and _8_   product: _48_

2. 9 × 0 = 0   factors: ____ and ____   product: ____

3. 8 × 7 = 56   factors: ____ and ____   product: ____

4. 6 × 9 = 54   factors: ____ and ____   product: ____

5. 1 × 3 = 3   factors: ____ and ____   product: ____

6-2 Symbols for Multiplication ·····················

We can write multiplication problems in different ways. Look at the example below.

$$4 \times 3 \text{ or } 4 \cdot 3 \text{ or } (4)(3) \text{ or } 4(3) \text{ or } (4)3$$

Write each multiplication problem in two different ways.

1. 6×2 _6 · 2_ OR _(6)(2)_ OR _6(2)_
      OR _(6)2_

2. $5 \cdot 3$ _____

3. $(9)(4)$ _____

4. 14×2 _____

5. $8 \cdot 4 \cdot 2$ _____

6. $6(3)(2)$ _____

7. $4 \cdot 6$ _____

8. $25 \times 3 \times 2$ _____

9. $(18)4$ _____

10. $(11) \times (9)$ _____

6-3 Commutative Property of Multiplication

Look at the following problems.

$$2 \cdot 5 = 10 \qquad 5 \cdot 2 = 10$$

The products are equal.

$$2 \cdot 5 = 5 \cdot 2$$

The *order* of multiplying numbers does not change the product.

RULE:

We can multiply numbers in any order. For all numbers a and b: $a \cdot b = b \cdot a$.

6-4 Associative Property of Multiplication

We can group $2 \cdot 3 \cdot 4$ in the following ways.

$$(2 \cdot 3)4 = \qquad 2(3 \cdot 4) =$$

$$(6)4 = 24 \qquad 2(12) = 24$$

The products are equal.

RULE:

If we *group* three or more numbers in different ways and multiply them together, the product does not change. For all numbers a, b, and c: $(a \cdot b) c = a (b \cdot c)$.

6-5 Multiplicative Identity Property of Multiplication

Look at the following problems.

$$4 \cdot 1 = 4$$

$$17 \cdot 1 = 17$$

RULE:

Multiplying any number by 1 does not change the value of the number. For all numbers a: $a \cdot 1 = a$.

6-6 Multiplicative Property of Zero

Look at the following problems.

$$6 \cdot 0 = 0$$

$$23 \cdot 0 = 0$$

RULE:

Multiplying any number by zero makes the product zero. For all numbers a: $a \cdot 0 = 0$.

What does it mean to multiply a number by zero? Look at the example below.

Notebooks cost $2 each.   3 notebooks cost $2 \times 3 = \$6$
2 notebooks cost $2 \times 2 = \$4$
0 notebooks cost $2 \times 0 = \$0$

Exercise 6

First, write the missing number. Then write the property shown—commutative, associative, multiplicative identity, or multiplicative property of zero.

1. $4 \cdot 2 = 2 \cdot 4 =$ ___8___   _commutative_

2. $16 \cdot 1 =$ ____   _____

3. $(8 \cdot 3)$ ____ $= 8(3 \cdot 4)$ _____

4. $95 = 95 \cdot$ ____   _____

5. $19(4 \cdot 2) = 19(2 \cdot$ ____$)$ _____

6. $(11 \cdot 4)0 =$ ____   _____

7. $1 \cdot m =$ ____   _____

8. $(9 \cdot m)n =$ ____ $(m \cdot n)$ _____

9. $p \cdot$ ____ $= 0$ _____

10. $11(6 \cdot r) = 11(\underline{\hspace{1cm}} \cdot 6)$ _____

11. $12 \cdot 0 = \underline{\hspace{1cm}} \cdot 12$ _____

12. $s \cdot \underline{\hspace{1cm}} = s$ _____

13. $a(b)0 = \underline{\hspace{1cm}}$ _____

14. $(4 \cdot p) \cdot \underline{\hspace{1cm}} = c(4 \cdot p)$ _____

15. $b(c \cdot d) = (b \cdot c) \underline{\hspace{1cm}}$ _____

6-7 Distributive Property of Multiplication · · · · · · · · · · · · · · · · · ·

Look at the illustration below.

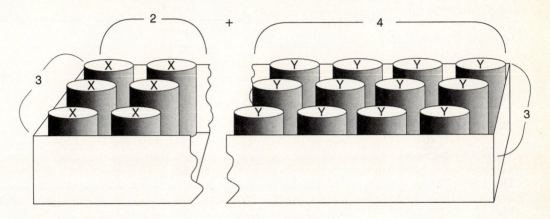

Altogether, there are $3(2 + 4) = 18$ cans. There are $3 \cdot 2 = 6x$ cans and $3 \cdot 4 = 12y$ cans. Therefore, . . .

$$3(2 + 4) = 3 \cdot 2 + 3 \cdot 4$$
$$3(6) = 6 + 12$$
$$18 = 18$$

This is an example of the distributive property of multiplication. Now look at the illustration below.

3 + 2

4 {●●● ○○} 4

Altogether, there are $4(3 + 2)$ circles. There are $4 \cdot 3$ black circles and $4 \cdot 2$ white circles. Therefore, . . .

$$4(3 + 2) = 4 \cdot 3 + 4 \cdot 2$$
$$4(5) = 12 + 8$$
$$20 = 20$$

71

RULE:

For all numbers *a*, *b*, and *c*: $a(b + c) = a \cdot b + a \cdot c$.

Exercise 7

Use the distributive property to complete the following problems. Use a separate sheet of paper, if necessary.

1. $8(2+4) =$ _____ $(8 \cdot 2) + (8 \cdot 4) = 16 + 32 = 48$ _____

2. $3(4 + 1) =$ _____

3. $9(6 + 2) =$ _____

4. $a(b + c) =$ _____

5. $(40 + 20)5 =$ _____

6. $7(m + n) =$ _____

7. $(6 \cdot 3) + (6 \cdot 2) =$ _____

8. $(9 \cdot 7) + (3 \cdot 7) =$ _____

9. $(4 \cdot 11) + (5 \cdot 11) =$ _____

10. $(9 \cdot x) + (4 \cdot x) =$ _____

11. $3(m + n) =$ _____

12. $(15 \cdot 12) + (15 \cdot 13) =$ _____

13. $(r \cdot x) + (r \cdot y) =$ _____

14. $p(t + s) =$ _____

15. $(4 \cdot 190) + (4 \cdot 190) =$ _____

6-8 Multiplying Two-Digit and Three-Digit Numbers by a One-Digit Number

How do we multiply two-digit and three-digit numbers by a one-digit number? Look at the following problem.

$$\begin{array}{r} 1\,3 \\ \times\ \ 2 \\ \hline \end{array}$$

We multiply the numbers in the ones place: $2 \times 3 = 6$.
We write the 6 in the ones place.

$$\begin{array}{r} 1\,3 \\ \times\ \ 2 \\ \hline 6 \end{array}$$

We multiply the 1 in the tens place by the 2 in the
ones place: $2 \times 1 = 2$. We write the 2 in the tens place.

$$\begin{array}{r} 1\,3 \\ \times\ \ 2 \\ \hline 2\,6 \end{array}$$

Look at the following problem.

$$
\begin{array}{r}
2\ 3\ 1 \\
\times \quad\ 3 \\
\hline
\end{array}
$$

We multiply the 1 in the ones place by 3: $3 \times 1 = 3$.

$$
\begin{array}{r}
2\ 3\ \textcircled{1} \\
\times \quad\ \textcircled{3} \\
\hline
3
\end{array}
$$

We multiply the 3 in the tens place by 3: $3 \times 3 = 9$.

$$
\begin{array}{r}
2\ \textcircled{3}\ 1 \\
\times \quad\ \textcircled{3} \\
\hline
9\ 3
\end{array}
$$

We multiply the 2 in the hundreds place by 3: $3 \times 2 = 6$.

$$
\begin{array}{r}
\textcircled{2}\ 3\ 1 \\
\times \quad\ \textcircled{3} \\
\hline
6\ 9\ 3
\end{array}
$$

Exercise 8

Multiply the following numbers. Write your answers in the spaces.

1. 13
    × 3
    ‾‾
    39

2. 42
    × 3

3. 51
    × 6

4. 33
    × 3

5. 24
    × 2

6. 23
    × 2

7. 44
    × 2

8. 14
    × 2

9. 42
    × 4

10. 63
    × 2

11. 83
    × 3

12. 21
    × 9

13. 64
    × 2

14. 221
    × 2

15. 142
    × 2

16. 323
    × 3

17. 443
    × 2

18. 133
    × 3

19. 543
    × 2

20. 421
    × 3

21. 213
    × 3

22. 112
    × 4

23. 203
    × 2

24. 231
    × 3

25. 201
    × 4

Some multiplication problems require carrying. Look at the following problem.

$$\begin{array}{r} 5\,6 \\ \times\quad 7 \\ \hline \end{array}$$

We multiply 7×6. The product is 42. We can only write one number in the ones place, so we write the 2 in the ones place and carry the 4 to the tens place digit.

We multiply 7×5. The product is 35. We add the 4 that we carried: $35 + 4 = 39$.

Now look at the following problem.

$$\begin{array}{r} 3\,0\,6 \\ \times\quad 5 \\ \hline \end{array}$$

We multiply 5×6. The product is 30. We write the 0 in the ones place and carry the 3 to the tens place digit.

We multiply 5×0. The product is 0. We add the 3 that we carried: $0 + 3 = 3$. We write the 3 in the tens place.

We multiply 5×3. The product is 15.

Exercise 9

Multiply the following numbers. Write your answers in the spaces.

1. $\begin{array}{r} 36 \\ \times\ 4 \\ \hline 144 \end{array}$

2. $\begin{array}{r} 56 \\ \times\ 7 \\ \hline \end{array}$

3. $\begin{array}{r} 44 \\ \times\ 3 \\ \hline \end{array}$

4. $\begin{array}{r} 72 \\ \times\ 8 \\ \hline \end{array}$

5. $\begin{array}{r} 66 \\ \times\ 8 \\ \hline \end{array}$

6. $\begin{array}{r} 87 \\ \times\ 9 \\ \hline \end{array}$

7. $\begin{array}{r} 42 \\ \times\ 9 \\ \hline \end{array}$

8. $\begin{array}{r} 15 \\ \times\ 6 \\ \hline \end{array}$

9. 59
   × 9

10. 67
   × 4

11. 25
   × 4

12. 67
   × 3

13. 53
   × 7

14. 88
   × 9

15. 85
   × 5

16. 467
   × 6

17. 294
   × 3

18. 908
   × 5

19. 385
   × 7

20. 538
   × 8

21. 734
   × 5

22. 509
   × 6

23. 921
   × 3

24. 565
   × 7

25. 988
   × 6

26. 734
   × 2

27. 832
   × 9

28. 208
   × 3

29. 874
   × 8

30. 620
   × 6

6-10 Multiplying Two Digits by Two Digits

How do we multiply a two-digit number by a two-digit number? Look at the following problem.

   2 1
   × 3 4

First, we multiply 4 × 21. This will be *product A* (4 × 21 = 84).

              2 1
           × 3 4
product A ⟶ 8 4

Next, we multiply 3 × 21. This will be *product B*
(3 × 21 = 63). We write the 3 in the tens place since we
are multiplying 3 tens times 1 one.

              2 1
           × 3 4
product A ⟶ 8 4
product B ⟶ 6 3

We add *product A* and *product B* together.
The sum will be the answer.

              2 1
           × 3 4
product A ⟶ 8 4
product B ⟶ 6 3
Answer ⟶   7 1 4

Write the following problems on a separate sheet of paper. Then multiply the numbers.

1.   32
  × 22
	6. 83
	  × 12
		11. 20
		  × 34
			16. 45
			  × 11

2.   31
  × 24
	7. 92
	  × 13
		12. 52
		  × 14
			17. 50
			  × 23

3.   42
  × 13
	8. 54
	  × 22
		13. 43
		  × 33
			18. 44
			  × 22

4.   63
  × 23
	9. 33
	  × 33
		14. 62
		  × 40
			19. 61
			  × 24

5.   72
  × 14
	10. 42
	  × 23
		15. 73
		  × 22
			20. 53
			  × 30

6-11 Multiplying Two-Digit Numbers by Two-Digit Numbers with Carrying

Sometimes when we multiply a two-digit number by a two-digit number, we have to carry. Look at the following problem.

$$\begin{array}{r} 6\,7 \\ \times\,2\,8 \end{array}$$

First, we multiply 8 × 7. We carry the 5 above the 6 to the tens place digit. We multiply 8 × 6 and add the 5 that we carried. This will be *product A*.

$$\begin{array}{r} \overset{5}{6}\,7 \\ \times\ \ 2\,8 \\ \hline \end{array}$$
product A ⟶ 5 3 6

Next, we multiply 2 × 7. We write the 4 in the tens place and carry the 1 to the tens place digit. We multiply 2 × 6 and add the 1 that we carried. This will be *product B*.

$$\begin{array}{r} \overset{1}{6}\,7 \\ \times\ \ 2\,8 \\ \hline \end{array}$$
product A ⟶ 5 3 6
product B ⟶ 1 3 4

We add *product A* and *product B* together. The sum will be the answer.

$$\begin{array}{r} 6\,7 \\ \times\ 2\,8 \\ \hline \end{array}$$
product A ⟶   5 3 6
product B ⟶ + 1 3 4
Answer ⟶   1 8 7 6

Write the following problems on a separate sheet of paper. Then multiply the numbers.

1. 34
   × 24

2. 45
   × 56

3. 53
   × 27

4. 73
   × 92

5. 26
   × 19

6. 76
   × 87

7. 93
   × 55

8. 81
   × 83

9. 13
   × 34

10. 77
    × 64

11. 82
    × 44

12. 63
    × 77

13. 92
    × 23

14. 75
    × 75

15. 55
    × 44

16. 32
    × 99

17. 29
    × 99

18. 28
    × 28

19. 35
    × 35

20. 99
    × 99

21. 45
    × 36

22. 84
    × 48

23. 23
    × 90

24. 64
    × 69

25. 89
    × 90

26. 35
    × 78

27. 66
    × 33

28. 59
    × 60

29. 91
    × 19

30. 44
    × 78

6-12 Multiplying Three-Digit Numbers by Two- and Three-Digit Numbers

How do we multiply a three-digit number by a two-digit or three-digit number? Look at the following problem.

```
  2 3 4
×   6 3
```

First, we multiply 3 × 234. This will be *product A*.

```
        2 3 4
      ×   6 3
product A →  7 0 2
```

Next, we multiply 6 × 234. This will be *product B*.

```
        2 3 4
      ×   6 3
product A →  7 0 2
product B → 1 4 0 4
```

We add *products A* and *B* together for the answer.

```
          2 3 4
       ×    6 3
product A ⟶      7 0 2
product B ⟶    1 4 0 4
Answer ⟶     1 4 7 4 2
```

Now look at the following problem.

```
   3 6 5
× 2 4 3
```

First, we multiply 3 × 365 (*product A*). Next, we multiply
4 × 365 (*product B*). Then we multiply 2 × 365 (*product C*).
We add *products A, B,* and *C* together for the answer.

```
            3 6 5
         ×   2 4 3
product A ⟶   1 0 9 5
product B ⟶  1 4 6 0
product C ⟶  7 3 0
Answer ⟶    8 8 6 9 5
```

Exercise 12

Write the following problems on a separate sheet of paper. Then multiply the numbers.

1. 342 × 25	**6.** 937 × 57	**11.** 722 × 45	**16.** 604 × 435
2. 980 × 34	**7.** 258 × 96	**12.** 609 × 69	**17.** 790 × 459
3. 546 × 49	**8.** 522 × 66	**13.** 344 × 78	**18.** 889 × 347
4. 688 × 55	**9.** 904 × 83	**14.** 922 × 88	**19.** 506 × 677
5. 732 × 99	**10.** 592 × 56	**15.** 811 × 55	**20.** 622 × 678

21.	403 × 344	24.	865 × 302	27.	566 × 143	29.	311 × 100
22.	322 × 498	25.	900 × 432	28.	760 × 301	30.	986 × 288
23.	123 × 123	26.	387 × 102				

6-13 Multiples of Ten

A **multiple of ten** is the product of 10 with any other whole number.

$2 \times 10 = 20$	$5 \times 10 = 50$	$8 \times 10 = 80$	$11 \times 10 = 110$
$3 \times 10 = 30$	$6 \times 10 = 60$	$9 \times 10 = 90$	$12 \times 10 = 120$
$4 \times 10 = 40$	$7 \times 10 = 70$	$10 \times 10 = 100$	$13 \times 10 = 130$

(20, 30, 40, 50, 60, 70, 80, 90, 100, 110, 120, 130, . . . are all multiples of ten.)

$100 \times 10 = 1,000$ $1,000 \times 10 = 10,000$ $10,000 \times 10 = 100,000$

(1,000, 10,000, 100,000, . . . are also multiples of ten.)

To multiply a number by a multiple of ten, first, we multiply the nonzero digits. Then we combine the zeros.

Example:

$$100 \times 1,000$$

Multiply 1×1: $1 \quad \times 1 \quad = 1$

Combine the zeros: 2 zeros and 3 zeros = 5 zeros

Answer: 100,000

1 and 5 zeros

Example:

$$30 \times 100$$

Multiply 3×1: $3 \quad \times 1 \quad = 3$

Combine the zeros: 1 zero and 2 zeros = 3 zeros

Answer: 3,000

3 and 3 zeros

Example:

$$74 \times 20 \times 1{,}000$$

Multiply $74 \times 2 \times 1$: $74 \times 2 \times 1 \quad = 148$

Combine the zeros: 1 zero and 3 zeros = 4 zeros

Answer: 1,480,000

148 and 4 zeros

Exercise 13

Write the following problems on a separate sheet of paper. Then multiply the numbers.

1. $6 \times 100 = \underline{600}$

2. $24 \times 10{,}000 =$

3. $100 \times 76 =$

4. $100 \times 840 =$

5. $10 \times 10{,}000 =$

6. $2{,}743 \times 10{,}000 =$

7. $1{,}000 \times 1{,}000 =$

8. $100 \times 3{,}450 =$

9. $2{,}300 \times 1{,}000 =$

10. $10 \times 100 \times 678 =$

11. $1{,}000 \times 890 \times 100 =$

12. $387{,}000 \times 1{,}000{,}000 =$

13. $65{,}000 \times 10 \times 1{,}000 =$

14. $1{,}000 \times 30 \times 300 =$

15. $1{,}000 \times 300 \times 20 =$

16. $450 \times 2{,}000{,}000 =$

17. $10 \times 60{,}000 \times 200 =$

18. $107{,}233 \times 10 \times 100 =$

19. $200 \times 14{,}000 \times 2{,}000 =$

20. $134 \times 3{,}000 \times 100 =$

21. $456{,}000 \times 300 \times 20{,}000 =$

22. $1{,}000 \times 40{,}000 \times 23{,}000 =$

23. $70{,}000 \times 400 \times 2{,}000{,}000 =$

24. $25{,}000 \times 300 \times 2{,}000{,}000 =$

25. $80{,}000 \times 2{,}000 \times 1{,}000 \times 200 =$

6-14 Solving Word Problems with Unnecessary Information

Some word problems have unnecessary information. We don't need the information to solve the problems.

Example:

My brother Jesse sold 4 paintings at the art fair. He sold each painting for $125. It took him 6 months to paint each one. How much money did he make from the sale of the paintings?

Unnecessary information: "It took him 6 months to paint each one." We don't need this information to solve the problem: How much money did he make from the sale of the paintings?

Answer: 125×4 paintings = $500

Read each word problem below. Then circle the letter next to the sentence with the unnecessary information.

1. Ruben collects baseball cards. He has 2,565 cards in all. He sold 35 cards last month for $5 each. How much money did he make?
   a. He has 2,565 cards in all.
   b. He sold 35 cards last month.
   c. He sold the cards for $5 each.

2. Luisa was born in 1973. She graduated from high school when she was 18 years old. She has lived in New York for 10 years. In what year did she graduate?
   a. Luisa was born in 1973.
   b. She graduated from high school when she was 18 years old.
   c. She has lived in New York for 10 years.

3. Lani drove 35 miles an hour. She drove for 5 hours. She rested for 2 hours. How far did she drive?
   a. Lani drove 35 miles an hour.
   b. She drove for 5 hours.
   c. She rested for 2 hours.

4. Tamala is 15 years old. She is 6 years older than her brother. Her father is 25 years older than she is. How old is her brother?
   a. Tamala is 15 years old.
   b. She is 6 years older than her brother.
   c. Her father is 25 years older than she is.

5. Percy began painting the house at 9:00 A.M. He finished one-half of the house at 2:00 P.M. He finished painting the house at 6:00 P.M. How many hours did he paint that day?
   a. Percy began painting the house at 9:00 A.M.
   b. He finished one-half of the house at 2:00 P.M.
   c. He finished painting the house at 6:00 P.M.

6-15 Solving Multiplication Word Problems

Multiplication can help us solve many word problems. It is faster than addition. Look at the problem below.

> Rachel works after school at Clothes For You. Her salary is $6 an hour. In 2 days, she worked 8 hours. What was her pay?

We can use addition to solve this problem.

Addition: $\underbrace{\$6 + \$6 + \$6 + \$6 + \$6 + \$6 + \$6 + \$6}_{\text{for 8 hours}} = \$48$

Or we can use multiplication to solve the problem.

Multiplication: $\$6 \times 8$ hours $= \$48$

Multiplication is a fast way to add.

Sometimes, multiplication problems include expressions that tell us to multiply. Look at the following problem.

> Kevin's salary is $300 a month. Tanner's salary is three times Kevin's salary. What is Tanner's salary?

> The expression *three times* tells us that we should multiply.

> $300 × 3 = $900

Exercise 15

Solve each problem below by using addition, subtraction, or multiplication (or a combination of the operations). Use only the necessary information. Write your answers on the lines. Show your work on a separate sheet of paper.

1. Hiroshi Asato was born in 1978. He has lived in the United States for 15 years. How old was he in 1990? ___*12 years old*___

2. Danielle loves to read. She reads 20 pages in 1 hour. Her favorite book has 270 pages. How many pages does she read in 6 hours? _____

3. Cody paints cars. He paints 16 cars a month. He asks $350 for each car he paints. How much does he earn by painting 7 cars? _____

4. A watermelon has 175 seeds. Each watermelon is 18 inches long. How many seeds do 5 watermelons have? _____

5. Our pet shop has 8 dogs, 4 cats, 6 rabbits, and 2 turtles. The turtles cost $5 each. How many animals are there altogether? _____

6. Brandon began studying at 4:00 P.M. He finished 2 pages of math, 3 pages of English, and 1 page of biology. He studied for 4 hours. What time did he stop studying? _____

7. An artist finished 1 painting in 30 weeks. He began in February. He painted 5 hours a week. How many hours did he paint altogether during the 30 weeks? _____

8. Scott runs 5 miles every week. He runs 35 minutes a day. How many miles does he run in 4 weeks? _____

9. Maria invited 18 friends to her party. Each person brought 1 friend. There were 17 boys. How many people were at the party, including Maria? _____

10. Logan earns $25 a week. He saves $9 a week. How much does he earn in 6 weeks? _____

Raymond Lopez works after school at The Pizza Pan restaurant. He is a waiter. Look at his weekly work schedule below. Then answer the questions. Write your answers on the lines. Show all your work on a separate sheet of paper.

Monday	Tuesday	Wednesday	Thursday	Friday	Saturday
5 hours	4 hours	6 hours	3 hours	7 hours	8 hours

1. When Raymond began working as a waiter, his hourly wage was $6 an hour. How much did he earn . . .

   a. every Wednesday? _____$36_____   **d.** every Saturday? _____
   b. every Monday? _____   **e.** every Friday? _____
   c. every Tuesday? _____

2. How much did Raymond earn in 1 week? _____

3. How much did Raymond earn in 4 weeks? _____

4. How much did Raymond earn in 24 weeks? _____

5. Sometimes, Raymond worked overtime (working more than 8 hours in one day). When he worked overtime, he received $3 more for each hour of overtime. One Saturday, Raymond worked 12 hours. How much did he earn that day? _____

6. Later, Raymond received a raise (a higher hourly wage) of $2 more an hour. What was his new hourly wage? _____

7. How much did Raymond earn in 1 week after his raise? _____

8. How much did he earn in 4 weeks after his raise? _____

9. Compare Raymond's weekly salary before and after his raise. How much more did he earn per week after his raise? _____

10. How much more did he earn every 4 weeks after his raise? _____

The Nelson family traveled to Japan last month. Mr. and Mrs. Nelson traveled with their two children, Rick, 16, and Lisa, 14. Answer the questions below about their trip. Write your answers on the lines. Show all your work on a separate sheet of paper.

1. Japanese money is called yen. If 1 American dollar equals 125 Japanese yen, how much would each of the following items cost in Japan?

	United States	**Japan**
a. a cup of coffee	$1	_125_ yen
b. dinner for one person	$15	_____ yen
c. a watch	$60	_____ yen
d. a camera	$130	_____ yen
e. a CD player	$230	_____ yen
f. a television set	$350	_____ yen
g. a new car	$21,000	_____ yen

2. The Nelsons stayed at the Cherry Blossom Hotel in Tokyo. The cost for one night was 15,625 yen. How much did they pay, in yen, for 2 weeks? _____

3. For lunch one day, Rick ordered a hamburger for 750 yen. Lisa ordered a ham sandwich for 875 yen. Mrs. Nelson ordered a salad for 1,250 yen, and Mr. Nelson ordered a steak sandwich for 1,500 yen. Mr. Nelson gave the waitress 6,000 yen. How much change, in yen, did he receive? _____

4. Mrs. Nelson went shopping in Tokyo and in Kyoto. She saw a dress she liked. In Tokyo, the dress cost 7,625 yen. In Kyoto, the same dress cost $58.

   a. Which was less, the dress in Tokyo for 7,625 yen or the dress in Kyoto for $58? _____

   b. How much less, in yen, was the dress? _____

5. Mr. and Mrs. Nelson wanted to rent a car to see the country. The children wanted to take the Bullet Train. Look at the costs for renting a car and taking the train. Then answer the questions below.

Rental Car	Bullet Train
car for 1 day: 4,375 yen	1 adult ticket for 1 week: 5,000 yen
car for 1 week: 17,500 yen	1 student ticket for 1 week: 2,500 yen

a. If the Nelsons rent a car for 2 weeks, how much will they pay in yen? _____

b. If the Nelsons buy train tickets for each person in the family for 2 weeks, how much will they pay in yen? (Rick and Lisa are students.) _____

c. Which is cheaper for the 2 weeks—renting a car or taking a train? _____

d. How much cheaper, in yen? _____

Have I Learned? (✓)

Work with a partner. Check what you have learned. Review what you need help with.

1. multiplication problem ☐

2. times ☐

3. equals ☐

4. product ☐

5. factors ☐

6. Commutative Property of Multiplication ☐

7. Associative Property of Multiplication ☐

8. Multiplicative Identity Property of Multiplication ☐

9. Multiplicative Property of Zero ☐

10. Distributive Property of Multiplication ☐

11. multiple of ten ☐

12. unnecessary information ☐

13. hourly wage ☐

14. overtime ☐

15. raise ☐

16. salary ☐

17. yen ☐

18. cheaper ☐

Exercise 1

On a separate sheet of paper, write the following multiplication problems using words.

1. $7 \times 10 = 70$ _Seven times ten equals_
seventy.

2. $3 \times 5 = 15$

3. $9 \times 8 = 72$

4. $6 \times 0 = 0$

5. $4 \times 1 = 4$

Exercise 2

On a separate sheet of paper, write the following problems. Then multiply the numbers.

1. $100 \times 82 =$ _8,200_

2. $5,320 \times 100 =$

3. $10,000 \times 1,000 =$

4. $100 \times 5,000 \times 600 =$

5. $70,000 \times 40 \times 5,000 =$

Exercise 3

For each multiplication problem, write the factors and the product.

1. $1 \times 15 = 15$ factors: _1_ and _15_   product: _15_

2. $8 \times 0 = 0$ factors: _____ and _____   product: _____

3. $10 \times 100 = 1,000$ factors: _____ and _____   product: _____

4. $7 \times 7 = 49$ factors: _____ and _____   product: _____

5. $6 \times 8 = 48$ factors: _____ and _____   product: _____

Exercise 4

On a separate sheet of paper, write the following problems. Then multiply the numbers.

1. $7 \times 7 =$ _49_

2. $6 \times 5 =$

3. $3 \times 13 =$

4. $23 \times 2 =$

5. $76 \times 6 =$

6. $55 \times 7 =$

7. $534 \times 9 =$

8. $874 \times 4 =$

9. $23 \times 45 =$

10. $75 \times 94 =$

11. $86 \times 52 =$

12. $245 \times 98 =$

13. $603 \times 95 =$

14. $576 \times 984 =$

15. $366 \times 843 =$

CHAPTER 7 Division

Look at the following **division** problem.

$$10 \div 2 = 5$$

We say: "Ten **divided by** two **equals** five."

The **quotient** is five. The **dividend** is ten. The **divisor** is two.

What is the quotient of 6 and 2? The quotient of 6 and 2 is 3.

Exercise 1

Complete each sentence. Write the correct word or words.

1. The _____*quotient*_____ of eight and four is two.

2. Twenty-four ____*divided by*____ three ____*equals*____ eight.

3. The quotient of ____*24*____ and eight is three.

4. Twelve _____ six equals two.

5. Thirty-six _____ four _____ nine.

6. Nine divided by three _____ three.

7. The quotient of twelve and three is _____.

8. The _____ of forty-two and seven

   _____ six.

9. _____ divided by seven _____ seven.

10. Fifty-four _____ nine _____ six.

Exercise 2

Answer each question. Write the correct number word.

1. What is the quotient of nine and three? ____*three*____

2. What is the quotient of forty and eight? _____

3. What is the quotient of thirty and five? _____

4. What is the quotient of twenty-one and three? _____

5. What is the quotient of sixteen and two? _____

6. What is the quotient of forty-five and five? _____

7. What is the quotient of twenty-seven and nine? _____

8. What is the quotient of eighteen and three? _____

9. What is the quotient of fifteen and fifteen? _____

10. What is the quotient of nineteen and one? _____

Exercise 3

Write the following division problems using words.

1. $12 \div 6 = 2$ _Twelve divided by six equals two._ OR _____

   The quotient of twelve and six is two. _____

2. $15 \div 5 = 3$ _____

3. $14 \div 7 = 2$ _____

4. $9 \div 9 = 1$ _____

5. $35 \div 7 = 5$ _____

6. $49 \div 7 = 7$ _____

7. $24 \div 3 = 8$ _____

8. $63 \div 7 = 9$ _____

9. $64 \div 8 = 8$ _____

10. $42 \div 7 = 6$ _____

Exercise 4

For each division problem, write the dividend, divisor, and quotient.

1. $20 \div 10 = 2$ dividend: _20_   divisor: _10_   quotient: _2_

2. $16 \div 8 = 2$ dividend: _____   divisor: _____   quotient: _____

3. $35 \div 7 = 5$ dividend: _____   divisor: _____   quotient: _____

4. $12 \div 4 = 3$ dividend: _____   divisor: _____   quotient: _____

5. $18 \div 9 = 2$ dividend: _____   divisor: _____   quotient: _____

We write division problems with the symbol ÷ or)⎺⎺⎺. Look at the ways we can write "eight divided by four."

8 ÷ 4 or 4)8

In the problem above, we want to know how many *times* 4 goes into 8. We can use multiplication to find the quotient.

4 × ? = 8

4 × 2 = 8

4 goes into 8 *two times*. Therefore, the quotient is 2. We write the quotient 2 above the dividend 8.

$$\begin{array}{r} 2 \\ 4\overline{)8} \end{array}$$

We then multiply the divisor (4) with the quotient (2): 4 × 2 = 8. We write the product 8 below the dividend and subtract it from the dividend.

$$\begin{array}{r} 2 \\ 4\overline{)8} \\ -8 \\ \hline 0 \end{array}$$

To check our answer, we multiply the divisor (4) with the quotient (2). The product should equal the dividend (8).

$$\begin{array}{rr} \text{quotient} & 2 \\ \times \quad \text{divisor} & \times\, 4 \\ \hline \text{dividend} & 8 \end{array}$$

Now look at the following problem.

4)24

4 × ? = 2. 2 is too small. We must use 24.
4 × ? = 24. 4 × 6 = 24.
We write the quotient 6 above the 4, not the 2, because we are using 24, not 2.

$$\begin{array}{r} 6 \\ 4\overline{)24} \\ -24 \\ \hline 0 \end{array}$$

We check our answer by multiplying the divisor (4) with the quotient (6). The product should equal the dividend (24).

$$\begin{array}{r} 6 \\ \times\, 4 \\ \hline 24 \end{array}$$

Now look at this problem.

4)636

4 × ? = 6. 4 × 1 = 4. 4 × 2 = 8. 2 is too large. We use 1. We write it above the 6, multiply 1 × 4, and subtract the product from 6.

We bring down the 3.

$$\begin{array}{r} 1 \\ 4\overline{)636} \\ -4 \\ \hline 23 \end{array}$$

$4 \times ? = 23.$ $4 \times 5 = 20.$ $4 \times 6 = 24.$ We use 5. We write 5 above the 3 and multiply 4×5. We write the product 20 below 23 and subtract.

We bring down the 6.

$$
\begin{array}{r}
15 \\
4\overline{)636} \\
-4 \\
\hline
23 \\
-20 \\
\hline
36
\end{array}
$$

$4 \times ? = 36.$ $4 \times 9 = 36.$ We write the 9 above the 6. We multiply 4×9 and subtract from 36.

The quotient, or answer, is 159.

$$
\begin{array}{r}
159 \\
4\overline{)636} \\
-4 \\
\hline
23 \\
-20 \\
\hline
36 \\
-36 \\
\hline
0
\end{array}
$$

We check our answer by multiplying the divisor (4) with the quotient (159). The product should equal the dividend (636).

$$
\begin{array}{r}
159 \\
\times \quad 4 \\
\hline
636
\end{array}
$$

Exercise 5

On a separate sheet of paper, divide the following numbers. Then check your answers.

1. $2\overline{)6}$ 6. $7\overline{)14}$ 11. $2\overline{)34}$

2. $5\overline{)45}$ 7. $5\overline{)10}$ 12. $4\overline{)84}$

3. $6\overline{)24}$ 8. $9\overline{)72}$ 13. $7\overline{)77}$

4. $3\overline{)9}$ 9. $8\overline{)56}$ 14. $2\overline{)46}$

5. $2\overline{)8}$ 10. $3\overline{)99}$ 15. $5\overline{)55}$

Exercise 6

On a separate sheet of paper, divide the following numbers. Then check your answers.

1. $8\overline{)648}$ 6. $4\overline{)444}$ 11. $7\overline{)308}$

2. $3\overline{)243}$ 7. $2\overline{)646}$ 12. $8\overline{)176}$

3. $7\overline{)105}$ 8. $3\overline{)552}$ 13. $9\overline{)792}$

4. $8\overline{)152}$ 9. $4\overline{)252}$ 14. $8\overline{)440}$

5. $6\overline{)150}$ 10. $3\overline{)198}$ 15. $6\overline{)366}$

On a separate sheet of paper, divide the following numbers. Then check your answers.

1. $2\overline{)4,568}$ 6. $3\overline{)1,941}$ 11. $4\overline{)1,476}$

2. $3\overline{)1,533}$ 7. $2\overline{)3,196}$ 12. $9\overline{)2,043}$

3. $5\overline{)3,550}$ 8. $9\overline{)1,944}$ 13. $4\overline{)1,064}$

4. $4\overline{)6,184}$ 9. $6\overline{)1,536}$ 14. $7\overline{)5,768}$

5. $9\overline{)1,584}$ 10. $6\overline{)1,308}$ 15. $3\overline{)7,731}$

Now look at the following problem.

$6\overline{)12,012}$

$6 \times ? = 12.$ $6 \times 2 = 12.$ We write the 2 above the 2, multiply, and subtract. We bring down the 0.

$$\begin{array}{r} 2 \\ 6\overline{)12,012} \\ -12 \\ \hline 0\,0 \end{array}$$

$6 \times ? = 0.$ $6 \times 0 = 0.$ We write the 0 above the 0 in the dividend. We bring down the 1.

$$\begin{array}{r} 2\,0 \\ 6\overline{)12,012} \\ -12 \\ \hline 0\,01 \end{array}$$

$6 \times ? = 1.$ $6 \times 1 = 6.$ 1 is too large. We use 0. We write the 0 above the 1, multiply, and subtract. We bring down the 2.

$$\begin{array}{r} 2\,00 \\ 6\overline{)12,012} \\ -12 \\ \hline 0\,01 \\ -0 \\ \hline 12 \end{array}$$

$6 \times ? = 12.$ $6 \times 2 = 12.$ We write the 2 above the 2 in the dividend. We multiply and subtract. The quotient is 2,002.

$$\begin{array}{r} 2,002 \\ 6\overline{)12,012} \\ -12 \\ \hline 0\,01 \\ -0 \\ \hline 12 \\ -12 \\ \hline 0 \end{array}$$

We check our answer by multiplying the divisor (6) with the quotient (2,002). The product should equal the dividend.

$$\begin{array}{r} 2,002 \\ \times \quad 6 \\ \hline 12,012 \end{array}$$

On a separate sheet of paper, divide the following numbers. Then check your answers.

1. $8\overline{)40,560}$ 6. $9\overline{)2,043}$ 11. $5\overline{)13,215}$

2. $2\overline{)97,148}$ 7. $4\overline{)99,916}$ 12. $4\overline{)27,340}$

3. $2\overline{)45,664}$ 8. $2\overline{)50,816}$ 13. $3\overline{)17,622}$

4. $9\overline{)51,075}$ 9. $5\overline{)1,115}$ 14. $8\overline{)51,096}$

5. $3\overline{)30,012}$ 10. $6\overline{)13,830}$ 15. $3\overline{)23,523}$

On a separate sheet of paper, divide the following numbers. Then check your answers.

1. $6\overline{)588,060}$ 6. $8\overline{)258,224}$ 11. $5\overline{)261,435}$

2. $9\overline{)54,036}$ 7. $9\overline{)221,022}$ 12. $2\overline{)159,972}$

3. $3\overline{)186,342}$ 8. $4\overline{)315,452}$ 13. $9\overline{)181,305}$

4. $7\overline{)161,784}$ 9. $5\overline{)160,025}$ 14. $8\overline{)293,584}$

5. $5\overline{)205,680}$ 10. $6\overline{)540,684}$ 15. $3\overline{)176,322}$

7-3 One-Digit Divisors with Remainders

Look at the following problem.

$$5\overline{)517}$$

Divide 517 by 5.

```
    103
5)517
   -5
   ---
    01
    -0
    ---
    17
   -15
    ---
     2
```

Notice that the last digit in the dividend is 7. There aren't any other digits to bring down. Therefore, there is a **remainder** of 2. We write this remainder as *r.2* next to the quotient.

```
    103 r.2
5)517
   -5
   ---
    01
    -0
    ---
    17
   -15
    ---
     2
```

To check our answer with a remainder, we multiply the
quotient without the remainder by the divisor. We then add
the remainder. The result should equal the dividend.

$$103 \longleftarrow \text{quotient without the remainder}$$
$$\times\ \ \ 5 \longleftarrow \text{divisor}$$
$$\overline{515}$$
$$+\ \ \ 2 \longleftarrow \text{remainder}$$
$$\overline{517} \longleftarrow \text{dividend}$$

Exercise 10

On a separate sheet of paper, divide the following numbers. Then check your answers.

1. $5\overline{)804}$
2. $9\overline{)715}$
3. $3\overline{)244}$
4. $8\overline{)345}$
5. $7\overline{)157}$

6. $6\overline{)785}$
7. $4\overline{)653}$
8. $2\overline{)313}$
9. $5\overline{)107}$
10. $4\overline{)769}$

11. $2\overline{)355}$
12. $8\overline{)887}$
13. $5\overline{)678}$
14. $9\overline{)342}$
15. $7\overline{)261}$

Exercise 11

On a separate sheet of paper, divide the following numbers. Then check your answers.

1. $3\overline{)7,241}$
2. $9\overline{)7,732}$
3. $9\overline{)97,561}$
4. $6\overline{)4,296}$
5. $7\overline{)6,519}$

6. $4\overline{)1,003}$
7. $9\overline{)6,352}$
8. $5\overline{)3,118}$
9. $8\overline{)2,014}$
10. $7\overline{)6,517}$

11. $6\overline{)7,394}$
12. $9\overline{)8,153}$
13. $6\overline{)40,827}$
14. $7\overline{)14,356}$
15. $9\overline{)90,908}$

Look at the following problem.

$$20\overline{)260}$$

$20 \times ? = 26.$ $20 \times 1 = 20.$ We write the 1 above the 6.
We multiply 1×20 and subtract the product from 26.
We bring down the 0.

$$\begin{array}{r} 1 \\ 20\overline{)260} \\ -20 \\ \hline 60 \end{array}$$

$20 \times ? = 60.$ $20 \times 3 = 60.$ We write the 3 above the 0.
We multiply 20×3 and subtract the product from 60.

$$\begin{array}{r} 13 \\ 20\overline{)260} \\ -20 \\ \hline 60 \\ -60 \\ \hline 0 \end{array}$$

We check our answer by multiplying the divisor (20) with the quotient (13).
The product should equal the dividend (260).

$$\begin{array}{r} 13 \\ \times\ 20 \\ \hline 00 \\ +\ 26 \\ \hline 260 \end{array}$$

Now look at the following problem.

$$12\overline{)4,567}$$

$12 \times ? = 45.$ $12 \times 3 = 36.$ $12 \times 4 = 48.$ 4 is too large.
3 is correct. We write the 3 above the 5. We multiply
and subtract. We then bring down the 6.

$$\begin{array}{r} 3 \\ 12\overline{)4,567} \\ -3\,6 \\ \hline 96 \end{array}$$

$12 \times ? = 96.$ $12 \times 8 = 96.$ We write the 8 above the 6,
multiply, and subtract. We bring down the 7.

$$\begin{array}{r} 38 \\ 12\overline{)4,567} \\ -3\,6 \\ \hline 96 \\ -96 \\ \hline 07 \end{array}$$

$12 \times ? = 7$. $12 \times 0 = 0$. $12 \times 1 = 12$. 1 is too large.
0 is correct. We write the 0 above the 7, multiply, and
subtract. The remainder is 7.

$$
\begin{array}{r}
380\,\text{r.}7 \\
12\overline{)4{,}567} \\
-3\,6 \\
\hline
96 \\
-96 \\
\hline
07 \\
-0 \\
\hline
7
\end{array}
$$

We check our answer by multiplying the divisor (12) with the quotient without the remainder (380). We then add the remainder (7). The answer should equal the dividend (4,567).

$$
\begin{array}{r}
380 \\
\times \quad 12 \\
\hline
760 \\
+\ 380 \\
\hline
4{,}560 \\
+ \quad 7 \\
\hline
4{,}567
\end{array}
$$

Exercise 12

On a separate sheet of paper, divide the following numbers. Then check your answers.

1. $25\overline{)250}$
2. $12\overline{)432}$
3. $15\overline{)300}$
4. $50\overline{)200}$
5. $11\overline{)143}$

6. $21\overline{)357}$
7. $15\overline{)915}$
8. $24\overline{)720}$
9. $30\overline{)900}$
10. $10\overline{)270}$

11. $22\overline{)704}$
12. $18\overline{)648}$
13. $54\overline{)756}$
14. $25\overline{)375}$
15. $12\overline{)420}$

Exercise 13

On a separate sheet of paper, divide the following numbers. Then check your answers.

1. $17\overline{)2{,}261}$
2. $12\overline{)1{,}056}$
3. $30\overline{)1{,}440}$
4. $36\overline{)1{,}296}$
5. $60\overline{)1{,}860}$

6. $10\overline{)5{,}500}$
7. $45\overline{)1{,}620}$
8. $35\overline{)1{,}225}$
9. $30\overline{)2{,}700}$
10. $10\overline{)4{,}730}$

11. $99\overline{)2{,}475}$
12. $78\overline{)1{,}404}$
13. $55\overline{)1{,}375}$
14. $75\overline{)1{,}950}$
15. $16\overline{)1{,}280}$

On a separate sheet of paper, divide the following numbers. Then check your answers.

1. $13\overline{)427}$ 6. $12\overline{)834}$ 11. $13\overline{)849}$

2. $52\overline{)893}$ 7. $30\overline{)837}$ 12. $22\overline{)845}$

3. $23\overline{)371}$ 8. $21\overline{)853}$ 13. $30\overline{)788}$

4. $20\overline{)678}$ 9. $11\overline{)840}$ 14. $15\overline{)349}$

5. $25\overline{)998}$ 10. $63\overline{)764}$ 15. $32\overline{)849}$

On a separate sheet of paper, divide the following numbers. Then check your answers.

1. $15\overline{)1,293}$ 6. $30\overline{)7,884}$ 11. $19\overline{)3,900}$

2. $25\overline{)3,992}$ 7. $62\overline{)5,998}$ 12. $15\overline{)29,304}$

3. $12\overline{)5,991}$ 8. $70\overline{)8,439}$ 13. $20\overline{)49,332}$

4. $31\overline{)1,119}$ 9. $68\overline{)4,051}$ 14. $11\overline{)39,992}$

5. $71\overline{)2,485}$ 10. $22\overline{)3,849}$ 15. $65\overline{)93,333}$

7-5 Inverse Operations

In Chapter 5, we learned that addition and subtraction are inverse, or opposite, operations. Multiplication and division are also inverse operations. Each multiplication problem has its inverse division problem, and each division problem has its inverse multiplication problem.

Now look at the following examples of inverse operations.

Multiplication	**Inverse Operation of Division**
$3 \times 2 = 6$	$6 \div 2 = 3$ and $6 \div 3 = 2$
$7 \times 3 = 21$	$21 \div 3 = 7$ and $21 \div 7 = 3$

Division	**Inverse Operation of Multiplication**
$10 \div 5 = 2$	$2 \times 5 = 10$ or $5 \times 2 = 10$
$12 \div 4 = 3$	$3 \times 4 = 12$ or $4 \times 3 = 12$

We can use inverse operations to check answers. We can use division to check our answers to multiplication problems. We can use multiplication to check our answers to division problems.

Problem	**Check**
$36 \times 3 = 108$	$108 \div 3 = 36$ or $108 \div 36 = 3$
$24 \div 6 = 4$	$4 \times 6 = 24$ or $6 \times 4 = 24$

Exercise 16

Check each problem by writing two inverse division problems.

1. $10 \times 2 = 20$ $\underline{20 \div 2 = 10}$ AND $\underline{20 \div 10 = 2}$

2. $7 \times 4 = 28$ _____

3. $4 \cdot 3 = 12$ _____

4. $6 \cdot 7 = 42$ _____

5. $(9)(8) = 72$ _____

6. $20 \times 3 = 60$ _____

7. $12 \cdot 3 = 36$ _____

8. $1 \cdot 9 = 9$ _____

9. $(8)4 = 32$ _____

10. $11 \times 2 = 22$ _____

11. $12 \times 4 = 48$ _____

12. $25(3) = 75$ _____

13. $24 \cdot 4 = 96$ _____

14. $15 \times 4 = 60$ _____

15. $(9)(7) = 63$ _____

16. $35 \times 2 = 70$ _____

17. $33(4) = 132$ _____

18. $50 \times 5 = 250$ _____

19. $22 \cdot 4 = 88$ _____

20. $18 \times 1 = 18$ _____

Exercise 17

Check each problem by writing two inverse multiplication problems.

1. $28 \div 7 = 4$ $\underline{4 \times 7 = 28}$ AND $\underline{7 \times 4 = 28}$

2. $54 \div 6 = 9$ _____

3. $75 \div 3 = 25$ _____

4. $88 \div 4 = 22$ _____

5. $125 \div 5 = 25$ _____

6. $340 \div 10 = 34$ _____

7. $542 \div 2 = 271$ _____

8. $712 \div 89 = 8$ _____

9. $236 \div 59 = 4$ _____

10. $228 \div 12 = 19$ _____

7-6 Using Inverse Operations to Find Missing Numbers

In Chapter 5, we used inverse operations to find missing numbers in addition and subtraction problems. We can use inverse operations to find missing numbers in multiplication and division problems.

Look at the following problem.

$$6 \times \underline{\hspace{1cm}} = 24$$

We can use the inverse operation of division to find the missing number.

$24 \div 6 = 4$

Answer: $6 \times 4 = 24$

Now look at this problem.

_____ $\div 6 = 5$

We can use the inverse operation of multiplication to find the missing number.

$5 \times 6 = 30$

Answer: $30 \div 6 = 5$

Exercise 18

Use the inverse division operation to find the missing numbers.

1. $10 \times$ __6__ $= 60$ __$60 \div 10 = 6$__

2. $8 \times$ _____ $= 56$ _____

3. $7 \times$ _____ $= 49$ _____

4. $25 \times$ _____ $= 200$ _____

5. $5 \times$ _____ $= 455$ _____

6. $3 \times$ _____ $= 201$ _____

7. _____ $\times 9 = 2,925$ _____

8. _____ $\times 8 = 624$ _____

9. $6 \times$ _____ $= 750$ _____

10. $6 \times$ _____ $= 5,304$ _____

11. $4 \times$ _____ $= 392$ _____

12. _____ $\times 9 = 261$ _____

13. $50 \times$ _____ $= 750$ _____

14. _____ $\times 20 = 800$ _____

15. $35 \times$ _____ $= 1,155$ _____

Exercise 19

Use the inverse multiplication operation to find the missing numbers.

1. __42__ $\div 7 = 6$ __$6 \times 7 = 42$__

2. _____ $\div 8 = 8$ _____

3. _____ $\div 12 = 3$ _____

4. _____ $\div 10 = 10$ _____

5. _____ $\div 8 = 25$ _____

6. _____ $\div 4 = 23$ _____

7. _____ $\div 7 = 19$ _____

8. _____ $\div 12 = 1$ _____

9. _____ $\div 15 = 80$ _____

10. _____ $\div 19 = 46$ _____

11. _____ $\div 16 = 77$ _____

12. _____ $\div 9 = 127$ _____

13. _____ $\div 18 = 455$ _____

14. _____ $\div 8 = 1,250$ _____

15. _____ $\div 22 = 0$ _____

In Chapter 6, we learned how to multiply numbers by multiples of ten. (We multiply the nonzero digits first and then combine the zeros.) Now we will learn how to divide numbers by multiples of ten.

To divide a multiple of ten by a multiple of ten, we cross out zeros in both the divisor and the dividend and then divide the numbers.

Example:

$24,000 \div 100 =$

The dividend 24,000 has 3 zeros. The divisor 100 has 2 zeros. We cross out the *lesser* number of zeros in *both* the divisor and the dividend.

We cross out 2 zeros. $24,0\cancel{0}\cancel{0} \div 1\cancel{0}\cancel{0}$

We then divide. $240 \div 1 = 240$

Example:

$1\underline{20,000} \div 6\underset{\smile}{00}$

↑ ↑

4 zeros   2 zeros

We cross out 2 zeros in both the divisor and the dividend.

$$120,0\cancel{0}\cancel{0} \div 6\cancel{0}\cancel{0}$$

We then divide. $1,200 \div 6 = 200$

Example:

$1,26\underline{0} \div 2\underset{\smile}{00}$

↑ ↑

1 zero   2 zeros

We cross out 1 zero from both the divisor and the dividend. Then we divide.

$1,26\cancel{0} \div 20\cancel{0}$

$126 \div 20 = 6 \text{ r. } 6$

Cross out the zeros and then divide. Use a separate sheet of paper, if necessary.

1. $350 \div 70 = $ _____5_____

2. $36,000 \div 600 = $ _____

3. $12,000 \div 60 = $ _____

4. $1,800 \div 90 = $ _____

5. $2,000 \div 200 = $ _____

6. $45,000,000 \div 9,000 = $ _____

7. $11,000 \div 1,000 = $ _____

8. $1,500,000 \div 3,000 = $ _____

9. $28,000 \div 700 = $ _____

10. $4,200,000 \div 60,000 = $ _____

11. $8,200,000 \div 2,000 = $ _____

12. $240,000 \div 1,200 = $ _____

13. $15,600,000 \div 3,000 = $ _____

14. $56,000 \div 1,400 = $ _____

15. $3,600 \div 1,800 = $ _____

16. $90,000,000 \div 30,000 = $ _____

17. $33,000 \div 1,100 = $ _____

18. $85,000 \div 5,000 = $ _____

19. $300 \div 120 = $ _____

20. $63,500 \div 2,000 = $ _____

21. $18,750 \div 100 = $ _____

22. $13,000 \div 70 = $ _____

23. $15,000 \div 400 = $ _____

24. $2,300 \div 60 = $ _____

25. $9,000 \div 800 = $ _____

26. $12,400 \div 500 = $ _____

27. $11,000,000 \div 6,000 = $ _____

28. $6,800 \div 270 = $ _____

29. $19,000 \div 700 = $ _____

30. $17,000,000 \div 3,000 = $ _____

7-8 Order of Operations

When we have a problem with more than one kind of operation (for example, addition and multiplication), which operation do we do first? Look at the following problem.

$$3 + 2 \times 6$$

Which answer is correct?

$$\underline{3 + 2} \times 6 = \qquad\qquad 3 + \underline{2 \times 6} =$$
$$\text{or}$$
$$5 \quad \times 6 = 30 \qquad\qquad 3 + \quad 12 \quad = 15$$

When we have a problem with more than one kind of operation, we must follow the Rules of Order.

Rules of Order

1. Always begin at the left side.

2. First, do all multiplication and division in the order in which they are presented. For example, if multiplication comes before division, do the multiplication first. If division comes before multiplication, do the division first.

3. Next, do all addition and subtraction in the order in which they are presented. For example, if addition comes before subtraction, do the addition first. If subtraction comes before addition, do the subtraction first.

If we apply the Rules of Order to the problem below, we multiply first and then we add.

$$3 + 2 \times 6 =$$

$$3 + \underline{2 \times 6} =$$
Multiply.

$$\underline{3 + 12} = 15$$
Add.

Now look at the next problem.

$$10 \div 5 + 3 + 4 \times 2 - 4$$

We begin at the left side and do all multiplication and division in the order in which they are presented.

$$\underline{10 \div 5} + 3 + 4 \times 2 - 4$$
Divide.

$$2 + 3 + \underline{4 \times 2} - 4$$
Multiply.

$$2 + 3 + 8 - 4$$

Then we do all addition and subtraction in the order in which they are presented.

$$\underline{2 + 3} + 8 - 4$$
Add.

$$\underline{5 + 8} - 4$$
Add.

$$\underline{13 - 4} = 9$$
Subtract.

On a separate sheet of paper, use the Rules of Order to solve the following problems.

1. $4 \times 4 - 3 \times 5 =$

2. $10 - 3 + 4 - 1 =$

3. $9 \times 4 - 30 \div 6 =$

4. $21 \div 7 + 3 =$

5. $12 - 4 \times 2 =$

6. $64 \div 8 \times 2 \div 4 =$

7. $8 + 4 \div 2 + 5 - 10 =$

8. $6 \times 5 - 5 \times 4 =$

9. $10 \div 2 - 3 + 6 \times 5 =$

10. $36 - 42 \div 7 \times 6 =$

11. $15 - 10 + 5 - 3 =$

12. $18 - 8 \div 2 - 4 \div 2 =$

13. $6 \times 3 - 5 \times 2 =$

14. $6 + 15 \div 5 - 20 \div 10 =$

15. $18 \times 2 - 9 \div 3 =$

16. $25 \div 5 \times 4 + 6 - 2 =$

17. $24 \div 8 - 2 =$

18. $12 + 20 \div 4 - 5 =$

19. $34 - 4 \div 4 + 16 \times 2 =$

20. $8 \times 8 + 9 \div 3 - 60 =$

On a separate sheet of paper, use the Rules of Order to solve the following problems.

1. $6 + 4 \div 2 \times 7 - 11 =$

2. $15 \div 3 \times 3 - 15 =$

3. $6 + 14 - 8 \div 4 - 3 \div 3 =$

4. $35 - 10 \times 3 + 2 \div 2 + 6 =$

5. $24 \div 8 + 3 \times 6 =$

6. $16 \times 2 - 1 =$

7. $10 \times 2 - 1 \times 5 =$

8. $12 - 4 \times 2 + 6 \div 3 + 3 =$

9. $7 \times 7 + 10 \div 2 - 20 =$

10. $56 \div 7 \times 3 - 5 \times 2 =$

11. $15 \times 3 - 2 \times 8 =$

12. $11 - 4 \times 2 + 6 \times 2 - 2 =$

13. $12 \div 4 \times 2 - 6 =$

14. $5 + 13 - 8 \div 4 - 4 \div 2 + 3 =$

15. $8 + 16 - 10 \div 2 - 7 \div 7 =$

16. $25 - 3 \times 5 + 8 \div 1 + 4 - 3 =$

17. $20 \div 4 - 5 \div 1 =$

18. $12 \div 6 + 3 + 2 \times 4 - 4 =$

19. $16 - 5 + 72 \div 9 + 4 \times 3 - 12 =$

20. $25 + 6 \div 2 \times 2 + 9 - 4 \div 2 =$

7-9 More Order of Operations

When there are parentheses ( ), **brackets** [ ], or **braces** { }, we use the following Rules of Order.

Rules of Order

1. Always begin at the left side.

2. First, do all operations inside the parentheses, brackets, or braces, in the order in which they are presented.

3. If there are parentheses inside brackets [( )] or braces {()}, do the operation in parentheses first, then do the operation in brackets or braces.

Example:

Add first.

$$[4 \times (3 + 5)]$$

Then multiply.

4. When there aren't any parentheses or brackets or braces left, follow the Rules of Order given in Section 7-8.

Example:

$17 - (3 + 1) \times 4$

$17 - \underbrace{(3 + 1)}_{\text{Add.}} \times 4$

$17 - \underbrace{4 \times 4}_{\text{Multiply.}}$

$17 - 16 = 1$

Example:

$3 + [3 \times (4 + 2)] \div 6$

$3 + [3 \times \underbrace{(4 + 2)}_{\text{Add.}}] \div 6$

$3 + \underbrace{[3 \times 6]}_{\text{Multiply.}} \div 6$

$3 + \underbrace{18 \div 6}_{\text{Divide.}}$

$3 + 3 = 6$

On a separate sheet of paper, use the Rules of Order to solve the following problems.

1. $6 + (2 - 1) =$
2. $7 \times (5 - 3) =$
3. $4 \times (5 + 1) - 4 \div 2 =$
4. $\{9 + (3 + 4)\} =$
5. $6 + \{4 - (6 - 4)\} =$
6. $15 - (4 + 4) =$
7. $8 \div (2 \times 2) \times 9 =$
8. $80 - [10 \times (3 + 2)] =$

9. $6 \times (3 + 5) =$
10. $17 + (2 + 4) =$
11. $9 + (6 \times 3) \div 6 =$
12. $2 \times [(4 + 6) - 3] =$
13. $65 - (15 + 2) =$
14. $(6 - 3) \times (9 - 6) =$
15. $55 - \{2 \times (13 + 4)\} =$

On a separate sheet of paper, use the Rules of Order to solve the following problems.

1. $6 \times 3 - (2 \times 6 + 3) =$
2. $(81 \div 9) \div 3 =$
3. $(7 - 3) \div (11 - 9) =$
4. $7 \times (3 - 2) \times 4 + 3 \times 2 =$
5. $4 + [(6 \times 2) + 3] =$
6. $96 \div (12 \times 4) \div 2 =$
7. $43 + (24 - 20) =$
8. $6 \times 7 - (4 + 9) =$

9. $4 \times (42 - 11) =$
10. $7 \times [(12 + 5) - 3 \times (19 - 14)] =$
11. $6 \times 3 + (4 \times 3 + 2 \times 6) =$
12. $7 \times (5 + 28) \div 7 =$
13. $171 - (17 + 4) \times 2 \times 3 - 30 =$
14. $3 \times (4 + 5) - 7 =$
15. $2 \times [(4 + 9) - 3 \times (2 - 0)] =$

Complete the sentences. Write words from the box below.

commutative	factors	multiply
distributive	inverse	product
divided by	multiplicative property of zero	quotient
divisor		

1. Multiplication and division are _____*inverse*_____ operations.

2. The _____ of 3 and 2 is 6.

3. $7 \times 3 = 3 \times 7$ is an example of the _____ property of multiplication.

4. The answer in a division problem is called the _____.

5. We read ÷ as _____.

6. 4 × 0 = 0 is an example of the _____.

7. The number we divide by is called the _____.

8. In 7 + 3 × 2, we _____ first.

9. The numbers we multiply together are called _____.

10. 8(2 + 6) = 8 × 2 + 8 × 6 is an example of the _____ property.

Have I Learned? (✓)

Work with a partner. Check what you have learned. Review what you need help with.

1. division ☐		**7.** remainder ☐
2. divided by ☐		**8.** inverse operations ☐
3. equals ☐		**9.** Order of Operations ☐
4. quotient ☐		**10.** brackets ☐
5. dividend ☐		**11.** braces ☐
6. divisor ☐		

7-10 Solving Division Word Problems

The words *each* and *per* in word problems tell us to use division to solve the problems.

Example:

Together, John and Tyler earn $324 in 1 week. If they earn equal amounts, how much money does each receive?

The word *each* tells us that this is a division problem. We divide by 2 because there are two people who receive equal amounts of money.

Answer: $324 ÷ 2 = $162 each

Example:

Stella stayed at a hotel for 7 days. The total bill was $511. How much did she pay per day?

The word *per* means *during each.* We divide by 7 to find the cost for **each** day.

Answer: $511 ÷ 7 = $73 per day

Corey is a manager of the restaurant at the Four Stars Hotel. This Saturday night, he will need to prepare the tables for Lafayette High School's Senior Dinner and Dance. Answer the questions below about the dinner and dance. Write your answers on the lines. Show all your work on a separate sheet of paper.

1. There will be 216 students for dinner at the restaurant. Each table will seat 9 people. How many tables will Corey need? _____24 tables_____

2. There will be 36 teachers at the dinner. The teachers will sit at their own tables. Each table will seat 9 people. How many tables will Corey need for the teachers only?
   _____

3. How many tables will there be altogether? _____

4. How many people will there be altogether? _____

5. Corey will divide 12 dozen flowers evenly among the student tables.

   a. How many flowers does he have in all? _____

   b. How many flowers will he need for each student table? _____

In solving the word problems in Exercise 26, we used the quotient alone as the answer. When we have division problems with remainders, we sometimes use the remainder alone. At other times, we use both the remainder and the quotient together for our answer.

Example:

There are 115 students who need to take a certain math class. Each classroom can only seat 30 students.

(a) How many classrooms will be needed?

To solve the problem, we use division.

$$
\begin{array}{r}
3 \\
30\overline{)115} \\
-90 \\
\hline
25
\end{array}
$$

3 classrooms of 30 students

25 students (remainder) need another classroom

Answer: 4 classrooms (3 + 1) will be needed to seat 115 students. We use the quotient (3) and the remainder (25) to get our answer.

(b) How many classrooms will be full (classrooms with 30 students)?

$$
\begin{array}{r}
3 \\
30\overline{)115} \\
-90 \\
\hline
25
\end{array}
$$

3 classrooms of 30 students

Answer: 3 classrooms will be full. We use the quotient only to get our answer.

(c) How many classrooms will not be full (will have fewer than 30 students)?

$$
\begin{array}{r}
3 \\
30\overline{)115} \\
-90 \\
\hline
25
\end{array}
$$

25 students in 1 classroom

Answer: 1 classroom of 25 students. We use the remainder only to get our answer.

The Hirata family is planning a camping trip. There are 34 members in the family, including uncles, aunts, and cousins. They are planning to go to Silver Lake for one week. Answer the questions below about the Hirata family's plans. Write your answers on the lines. Show all your work on a separate sheet of paper.

1. The Hiratas are planning to travel by car. Each car seats 5 people. How many cars will they need? _____ *7 cars* _____

2. The Hiratas are going to bring tents for sleeping. Each tent can sleep up to 6 people.

   a. How many tents will they need? _____

   b. How many tents will be full? _____

   c. How many tents will not be full? _____

3. Yori Hirata is going to bring 36 poles to hold up the tents. How many poles will he use for each tent? _____

4. The Hirata children are going to hike around the lake. They are going to divide into groups of 6. There are 21 Hirata children altogether.

   a. How many full groups (groups of 6) will there be? _____

   b. How many children will be in a group of fewer than 6? _____

   c. How many groups will they need altogether? _____

5. Nari Hirata is going to buy apples for everyone. She is going to buy 70 apples altogether.

   a. How many apples will each person have to eat? _____

   b. How many extra apples will there be? _____

6. Keiko Hirata is going to buy bottles of water for everyone. She estimates that each person will drink 4 bottles of water. How many bottles will she need? _____

7. The bottles come in 6-packs (6 bottles in a pack). How many 6-packs will she need to buy? _____

8. The Hirata family is going to rent boats at the lake. Each boat can hold up to 7 people.

   a. How many boats will they need? _____

   b. How many boats will be full? _____

   c. How many people will be in a boat that has fewer than 7 people? _____

9. Each boat costs $18 a day to rent.

   a. How much will the Hirata family spend on boat rentals for 1 day? _____

   b. If the Hirata family has $300 to spend on boat rentals, for how many days will they be able to rent boats? _____

10. Six of the Hirata children are going to go horseback riding. Horseback riding costs $25 per hour per child. If the 6 Hirata children go horseback riding for one hour, how much will it cost them altogether? _____

Exercise 1

On a separate sheet of paper, write the following division problems using words.

1. $12 \div 6 = 2$ *Twelve divided by six equals two.*

3. $15 \div 5 = 3$

5. $72 \div 8 = 9$

2. $24 \div 3 = 8$

4. $21 \div 7 = 3$

Exercise 2

On a separate sheet of paper, divide the following numbers. Then check your answers. Rewrite the problems first, if necessary.

1. $345 \div 5 =$

5. $205 \div 4 =$

8. $1{,}650 \div 25 =$

2. $236 \div 4 =$

6. $34{,}003 \div 8 =$

9. $7{,}566 \div 20 =$

3. $5{,}004 \div 6 =$

7. $216 \div 12 =$

10. $60{,}544 \div 90 =$

4. $796 \div 5 =$

Exercise 3

On a separate sheet of paper, use inverse operations to find the missing numbers.

1. $12 \times \underline{\quad\quad} = 3{,}660$

3. $\underline{\quad\quad} + 742 = 3{,}245$

5. $\underline{\quad\quad} - 34 = 214$

2. $\underline{\quad\quad} \div 15 = 23$

4. $609 + \underline{\quad\quad} = 1{,}233$

Exercise 4

Multiply or divide by combining or crossing out zeros. Use a separate sheet of paper, if necessary.

1. $2{,}300{,}000 \div 1{,}000 = \underline{\quad 2{,}300 \quad}$

4. $16{,}000{,}000 \div 800 = \underline{\quad\quad\quad}$

2. $4{,}500 \times 100 = \underline{\quad\quad\quad\quad}$

5. $2{,}500 \times 200 \times 3{,}000 = \underline{\quad\quad\quad}$

3. $340 \times 2{,}000{,}000 = \underline{\quad\quad\quad}$

Exercise 5

On a separate sheet of paper, use the Rules of Order to solve the following problems.

1. $64 \div 8 \times 2 \div 4 =$

4. $\{8 \times (15 - 4)\} =$

2. $34 - 4 \div 4 + 16 \times 2 =$

5. $8 \times [(10 + 3) - 3 \times (18 - 16)] =$

3. $\{9 \times (3 + 4)\} =$

Number Theory

In this unit, you will learn . . .

- the number line

- negative integers and positive integers

- additive inverses

- whole numbers

- even integers and odd integers

- prime numbers

- composite numbers

- prime factors

- bases and exponents

- using base ten and exponents

- the zero exponent

- expanded notation

CHAPTER 8 Integers

8-1 The Number Line

Look at the number line below.

The number line continues to the right and to the left. There is no end to the number line.

Now look at the number line below. The numbers on the number line are called **integers**. There is an infinite number of integers on a number line. That means there is no end to the number of integers. Notice that there are **negative** and **positive integers**.

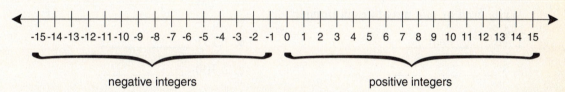

Every positive integer has an opposite negative integer, except 0. A positive integer and its opposite negative integer are called **additive inverses**.

Examples:
−1 and 1 are additive inverses.
−30 and 30 are additive inverses.

Exercise 1

Write the additive inverse of each integer.

1. −7 _____7_____
2. 19 _____
3. −33 _____
4. −45 _____
5. 100 _____

6. 98 _____
7. −67 _____
8. 1,344 _____
9. −876 _____
10. 1,020 _____

Now look at the number line below. The positive integers (0, 1, 2, 3, . . .) are also called whole numbers.

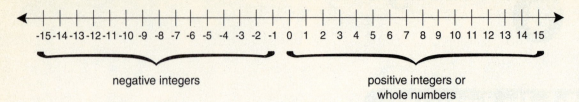

negative integers

positive integers or
whole numbers

Even integers are whole numbers that end with a 0, 2, 4, 6, or 8, except 0.

Odd integers are whole numbers that end with a 1, 3, 5, 7, or 9.

Even and odd integers can also be negative:

Even negative integers: −2, −4, −6, −8, . . .
Odd negative integers: −1, −3, −5, −7, . . .

Exercise 2

Write *even* or *odd* next to each integer.

1. 16 _____even_____

2. 3 _____

3. −4 _____

4. 20 _____

5. 11 _____

6. 123 _____

7. −200 _____

8. 1,609 _____

9. 1,151 _____

10. 2,300 _____

11. −1,000 _____

12. 2,001 _____

13. 4,500 _____

14. 600,000 _____

15. 2,235 _____

Write integers to answer the following questions.

1. What is the odd integer between 10 and 12? _____//_____

2. What is the even integer between −3 and −1? _____

3. Is your address number an even or odd number? _____

4. What is the next even integer after 98? _____

5. What is the next odd integer after 637? _____

6. Is your age an even or odd number? _____

7. How many odd integers are there between 36 and 49? _____

8. How many even integers are there between −1 and 15? _____

9. Name all the negative even integers between −5 and −19. _____

   _____

10. Name all the negative odd integers between −33 and −52. _____

   _____

8-2 Comparing Integers

Look at the following number line.

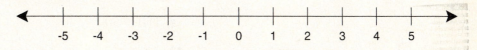

On the number line, the integers on the right are greater than the integers on the left.

Examples:
3 is greater than 1.
1 is greater than −3.
−1 is greater than −2.

The integers on the left are less than the integers on the right.

Examples:
2 is less than 4.
0 is less than 1.
−4 is less than −3.

The symbol for *is greater than* is >.

Examples:

$4 > 2$

$-6 > -12$

The symbol for *is less than* is <.

Examples:

$7 < 9$

$-1 < 2$

The symbol for *is equal to* is =.

Examples:

$3 = 3$

$-5 = -5$

Exercise 4

Work with a partner. Say the following expressions aloud.

1. $14 < 20$ *Fourteen is less than twenty.*
2. $6 < 14$
3. $19 < 25$
4. $0 = 0$
5. $-2 < 1$

6. $0 > -3$
7. $-16 < -11$
8. $45 > 44$
9. $150 > 50$
10. $-5 < -2$

Exercise 5

Write the symbol <, >, or = for each item below.

1. $0 \underline{\ >\ } -5$
2. $-15 \underline{\quad} -12$
3. $29 \underline{\quad} 29$
4. $-94 \underline{\quad} -95$
5. $675 \underline{\quad} 657$

6. $-410 \underline{\quad} 401$
7. $-2 \underline{\quad} 0$
8. $15 \underline{\quad} 15$
9. $-11 \underline{\quad} -30$
10. $0 \underline{\quad} -6$

Exercise 6

Write positive or negative integers to answer the questions below.

1. Write two odd integers greater than 95. _____ *97 and 99* _____

2. Write two even integers greater than 27. _____

116

3. Write two even positive integers less than 6. _____

4. Write two odd negative integers greater than −5. _____

5. Write two even negative integers less than −15. _____

6. Write two even integers greater than 26 and less than 31. _____

7. Write three odd integers greater than 0 and less than 7. _____

8. Write two even negative integers greater than −10 and less than −5. _____

9. Write two odd negative integers greater than −20 and less than −16. _____

10. Write an odd integer less than 2 and greater than −1. _____

Exercise 7

Write each group of integers in order, from smallest to greatest.

1. 7, 0, 4, −1 _____−1, 0, 4, 7_____   **11.** 6, 9, −6, −9 _____

2. 9, −3, −2, 6 _____   **12.** 6, −7, 4, −8 _____

3. 3, −8, −2, −7 _____   **13.** −4, −7, 0, 1 _____

4. −3, −6, 5, −4 _____   **14.** −4, −6, −3, −10 _____

5. 9, 14, −5, −9 _____   **15.** −3, −5, 3, 5 _____

6. −6, 6, 3, −3 _____   **16.** 12, −8, −3, 6 _____

7. −7, 5, −2, 0 _____   **17.** 19, −24, −18, 23 _____

8. −4, −2, 6, 1 _____   **18.** 0, −1, −3, 4 _____

9. 14, −7, −5, 5 _____   **19.** −15, −19, −13, −10 _____

10. −9, −8, −10, −12 _____   **20.** 14, 12, 0, −14 _____

Have I Learned? (✓)

Work with a partner. Check what you have learned. Review what you need help with.

1. number line ☐   **9.** odd integers ☐

2. integers ☐   **10.** is greater than ☐

3. infinite ☐   **11.** is less than ☐

4. negative integers ☐   **12.** is equal to ☐

5. positive integers ☐   **13.** > ☐

6. additive inverse ☐   **14.** < ☐

7. whole numbers ☐   **15.** = ☐

8. even integers ☐

Exercise 1

Write the additive inverse of each integer.

1. 15 _____*−15*_____   **3.** 100 _____   **5.** −2,388 _____

2. −3 _____   **4.** 35 _____

Exercise 2

Write *even* or *odd* next to each integer.

1. 10 _____*even*_____   **3.** 1,800 _____   **5.** 2,787 _____

2. 100 _____   **4.** 333 _____

Exercise 3

On a separate sheet of paper, write the following expressions using words.

1. 4 > 2 ___*Four is greater than two.*___   **4.** −9 < 0

2. 9 < 18   **5.** 25 = 25

3. −4 > −15

Exercise 4

Write the symbol <, >, or = for each item below.

1. 37 __*<*__ 45   **6.** 950 _____ 905

2. −15 _____ 0   **7.** −55 _____ 55

3. 9 _____ 19   **8.** −222 _____ −222

4. 0 _____ −12   **9.** 98 _____ −98

5. −24 _____ −55   **10.** 416 _____ 416

Exercise 5

Write each group of integers in order, from smallest to greatest.

1. 12, 6, 0, 7 _____*0, 6, 7, 12*_____   **6.** −45, −66, −13, −54 _____

2. −4, 7, −5, 10 _____   **7.** 8, −7, 0, −9 _____

3. 34, 43, −13, −4 _____   **8.** −11, −10, −12, −9 _____

4. −19, 0, −45, −8 _____   **9.** 34, 43, 54, 45 _____

5. 456, 355, 534, 435 _____   **10.** −6, −16, 9, 0 _____

CHAPTER 9 Prime Numbers, Bases, and Exponents

9-1 Prime Numbers

In Chapter 6, we studied factors. Factors are the numbers we multiply together to result in a product.

Example:

What are the factors of 8?

$8 = 1 \times 8$ $\qquad\qquad$ $8 = 2 \times 4$

The factors of 8 are 1, 8, 2, and 4. There are four factors of 8.

Some numbers have only two factors. Other numbers have more than two factors.

Example:

$7 = 1 \times 7$ $\qquad\qquad$ $12 \begin{cases} = 1 \times 12 \\ = 2 \times 6 \\ = 3 \times 4 \end{cases}$

The number 7 has only two factors. The number 12 has six factors.

Exercise 1

On a separate sheet of paper, make a chart like the one below. Then write all the factors for each number and how many factors there are.

Factors	How many?	Factors	How many?
1. 14 $1 \times 14, 2 \times 7$	4	11. 24	
2. 40		12. 35	
3. 48		13. 100	
4. 11		14. 23	
5. 28		15. 56	
6. 36		16. 13	
7. 5		17. 99	
8. 12		18. 33	
9. 19		19. 150	
10. 27		20. 80	

A **prime number** is a whole number greater than 1 that has exactly two factors. The factors are 1 and the number itself. Look at these examples of some prime numbers and their factors.

$$2 = 1 \times 2 \qquad\qquad 7 = 1 \times 7$$
$$3 = 1 \times 3 \qquad\qquad 11 = 1 \times 11$$
$$5 = 1 \times 5 \qquad\qquad 13 = 1 \times 13$$

Because there are an infinite number of integers, there are also an infinite number of prime numbers.

A **composite number** is a whole number greater than 1 with more than two factors. Look at these examples of composite numbers and their factors.

$$4 = 1 \times 4 \qquad 6 = 1 \times 6 \qquad 8 = 1 \times 8 \qquad 9 = 1 \times 9$$
$$= 2 \times 2 \qquad\quad = 2 \times 3 \qquad\quad = 2 \times 4 \qquad\quad = 3 \times 3$$

There are an infinite number of composite numbers.

The number 1 is neither a prime number nor a composite number.

Exercise 2

Write *prime* or *composite* next to each number below.

1. 10 ___composite___
2. 11 _____
3. 15 _____
4. 2 _____
5. 33 _____
6. 27 _____
7. 21 _____

8. 17 _____
9. 22 _____
10. 29 _____
11. 39 _____
12. 3 _____
13. 9 _____
14. 5 _____

15. 23 _____
16. 45 _____
17. 19 _____
18. 100 _____
19. 7 _____
20. 14 _____

Exercise 3

Follow the directions or answer the questions.

1. Name all the prime numbers between 1 and 20. ___2, 3, 5, 7, 11, 13, 17, 19___

2. What prime number is greater than 30 and less than 35? _____

3. How many prime numbers are there between 10 and 20? _____

4. How many prime numbers are there altogether? _____

5. Name all the composite numbers between 20 and 30. _____

120

When the factors of a number are prime numbers, they are called **prime factors**. Look at these examples of prime factors.

$$6 = 3 \times 2$$
$$35 = 5 \times 7$$
$$21 = 7 \times 3$$

We can write prime factors for composite numbers, for example, for the numbers 24, 16, and 20.

$$24 = 2 \times 2 \times 2 \times 3$$
$$16 = 2 \times 2 \times 2 \times 2$$
$$20 = 2 \times 2 \times 5$$

We *cannot* write prime factors for prime numbers.

$$2 = 1 \times 2 \qquad\qquad 5 = 1 \times 5$$
$$7 = 1 \times 7 \qquad\qquad 13 = 1 \times 13$$
$$11 = 1 \times 11 \qquad\quad 17 = 1 \times 17$$

1 is *not* a prime number.

Since 1 is not a prime number—and since 1 is a factor for every prime number—we cannot write prime factors for prime numbers.

Exercise 4

Write two factors for each number. Use prime factors.

1. 15 _____ 3×5 _____   6. 9 _____   11. 33 _____

2. 22 _____   7. 14 _____   12. 65 _____

3. 21 _____   8. 55 _____   13. 10 _____

4. 6 _____   9. 35 _____   14. 49 _____

5. 25 _____   10. 26 _____   15. 14 _____

There is an easy way to find the prime factors of a composite number. We use a **factor tree**. The lines / \ are called the branches of the tree.

Examples:

Follow these steps to make a factor tree:

1. For a composite number, write two factors. Draw two branches between the number and factors. Look at the example below.

2. If any factor is composite, write two more factors, with branches. Bring down any prime factor. Look at the example below.

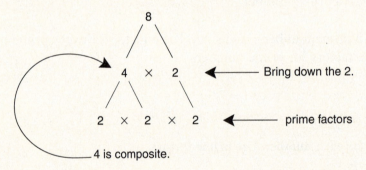

When all the numbers on the last line are prime, you have found the prime factors of the composite number.

On a separate sheet of paper, find the prime factors for each number by drawing a factor tree.

1. 20	**8.** 22	**14.** 96	**20.** 45
2. 25	**9.** 100	**15.** 75	**21.** 80
3. 30	**10.** 35	**16.** 55	**22.** 90
4. 36	**11.** 50	**17.** 56	**23.** 125
5. 60	**12.** 16	**18.** 28	**24.** 200
6. 24	**13.** 63	**19.** 64	**25.** 150
7. 39			

9-3 Bases and Exponents

The prime factors of 8 are $2 \times 2 \times 2$. We can write $2 \times 2 \times 2$ in a shorter form: 2^3. We read 2^3 as "Two to the third power." In 2^3, the number 2 is called the **base**. The number 3 is called the **exponent**. The exponent tells us how many times the number, or base, is used as a factor. (In 2^3, 2 is used as a factor 3 times.)

Now look at how we read the following expressions.

2^0 = "two to the zero power"
2^1 = "two to the first power"
2^2 = "two to the second power" or "two squared"
2^3 = "two to the third power" or "two cubed"
2^4 = "two to the fourth power"

We read the base as a cardinal number and the exponent as an ordinal number.

Exercise 6

Work with a partner. Read the following expressions aloud.

1. 4^3 _four to the third power_ OR _four cubed_	**6.** 6^2	**11.** 2^{10}
2. 3^5	**7.** 3^0	**12.** 4^8
3. 9^2	**8.** 10^3	**13.** 7^4
4. 7^1	**9.** 9^7	**14.** 3^6
5. 8^5	**10.** 10^2	**15.** 10^0

Rewrite the expressions below using bases and exponents.

1. $7 \cdot 7 \cdot 7 =$ _____ 7^3 _____

2. $5 \cdot 5 \cdot 5 =$ _____

3. $4 \cdot 4 =$ _____

4. $9 =$ _____

5. $3 \cdot 3 \cdot 3 \cdot 3 =$ _____

6. $x \cdot x \cdot x =$ _____

7. $2 \cdot 2 \cdot 2 \cdot 2 \cdot 2 =$ _____

8. $10 \times 10 =$ _____

9. $m \cdot m \cdot m \cdot m =$ _____

10. $15 =$ _____

11. $c \cdot c + k \cdot k =$ _____

12. $y \cdot y \cdot y \cdot y \cdot y \cdot y =$ _____

13. $4 \cdot 4 \cdot 4 \cdot 4 \cdot 4 \cdot 4 \cdot 4 \cdot 4 =$ _____

14. six squared = _____

15. nine to the seventh power = _____

16. twelve cubed = _____

17. sixteen to the third power = _____

18. y to the eleventh power = _____

19. n cubed = _____

20. a to the b power = _____

21. $m \cdot m \cdot m + n \cdot n \cdot n \cdot n \cdot n =$ _____

22. r to the s power = _____

23. x squared = _____

24. $20 \cdot 20 \cdot 20 \cdot 20 \cdot 20 \cdot 20 =$ _____

25. five cubed = _____

26. two to the eighth power = _____

27. x cubed plus y squared = _____

28. four to the zero power = _____

29. fourteen to the second power = _____

30. ten cubed plus nine squared = _____

On a separate sheet of paper, multiply to find the answers.

1. $7^3 = 7 \times 7 \times 7 = 343$

2. $3^5 =$

3. $19^2 =$

4. $6^4 =$

5. $13^3 =$

6. $1^8 =$

7. $10^3 =$

8. $12^2 =$

9. $4^3 =$

10. $10^8 =$

11. $8^4 =$

12. $3^4 =$

13. $6^5 =$

14. $2^8 =$

15. $9^4 =$

16. $5^4 =$

17. $36^2 =$

18. $5^5 =$

19. $100^3 =$

20. $30^4 =$

21. $3^3 =$

22. $4^5 =$

23. $1^5 =$

24. $25^3 =$

25. $50^3 =$

26. $9^2 =$

27. $2^9 =$

28. $10^1 =$

29. $20^3 =$

30. $15^3 =$

In Chapter 6, we learned how to multiply numbers quickly by multiples of ten.

To multiply numbers by multiples of ten, we first multiply the nonzero digits and then combine the zeros.

Example:
$100 \times 1,000$
Multiply 1×1: $1 \times 1 = 1$
Combine the zeros: 2 zeros + 3 zeros = 5 zeros
Answer: 100,000
                     1 and 5 zeros

Now we can use base ten and exponents in our answers when we multiply numbers by multiples of ten.

Example:
$1,000 \times 100 = 100,000 = 10^5$
(The exponent 5 tells us that there are 5 zeros.)

Example:
$1,000 \times 100,000 = 10^8$
(The exponent 8 tells us that there are 8 zeros.)

Remember, when the base is ten, the exponent tells us the number of zeros.

Exercise 9

On a separate sheet of paper, write the answers using base ten and an exponent.

1. $10 \times 10 = \underline{\quad 10^2 \quad}$
2. $100 \times 10 =$
3. $1,000 \times 1,000 =$
4. $100 \times 1,000 =$
5. $100 \times 10,000 =$

6. $100 \times 100 \times 100 =$
7. $1,000 \times 10 =$
8. $100,000,000 \times 10 =$
9. $100 \times 10 \times 1,000 =$
10. $100 \times 1,000 \times 10 =$

11. $100,000 =$
12. $1,000,000,000 =$
13. $10 =$
14. $100 \times 1,000 \times 100,000 =$
15. $1,000,000,000,000,000 =$

9-5 The Zero Exponent

The **zero exponent** is a special exponent. It makes all numbers equal to 1.

Examples:

$3^0 = 1$ $5^0 = 1$ $x^0 = 1$
$10^0 = 1$ $1^0 = 1$ $m^0 = 1$

125

Now, using what we know about bases and exponents, let's simplify the following expression.

$$4^2 + 4^0 =$$
$$\overbrace{4 \times 4} + 1 =$$
$$16 + 1 = 17$$

Exercise 10

On a separate sheet of paper, simplify the following expressions.

1. $5^0 + 5^1 = $ *1 + 5 = 6*

2. $2^0 + 2^2 =$

3. $4^0 =$

4. $10^5 =$

5. $3^3 - 3^1 =$

6. $2^4 =$

7. $9^0 - 2^0 =$

8. $8^2 + 8^0 =$

9. $5^3 =$

10. $10^3 + 2^0 =$

11. $5^2 + 5^2 =$

12. $20^0 =$

13. $10^4 + 10^0 =$

14. $9^2 + 7^2 + 10^2 =$

15. $2^4 + 2^3 + 2^0 =$

16. $10^4 + 10^2 + 10^1 + 10^0 =$

17. $20^2 + 3^2 =$

18. $8^2 + 4^3 + 10^2 =$

19. $10^3 + 2^3 + 5^0 =$

20. $8^0 + 17^0 + 4^0 =$

21. $10^6 + 10^0 =$

22. $3^4 + 3^1 =$

23. $2^0 + 1^0 + 2^1 =$

24. $x^0 - y^0 =$

25. $5^1 + 7^0 - 3 =$

LISTENING

Your teacher will say expressions aloud. Listen. Then circle the letter next to the correct expression.

1. a. 40^2
   b. 4^2 (circled)
   c. 4^1

2. a. $70 > 30$
   b. $17 > 32$
   c. $17 < 32$

3. a. $16 < 12$
   b. $16 > 12$
   c. $12 > 16$

4. a. 5^{30}
   b. 5×30
   c. $5 + 30$

5. a. $11 = m$
   b. $11 \times m$
   c. $11 + m$

6. a. $t - 14$
   b. $14 > t$
   c. $14 < t$

7. a. $x^3 + y^2$
   b. $x^2 + y^2$
   c. $x^2 + y^3$

8. a. $8^2 + 3^2$
   b. $8^3 + 3^3$
   c. $8^2 + 2^3$

9. a. $s\overline{)r}$
   b. $r\overline{)s}$
   c. $s \div r$

10. a. 3×3
   b. 3^2
   c. 2^3

11. a. $10^5 - 100$
   b. $10^5 - 10^2$
   c. $10^5 - 100^2$

12. a. $b \times 4$
   b. b^4
   c. 4^b

13. a. $-6 < -9$
   b. $-6 > -9$
   c. $-6 > 9$

14. a. $m^2 > m^3$
   b. $m^3 < m^2$
   c. $m^3 > m^2$

15. a. $-40 < -14$
   b. $-14 < -40$
   c. $-40 > -14$

16. **a.** 6^0
 b. 0^6
 c. 6^6

17. **a.** $4^3 = 81$
 b. $3^4 = 81$
 c. $3^4 = 18$

18. **a.** 10^{60}
 b. 10^6
 c. 10^{16}

19. **a.** $x^2 > y^3$
 b. $x^2 < y^3$
 c. $x \times 2 < y^3$

20. **a.** $3^{10} = 100$
 b. $10^3 = 100$
 c. $10 \times 3 = 100$

Exercise 11

Complete each sentence. Circle the letter next to the correct answer.

1. In 10^2, the exponent is _____.
 a. 10
 b. 2
 c. 3

2. Zero is _____.
 a. neither positive nor negative
 b. a negative integer
 c. a positive integer

3. The additive inverse of -3 is _____.
 a. 3
 b. -3
 c. 0

4. Whole numbers are _____.
 a. negative and positive integers
 b. negative integers
 c. positive integers

5. 14 is _____.
 a. an odd integer
 b. an even integer
 c. a negative integer

6. A prime number has _____.
 a. one factor
 b. two factors
 c. more than two factors

7. 1 is _____.
 a. a prime number
 b. a composite number
 c. neither prime nor composite

8. 20 is a _____.
 a. composite and even integer
 b. composite and odd integer
 c. prime and even integer

9. We say or read exponents as _____.
 a. cardinal numbers
 b. ordinal numbers
 c. round numbers

10. A number with a zero exponent is _____.
 a. equal to zero
 b. equal to the number
 c. equal to one

9-6 Expanded Notation

We can write the number 52 in **expanded notation**:

$$52 = (5 \times 10) + (2 \times 1)$$

There are 5 tens and 2 ones in the number 52.

How do we write the number 427 in expanded notation?

$$427 = (4 \times 100) + (2 \times 10) + (7 \times 1)$$

There are 4 hundreds, 2 tens, and 7 ones in the number 427.

On a separate sheet of paper, write the following numbers in expanded notation.

1. $12 = \underline{(1 \times 10) +}$
   $\underline{(2 \times 1)}$

2. $26 =$

3. $7 =$

4. $68 =$

5. $219 =$

6. $306 =$

7. $999 =$

8. $2{,}121 =$

9. $3{,}456 =$

10. $12{,}904 =$

11. $125{,}840 =$

12. $230{,}090 =$

13. $4{,}609{,}031 =$

14. $104 =$

15. $4{,}070 =$

We can use base ten with exponents to write numbers in expanded notation.

Examples:
$3{,}521 = (3 \times 10^3) + (5 \times 10^2) + (2 \times 10^1) + (1 \times 10^0)$
$206 = (2 \times 10^2) + (0 \times 10^1) + (6 \times 10^0)$

Remember, the zero exponent makes all numbers equal to one.

Example:
$(2 \times 10^0) = 2 \times 1 = 2$

Write the following numbers in expanded notation, using base ten with exponents. Use a separate sheet of paper.

1. $90 = \underline{(9 \times 10^1) +}$
   $\underline{(0 \times 10^0)}$

2. $29 =$

3. $10 =$

4. $1 =$

5. $980 =$

6. $600 =$

7. $704 =$

8. $4{,}001 =$

9. $5{,}387 =$

10. $1{,}600 =$

11. $60{,}525 =$

12. $12{,}401 =$

13. $75{,}300 =$

14. $190{,}026 =$

15. $143{,}974 =$

16. $2{,}366{,}747 =$

17. $23{,}574{,}077 =$

18. $254{,}664{,}922 =$

19. $652{,}387 =$

20. $4{,}694{,}123 =$

Complete the sentences on the next page. Write the correct words or numbers from the box.

factor	exponent	greater than	2
between	even	beginning	equal to
negative	infinite	less than	end
left	integer	1	odd
additive inverse	base	power	whole numbers
positive			

1. A number line has no ___beginning___ and no ___end___.

2. We read x^3 as "x cubed" or "x to the third _____."

3. Zero is a _____ integer.

4. A _____ integer is less than zero.

5. There are an _____ number of integers on the number line.

6. −27 is the _____ _____ of 27.

7. An _____ integer can be divided by 2 with no remainder.

8. In "two to the third power," the _____ is 2.

9. To write $m \times m$ with an exponent, we use m as the base and _____ as the exponent.

10. −7 is a negative _____ integer.

11. −4 is _____ _____ −3.

12. −2 comes _____ −3 and −1.

13. When two integers have the same value, they are _____ _____ each other.

14. A number with a zero exponent is always equal to _____.

15. 6 is less than 7 because 6 is to the _____ of 7 on the number line.

16. In "five cubed," the _____ is 3.

17. 16 is an example of a positive _____.

18. 2 is a _____ of 8.

19. 1 is _____ _____ 0.

20. Positive integers are also called _____ _____.

Have I Learned? (✓)

Work with a partner. Check what you have learned. Review what you need help with.

1. factors ☐
2. prime number ☐
3. composite number ☐
4. prime factors ☐
5. factor tree ☐

6. base ☐
7. exponent ☐
8. zero exponent ☐
9. expanded notation ☐

Exercise 1

On a separate sheet of paper, find the prime factors for each number by drawing a factor tree.

1. 45

2. 24

3. 100

4. 33

5. 50

Exercise 2

On a separate sheet of paper, write the following expressions using words.

1. 3^2 _three squared_ OR _three to the_
   second power

2. 10^3

3. 2^4

4. 9^6

5. 100^1

Exercise 3

Rewrite the expressions below using bases and exponents.

1. $3 \times 3 \times 3 \times 3 =$ _____ 3^4 _____

2. $10 \cdot 10 \cdot 10 \cdot 10 \cdot 10 =$ _____

3. $7 =$ _____

4. $5 \times 5 \times 5 =$ _____

5. $m \cdot m \cdot m \cdot m \cdot m \cdot m \cdot m \cdot m =$ _____

6. $a \cdot a + b \cdot b \cdot b \cdot b =$ _____

7. twenty cubed = _____

8. nine squared = _____

9. $4 \cdot 4 \cdot 4 \cdot 4 + 2 \cdot 2 =$ _____

10. $x \cdot x =$ _____

11. y cubed plus n squared = _____

12. $2 \cdot 2 \cdot 2 \cdot 2 \cdot 2 \cdot 2 \cdot 2 \cdot 2 \cdot 2 =$ _____

13. t to the y power = _____

14. six to the first power = _____

15. r squared plus b cubed = _____

Exercise 4

Simplify the following expressions.

1. $7^2 =$ _____ 49 _____

2. $10^5 =$ _____

3. $2^4 =$ _____

4. $19^0 =$ _____

5. $3^5 + 3^2 =$ _____

6. $10^3 - 10^2 =$ _____

7. $4^2 + 4^1 =$ _____

8. $2^3 + 2^2 + 2^0 =$ _____

9. $9^2 + 9^1 - 9^0 =$ _____

10. $3^4 + 8^0 - 2^2 =$ _____

UNIT 4

Operations with Decimal Numbers

In this unit, you will learn . . .

- tenths
- hundredths
- thousandths
- more decimal places
- how to write integers as decimals
- how to add decimals
- how to use decimals to express money
- how to subtract decimals
- how to use inverse operations to find missing decimals
- how to round off decimals
- how to multiply decimals
- how to divide with decimals
- how to solve problems with decimals
- how to find the average, or mean

10-1 Tenths •••

Look at the integers on the following number line.

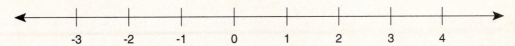

We do not see divisions between 0 and 1, 1 and 2, 2 and 3, and so on, but we can make an infinite number of divisions, or points, between each integer. Look at the following number line.

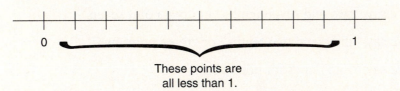

These points are all less than 1.

Now let's make 10 equal divisions between 0 and 1.

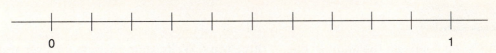

In the number line above, each division, or point, is called a **tenth**. Look at the following number line.

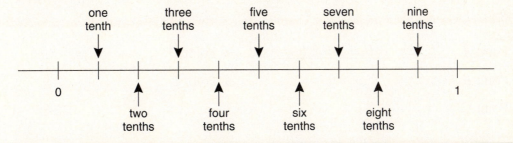

We refer to the numbers as **decimal numbers**, or **decimals**.

We say or write:	As a decimal, we write:	We can also say:
one tenth	.1	"point one"
two tenths	.2	"point two"
three tenths	.3	"point three"
four tenths	.4	"point four"
five tenths	.5	"point five"
six tenths	.6	"point six"
seven tenths	.7	"point seven"
eight tenths	.8	"point eight"
nine tenths	.9	"point nine"

To write a number as tenths, we write the number to the right of the **decimal point**, in the **tenths place**.

Example:

$$. \underline{6}$$

↑ ↑
decimal point   tenths place

We say, "six tenths" or "point six."

Look at the following number line.

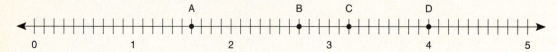

Point *A* = 1.6   We say, "one and six tenths" or "one point six."

We always read the decimal point as "and."

Point *B* = 2.7   We say, "two and seven tenths" or "two point seven."

Point *C* = 3.2   We say, "three and two tenths" or "three point two."

Point *D* = 4.0   We say, "four" or "four point zero."

Exercise 1

Identify the points on the number line in three ways. Write your answers on a separate sheet of paper.

1. Point *A* *.2; two tenths; point two*

2. Point *B*

3. Point *C*

4. Point *D*

5. Point *E*

Exercise 2

Write the following expressions as decimals.

1. six tenths _____.6_____

2. nine tenths _____

3. seven and eight tenths _____

4. eight point seven _____

5. three and three tenths _____

6. six point zero _____

7. fifty and four tenths _____

8. nine point one _____

9. sixty and two tenths _____

10. three point zero _____

Compare the decimals. Use < or >.

1. .8 __>__ .7

2. .2 _____ .5

3. 6.3 _____ 6.1

4. 5.3 _____ 5.9

5. 7.4 _____ 7.0

6. .9 _____ 1.0

7. 11.4 _____ 1.4

8. 24.9 _____ 25.0

9. 6.1 _____ 5.9

10. 10.9 _____ 9.1

10-2 Hundredths

Let's make 100 equal divisions between 0 and 1.

In the number line above, each division, or point, is called a **hundredth**. Look at the following number line.

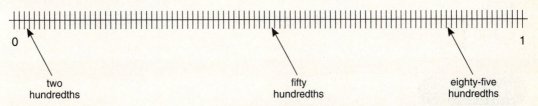

We say or write:	As a decimal, we write:	We can also say:
one hundredth	.01	"point zero one"
two hundredths	.02	"point zero two"
twelve hundredths	.12	"point one two"
twenty hundredths	.20	"point two zero"
twenty-one hundredths	.21	"point two one"
sixty-four hundredths	.64	"point six four"
ninety-eight hundredths	.98	"point nine eight"
ninety-nine hundredths	.99	"point nine nine"

Look at the following number line.

Point A = 1.32   We say, "one and thirty-two hundredths" or "one point three two."

Point B = 1.66   We say, "one and sixty-six hundredths" or "one point six six."

We always read the decimal point as "and," and we always use the place name at the end of the decimal: "one *and* thirty-two *hundredths*," "one *and* sixty-six *hundredths*."

To write a number as hundredths, we write the last digit of the number to the right of the decimal point in the **hundredths place**.

Example:

$$. \;\; \underline{2} \;\; \underline{3}$$

decimal point   tenths place   hundredths place

We say, "twenty-three hundredths" or "point two three."

Exercise 4

Work with a partner. Say the following numbers aloud.

1. .09   *nine hundredths;*
    point zero nine

2. .06

3. .19

4. .90

5. 3.40

6. 9.01

7. 16.10

8. 8.22

9. .95

10. 1.00

11. 45.05

12. 18.80

13. 9.91

14. 102.02

15. 200.02

Exercise 5

Write the following expressions as decimals.

1. seven hundredths _____ .07 _____

2. four hundredths _____

3. thirteen hundredths _____

4. ten hundredths _____

5. ninety hundredths _____

6. point zero one _____

7. five and three hundredths _____

8. two point one one _____

9. nineteen and eleven hundredths _____

10. seven point zero one _____

11. twelve point seven two _____

12. thirteen and nineteen hundredths _____

13. fifty-five point three six _____

14. ten and ten hundredths _____

15. eighteen and one hundredth _____

16. seven point zero zero _____

17. thirty and two hundredths _____

18. ninety-five point six two _____

19. forty-three and four hundredths _____

20. one hundred and one hundredth _____

10-3 Equivalent Decimals in Tenths and Hundredths

Compare   .3 with .30

three tenths   thirty hundredths

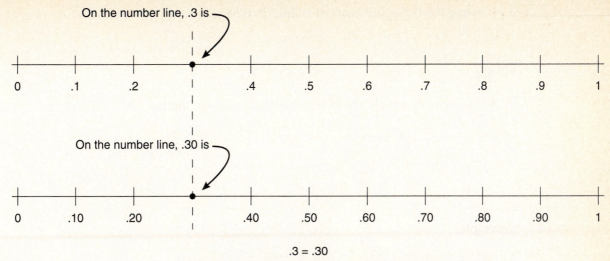

On the number line, .3 is

| + | | + | | + | | + | | + | | + | | + | | + | | + | | + | |
| 0 | .1 | .2 | | .4 | .5 | .6 | .7 | .8 | .9 | 1 |

On the number line, .30 is

| + | | + | | + | | + | | + | | + | | + | | + | | + | | + | |
| 0 | .10 | .20 | | .40 | .50 | .60 | .70 | .80 | .90 | 1 |

.3 = .30

They are **equivalent decimals**, or equal decimals.

To change a decimal in tenths to an equivalent decimal in hundredths, write a zero in the hundredths place.

Example:

tenths	→	hundredths	
.2	→	.2<u>0</u>	(.2 = .20)
1.6	→	1.6<u>0</u>	(1.6 = 1.60)

Exercise 6

Change the decimals in tenths to equivalent decimals in hundredths. Write your answers on the lines.

1. .9 _____.90_____
2. .7 _____
3. 6.2 _____
4. 19.0 _____
5. .1 _____

6. 11.3 _____
7. .2 _____
8. 12.4 _____
9. 100.1 _____
10. 23.0 _____

11. 55.5 _____
12. 73.7 _____
13. 256.1 _____
14. 48.8 _____
15. 100.9 _____

10-4 Comparing Decimals in Tenths and Hundredths

How do we compare decimals in tenths with decimals in hundredths?

Example:

Compare .6 with .67

six tenths   sixty-seven hundredths

1. Change the decimal in tenths to hundredths.

.6   .67
↓
.60   .67

2. When both decimals are in hundredths, compare them.

.60 < .67
   so
.6 < .67

Example:

Compare 1.2 with 1.20.

1. Change 1.2 to hundredths.   **2.** Compare the two decimals.

1.2   1.20   1.20 = 1.20
↓   so
1.20   1.20   1.2 = 1.20

Exercise 7

Compare the decimals. Write <, >, or =.

1. .7 _<_ .76   **6.** 4.01 _____ 4.1   **11.** .1 _____ .10

2. .3 _____ .31   **7.** 17.0 _____ 17.00   **12.** 72.9 _____ 72.91

3. 1.0 _____ 1.2   **8.** 11.00 _____ 11.2   **13.** 9.6 _____ 9.59

4. 9.47 _____ 9.3   **9.** .4 _____ .43   **14.** 6.2 _____ 6.21

5. 6.9 _____ 6.87   **10.** .29 _____ .3   **15.** 21.32 _____ 21.3

10-5 Thousandths

Look at the following number line.

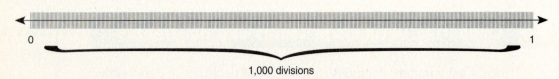

1,000 divisions

If there are 1,000 divisions between 0 and 1, each point is called a **thousandth**. Look at the following number line.

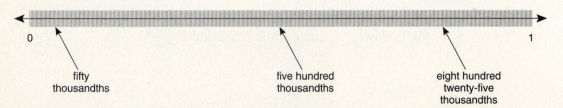

fifty
thousandths

five hundred
thousandths

eight hundred
twenty-five
thousandths

138

We say or write:	As a decimal, we write:	We can also say:
one thousandth	.001	"point zero zero one"
two thousandths	.002	"point zero zero two"
sixty thousandths	.060	"point zero six zero"
one hundred six thousandths	.106	"point one zero six"
nine hundred fifty thousandths	.950	"point nine five zero"

Look at the following number line.

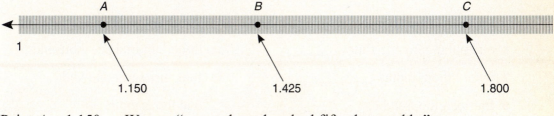

Point *A* = 1.150   We say, "one and one hundred fifty thousandths" or "one point one five zero."

Point *B* = 1.425   We say, "one and four hundred twenty-five thousandths" or "one point four two five."

Point *C* = 1.800   We say, "one and eight hundred thousandths" or "one point eight zero zero."

We always read the decimal point as "and," and we always use the place name at the end of the decimal: "one *and* one hundred fifty *thousandths*," "one *and* four hundred twenty-five *thousandths*," "one *and* eight hundred *thousandths*."

To write a number as thousandths, we write the last digit of the number to the right of the decimal point in the **thousandths place**.

Example:

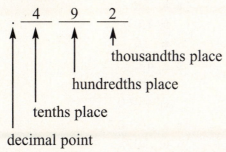

We say, "four hundred ninety-two thousandths" or "point four nine two."

Exercise 8

Work with a partner. Say the following numbers aloud.

1. .003	**5.** .599	**9.** 21.200	**13.** 1.999
2. .010	**6.** 2.072	**10.** 64.350	**14.** 17.090
3. .025	**7.** 1.002	**11.** 173.001	**15.** 81.003
4. .102	**8.** 13.020	**12.** 214.035	

Write the following expressions as decimals.

1. seventeen thousandths ___.017___

2. three thousandths _____

3. point zero six four _____

4. four and nineteen thousandths _____

5. six _____

6. one point zero one four _____

7. ninety thousandths _____

8. fourteen thousandths _____

9. fifty-two and thirty thousandths _____

10. six hundred eleven thousandths _____

11. four seven point zero zero nine _____

12. eight and eighty thousandths _____

13. ten thousandths _____

14. three hundred six thousandths _____

15. four thousand one and

one thousandth _____

LISTENING

Your teacher will read decimals aloud. Listen. Then circle the letter next to the correct decimal.

1. a. 4.03
   b. 43.3
   c. 4.3

2. a. .704
   b. .74
   c. 7.04

3. a. 1.09
   b. 1.19
   c. 1.90

4. a. .613
   b. .630
   c. 600.13

5. a. 3.14
   b. 3.40
   c. 3.040

6. a. .1
   b. .001
   c. .01

7. a. 7.006
   b. 7.060
   c. 7.0006

8. a. .50
   b. 15.1
   c. .15

9. a. 45.9
   b. 45.09
   c. 459.0

10. a. 500.07
    b. .507
    c. .0507

10-6 Equivalent Decimals in Tenths, Hundredths, and Thousandths

Compare   .4   .40   with   .400

four   forty   four hundred
tenths   hundredths thousandths

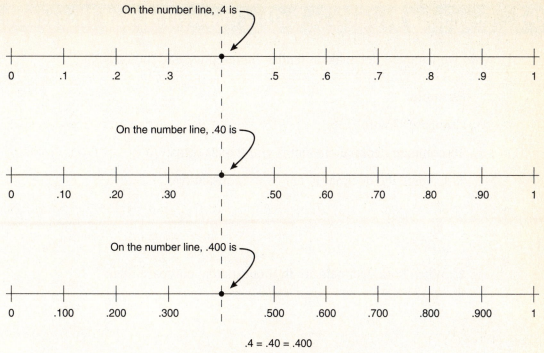

.4 = .40 = .400
They are equivalent, or equal, decimals.

To change a decimal in tenths to an equivalent, or equal, decimal in thousandths, write two more zeros, one in the hundredths place and one in the thousandths place.

Example:

tenths → thousandths
.3 → .3<u>00</u>   (.3 = .300)

To change a decimal in hundredths to an equivalent, or equal, decimal in thousandths, write one more zero in the thousandths place.

Example:

hundredths → thousandths
1.25 → 1.25<u>0</u>   (1.25 = 1.250)

Exercise 10

Write the following decimals as thousandths.

1. 7.3 ___7.300___
2. 1.6 _____
3. 17.21 _____
4. 9.0 _____
5. 56.11 _____

6. 2.4 _____
7. 243.2 _____
8. 97.12 _____
9. 51.20 _____
10. 6.91 _____

11. 2.63 _____
12. 193.7 _____
13. 2.67 _____
14. 19.8 _____
15. 1.71 _____

How do we compare decimals in tenths, hundredths, and thousandths?

Example:

Compare .7 with .736.

To compare decimals in tenths and thousandths:

1. Change the decimal in tenths to thousandths.

   .7   .736

   ↓

   .700   .736

2. When both decimals are in thousandths, compare them.

   .700   <   .736

                 so

   .7   <   .736

Example:

Compare .63 with .621.

Change .63 to thousandths, and then compare the two decimals.

   .63   .621

   ↓

   .630   >   .621

                 so

   .63   >   .621

Exercise 11

Compare the decimals. Write <, >, or =.

1. .73 __>__ .725

2. 1.6 _____ 1.614

3. 2.9 _____ 2.891

4. 31.24 _____ 31.239

5. 2.006 _____ 2.6

6. .071 _____ .07

7. 19.3 _____ 19.300

8. .670 _____ .6

9. .41 _____ .419

10. 1.300 _____ 1.3

11. 17.91 _____ 17.199

12. 8.1 _____ 8.111

13. .973 _____ .9

14. .240 _____ .2

15. .100 _____ 1.10

16. 19.014 _____ 19.2

17. 3.066 _____ 4.7

18. .77 _____ .7

19. .6 _____ .60

20. 3.2 _____ 3.19

21. .456 _____ .5

22. .009 _____ .109

23. .98 _____ .9

24. .554 _____ .5

25. 20.5 _____ 20.500

We have studied decimals in tenths, hundredths, and thousandths.

Example:

tenths:	.2	. ____
	3.4	↑
		tenths place

hundredths:	.64	. ____ ____
	9.07	↑
		hundredths place

thousandths:	.774	. ____ ____ ____
	9.001	↑
		thousandths place

There are many more decimal places to learn. Look at the following diagram.

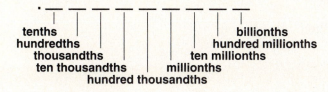

```
. _ _ _ _ _ _ _ _ _ _
```
tenths
hundredths
    thousandths
    ten thousandths
        hundred thousandths
                millionths
            ten millionths
            hundred millionths
            billionths

Example:

What is the place name of the underlined number below?

6.324<u>9</u>

Answer: ten thousandths place

Exercise 12

Write the place name of each underlined number below.

1. 6.<u>3</u>974 _____*tenths*_____
2. .936<u>4</u> _____
3. 1.29664<u>1</u> _____
4. 24.1<u>9</u>36 _____
5. 11.0060<u>1</u> _____
6. .000016<u>7</u> _____
7. 4.3<u>0</u>96 _____
8. 2.1467804<u>1</u> _____
9. 19.24<u>6</u>3 _____
10. 1.3974<u>2</u> _____

11. 3.<u>2</u>147 _____
12. 6.1589<u>2</u> _____
13. 103.4<u>9</u>604 _____
14. 72.63214<u>7</u> _____
15. 2.904<u>0</u>76 _____
16. .4963<u>4</u>2 _____
17. .3<u>4</u>982 _____
18. 17.24673589<u>6</u> _____
19. .429165<u>1</u> _____
20. 6.3621748<u>9</u> _____

How do we read or say decimals?

Example:

How do we read or say the decimal 4.3261?

4.326<u>1</u>

The decimal ends in the ten thousandths place. We read or say the decimal as

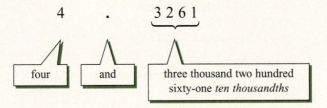

4   .   3 2 6 1

four   and   three thousand two hundred sixty-one *ten thousandths*

REMEMBER:

We always read the decimal point as "and."
We always say the place name at the end of the number.

OR

We can say, "four point three two six one."

Example:

How do we read or say the decimal 2.0040?

2.0004<u>0</u>

The decimal ends in the hundred thousandths place. We read or say the decimal as "two and forty hundred thousandths" or "two point zero zero zero four zero."

Exercise 13

Say the decimals aloud and write them out on a separate sheet of paper.

1. 6.243 *six and two hundred forty-three thousandths*

2. .0009

3. 19.32

4. 9.42610

5. .00013

6. 6.301

7. 14.0000020

8. 6.195

9. .37

10. 195.2

11. 143.6731

12. 2123.4

13. 9.00276

14. 9.000900

15. .700010

Exercise 14

Write the following expressions as decimals.

1. seven and six hundredths _____7.06_____

2. two and nine hundred fifty-five thousandths _____

3. seventy-five ten thousandths _____

4. eleven and seven tenths _____

5. nine hundred ninety-five ten millionths _____

6. one and nine hundredths _____

7. four thousand sixty-three and nine tenths _____

8. eighty-two and sixteen hundred thousandths _____

9. forty and eleven thousandths _____

10. seven hundred sixty-one and three billionths _____

11. ninety-eight hundred millionths _____

12. seventy thousandths _____

13. six tenths _____

14. nineteen hundred thousandths _____

15. two and six hundred fifty thousand millionths _____

Exercise 15

On a separate sheet of paper, write the decimals in order, from smallest to greatest.

1. 6.21, .621, 621.0, 6.211, 62.1

2. .0413, .0431, .04013, .0341, .0423

3. .98, 9.2, .99, 9.1, 98.1

4. .88, .8, 8.0, .08, 80.0

5. 7.63, 6.73, .763, 76.3, 67.3

6. 1.271, 12.71, .1271, 127.1, .01271

7. .781, 78.1, 7.81, .718, 78.11

8. .00123, .00321, .0213, .0123, .0321

9. 16.1, .161, 1.61, .016, 1610.0

10. .065, .0065, .056, .0056, .650

11. 5.11, 51.1, .511, .0511, 511.0

12. .998, 9.98, .9978, .099, .989

13. .764, .746, .765, .757, .756

14. .11274, .11724, .11247, .11742, .12741

15. 128.32, 128.23, 182.32, 128.41, 128.14

Have I Learned? (✓)

Work with a partner. Check what you have learned. Review what you need help with.

1. tenth ☐
2. decimal numbers (decimals) ☐
3. decimal point ☐
4. tenths place ☐
5. hundredth ☐

6. hundredths place ☐
7. equivalent decimals ☐
8. thousandth ☐
9. thousandths place ☐
10. ten thousandths ☐

11. hundred thousandths ☐
12. millionths ☐
13. ten millionths ☐
14. hundred millionths ☐
15. billionths ☐

Exercise 16

Complete the puzzle. First, answer the questions or complete the sentences on the next page. Then write the words in the boxes. Write one letter in a box. Reminder: Some words go across ➤; other words go down ↓.

```
                              ¹T  ²E  N  ³S
                                             ⁴
 ⁵         ⁶                    ⁷
    ⁸                        ⁹
¹⁰
                    ¹¹              ¹²
¹³      ¹⁴      ¹⁵
¹⁶      ¹⁷              ¹⁸
              ¹⁹      ²⁰
```

1. What is the place name between the ones place and the hundreds place?

   the _____ *tens* _____ place

7. We read the sign in a subtraction problem as _____.

8. A prime number less than 20 is _____.

10. We _____ a problem when we find the answer to the problem.

11. The number we multiply to get a product is called a _____.

13. ✐ This is called a decimal _____.

16. The number 3 is not an even number. It is an _____ number.

17. There is no end to a number line. It is _____.

18. A prime number has two factors—itself and the number _____.

19. We read the sign in an addition problem as _____.

20. ✐ This is called a _____ point.

2. 2, 4, 6, 8, . . . are called _____ numbers.

3. The answer to an addition problem is called the _____.

4. The answer to a division problem is called the _____.

5. A number between −1 and 1 is _____.

6. The number 6 is _____ than 7.

8. A prime number less than 15 is _____.

9. If two numbers have the same value, they are _____.

12. When we change the number 29 to 30, we are _____ to the nearest tens place.

13. The answer to a multiplication problem is called the _____.

14. Another word for "two times" is _____.

15. When we multiply a number by 2, we double the number; when we multiply by 3, we _____ the number.

Exercise 1

On a separate sheet of paper, use words to write the decimals in two ways.

1. 3.4 *three point four; three and*
   four tenths
2. .74
3. 19.567
4. .875
5. 2.0090

6. .034001
7. 3.60486
8. .08
9. .002
10. 1.516904

Exercise 2

On a separate sheet of paper, write the following expressions as decimals.

1. five tenths __.5__
2. sixteen thousandths
3. two and three hundredths
4. ten and thirty ten thousandths
5. seven hundred sixty millionths

6. thirty hundred thousandths
7. one tenth
8. six and fifty ten thousandths
9. twelve and thirty-four thousandths
10. eighty-seven hundredths

Exercise 3

On a separate sheet of paper, write the place names of the underlined numbers below.

1. .4<u>5</u>7 __hundredths__
2. 3.9<u>5</u>84
3. 3.<u>5</u>
4. .245684<u>9</u>

5. .5674<u>3</u>
6. .00000<u>1</u>
7. 144.334<u>5</u>
8. .<u>4</u>7566

9. 67.7<u>8</u>55
10. 5.20<u>7</u>

Exercise 4

Compare the decimals. Write <, >, or =.

1. 5.6 __<__ 5.63
2. .45 _____ .450
3. 34.607 _____ 34.660
4. 5.45 _____ 5.4
5. .567 _____ .6

6. .5900 _____ .59
7. .670 _____ .6710
8. .878 _____ .91
9. .129 _____ .1290
10. 8.23 _____ 9.20

11. 4.556 _____ 4.55
12. .449 _____ .45
13. .6700 _____ .670
14. .7112 _____ .71121
15. 1.009 _____ 1.0010

CHAPTER 11 Adding and Subtracting Decimals

11-1 Writing Integers as Decimals

We can write any integer as a decimal. We write a decimal point to the right of the integer and one or more zeros.

Integer	Decimal
3 $\longrightarrow$	3.0
	3.00
	3.000

$$3 = 3.0 = 3.00 = 3.000 \ldots$$

These are all equivalent decimals. We can write any number of zeros after the decimal point. Writing a zero or zeros after the decimal point does not change the value of the decimal.

Example:

We can write 62 as a decimal that ends in the thousandths place.

$$62 \longrightarrow 62.000$$

Since we want the decimal to end in the thousandths place, we write a decimal point and three zeros. We read the decimal as "sixty-two" or "sixty-two point zero zero zero."

Exercise 1

Write the following integers as decimals that end in the . . .

tenths place	hundredths place	thousandths place
1. 16 = _____16.0_____	**8.** 24 = _____	**15.** 63 = _____
2. 9 = _____	**9.** 10 = _____	**16.** 7 = _____
3. 1 = _____	**10.** 365 = _____	**17.** 21 = _____
4. 122 = _____	**11.** 2 = _____	**18.** 724 = _____
5. 89 = _____	**12.** 926 = _____	**19.** 90 = _____
6. 12 = _____	**13.** 1,341 = _____	**20.** 4,230 = _____
7. 906 = _____	**14.** 2,090 = _____	

How do we add decimals? Look at the following examples.

Example:

$7 + 3.2 + 1.6$

1. We rewrite the decimals so that the decimal points are in line. We then change the integer 7 to a decimal ending in the tenths place, since 3.2 and 1.6 end in the tenths place.

$$
\begin{array}{r}
7.0 \\
3.2 \\
+\ 1.6 \\
\end{array}
$$

Notice that the decimal points are in line.

2. Next, we add.

$$
\begin{array}{r}
7.0 \\
3.2 \\
+\ 1.6 \\
\hline
\textbf{Answer:}\quad 11.8 \\
\end{array}
$$

Example:

$4.2 + 21.32 + 12$

First, we line up the decimal points. Since 21.32 ends in the hundredths place, we change 4.2 to a decimal ending in the hundredths place (4.20), and we change 12 to a decimal ending in the hundredths place (12.00). Then we add.

$$
\begin{array}{r}
4.20 \\
21.32 \\
+\ 12.00 \\
\hline
\textbf{Answer:}\quad 37.52 \\
\end{array}
$$

Notice that the decimal points are in line.

Exercise 2

On a separate sheet of paper, rewrite the decimals and add them.

1. $6.3 + .9 + 4.7 =$

2. $17.27 + 8.83 + .96 =$

3. $317.29 + 19.56 + .74 =$

4. $.86 + 92 + 8.2 =$

5. $7.4 + 11 + .19 =$

6. $.236 + 1.4 + 8 =$

7. $14.1 + 82.47 + .9 =$

8. $7.6 + 2 + 1.105 =$

9. 4.34 + .793 + 6 =

10. 8.8 + .75 + 14.2 =

11. 19.3 + .145 + 89 =

12. 7.5 + 845 + 16.97 =

13. .54 + 11 + 1.9 =

14. .9 + 12.6 + 144 + 6 =

15. 62.4 + 12 + 8.6 + .7 =

16. 473 + 26.9 + .14 + .23 =

17. 4 + 6.3 + .27 + .8 =

18. .896 + 72 + 1.3 + .11 =

19. 2.975 + .26 + 84 + .95 =

20. 95.4 + .237 + 8.6 + 54 =

21. 62.4 + 9 + .596 =

22. .0071 + 13 + 2.43 + .4 =

23. 16.32 + 9.2 + .334 + 2 =

24. 75 + .263 + 1.1 + .556 =

25. .45 + 9.9 + 181.3 + .65 =

26. .29 + 4.6 + 23 + .01 =

27. 4.312 + .8 + 7.15 + .49 =

28. 88.9 + 176.4 + 16 + .5 =

29. 2.223 + .0021 + .45 + 33 =

30. .453 + 6 + 5.44 + .077 + 22 =

Exercise 3

Mr. and Mrs. Ramos went on a bicycle trip around Lake Willow last month. They began their tour at Point Linda. First, look at the illustration. Then answer the questions on the next page. Write your answers on the lines. Show your work on a separate sheet of paper.

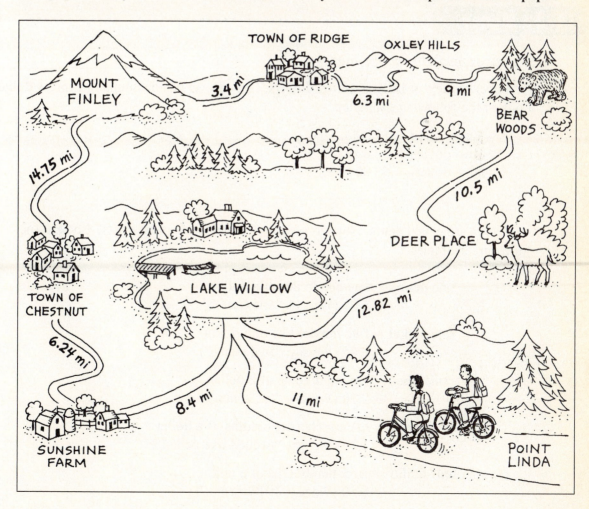

1. Mr. and Mrs. Ramos began their trip at Point Linda on a Sunday. They bicycled to Lake Willow and then on to Chestnut. How many miles did they travel altogether on Sunday? _25.64 miles_

2. On Monday, Mr. and Mrs. Ramos rode from Chestnut to Mount Finley. Then they returned to Chestnut in the evening. How many miles did they travel altogether on Monday? _____

3. Mrs. Ramos wanted to visit Bear Woods on Tuesday. Mr. and Mrs. Ramos rode to Bear Woods from Chestnut.

   a. Which way is closer—from Chestnut to Bear Woods through Mount Finley, or from Chestnut to Bear Woods through Lake Willow? _____

   b. How much closer (in miles) is this route? _____

4. On Wednesday, Mr. and Mrs. Ramos spent a day and a night at Lake Willow for fishing and swimming. Then on Thursday, they rode to Oxley, then back to Deer Place, where they had dinner. How many miles did they ride altogether on Thursday?

   _____

5. On Friday, Mrs. Ramos rode from Deer Place to Mount Finley, through Bear Woods. Mr. Ramos rode from Deer Place to Mount Finley, through Lake Willow. Who arrived there first—Mrs. Ramos or Mr. Ramos? _____

11-3 Money

We use decimals to express **money**.

Paper money, or **bills**, is called **dollars**. How do we use decimals to express dollars? Look at the following examples.

$$\begin{aligned} \text{one dollar} &= \$1.00 \\ \text{two dollars} &= \$2.00 \\ \text{three dollars} &= \$3.00 \end{aligned}$$

Coins are called **cents**. How do we use decimals to express cents? Look at the following examples.

one **penny** = one hundredth of a dollar
= $.01 (We say, "one cent.")

one **nickel** = five hundredths of a dollar
= $.05 (We say, "five cents.")

one **dime** = ten hundredths of a dollar
= $.10 (We say, "ten cents.")

one **quarter** = twenty-five hundredths of a dollar
= $.25 (We say, "twenty-five cents.")

one **half-dollar** = fifty hundredths of a dollar
= $.50 (We say, "fifty cents.")

How do we use decimals to express both dollars and cents? Look at the following example.

Example:

We write $1.24.

We say, "one dollar and twenty-four cents" or "one twenty-four."

Exercise 4

Work with a partner. Say the following amounts aloud.

1. $3.45 *three dollars and forty-five*
   cents OR *three forty-five*

2. $.15

3. $4.50

4. $.95

5. $10.00

6. $15.95

7. $.99

8. $35.66

9. $75.25

10. $19.99

11. $100.00

12. $345.55

13. $560.80

14. $888.88

15. $744.98

There are different ways to show cents amounts. Look at the following examples.

Example:

$.18 = 18 pennies (18 coins) or
$.18 = 3 nickels and 3 pennies (6 coins) or
$.18 = 1 dime, 1 nickel, and 3 pennies (5 coins)

This combination of coins (5 coins) shows the least number of coins that we can use to express $.18.

Example:

$.76 = 76 pennies (76 coins) or
$.76 = 7 dimes, 1 nickel, and 1 penny (9 coins) or
$.76 = 3 quarters and 1 penny (4 coins) or
$.76 = 1 half-dollar, 1 quarter, and 1 penny (3 coins)

This combination of coins (3 coins) shows the least number of coins that we can use to express $.76.

List the combination of coins for each cents amount. Use the *least* number of coins.

	Pennies	Nickels	Dimes	Quarters	Half-Dollars	Total Number of Coins
1. $.13	3	–	1	–	–	4
2. $.68						
3. $.59						
4. $.95						
5. $.27						
6. $.82						
7. $.99						
8. $.47						
9. $.62						
10. $.70						
11. $.34						
12. $.69						
13. $.78						
14. $.19						
15. $.91						

Mr. and Mrs. Ramos stayed at a campground in Chestnut for three nights. Answer the questions below about their visit. Write your answers on the lines. Show your work on a separate sheet of paper.

1. The campground charges $18.00 for the first person in a group per night. For others in the same group, it charges $8.00 per person for each night.

   a. How much did Mr. and Mrs. Ramos pay for one night? *$26.00*

   b. How much did they pay for three nights? _____

2. Mr. and Mrs. Ramos ate their meals at the Café Chestnut. Here are their food bills.

	Breakfast	Lunch	Dinner
Day 1	$9.25	$14.95	$24.80
Day 2	$8.95	$15.33	$23.55
Day 3	$10.25	$14.15	$21.36

   a. How much did they pay for breakfast for three days? _____

   b. How much did they pay for lunch for three days? _____

   c. How much did they pay for dinner for three days? _____

d. Did they spend more money for all three meals (breakfast, lunch, and dinner) on Day 2 or Day 3? _____

e. What was their total food bill for all three days? _____

3. Additional items and their costs for the trip included the following ones:

Bicycle tires $18.00
First-aid kit $23.50
Extra food $19.85

How much did they pay for the additional items? _____

4. Mr. and Mrs. Ramos made three long-distance phone calls from the Café Chestnut. They cost $5.28, $2.46, and $4.97. How much did they pay for the three phone calls? _____

5. How much did they spend altogether for the campground, food, and additional items? _____

11-4 Subtracting Decimals

How do we subtract decimals? Look at the following examples.

Example:

6 – 4.3

We rewrite the decimals so that the decimal points are in line. We then change the integer 6 to a decimal ending in the tenths place, since 4.3 ends in the tenths place. Then we subtract.

$$\begin{array}{r} 6.0 \\ -\ 4.3 \\ \hline \end{array}$$
Answer: 1.7

Notice that the decimal points are in line.

Example:

.6 – .3211

We rewrite the decimals so that the decimal points are in line. Since .3211 is a decimal ending in the ten thousandths place, we write .6 as a decimal ending in the ten thousandths place. We write three zeros: .6000. Then we subtract.

$$\begin{array}{r} .6000 \\ -\ .3211 \\ \hline \end{array}$$
Answer: .2789

Notice that the decimal points are in line.

On a separate sheet of paper, rewrite the decimals and subtract them.

1. 43.6 – 3.2 =

2. 95.6 – 14.7 =

3. 6.3 – 3.8 =

4. 78.4 – 19.9 =

5. 24 – 5.8 =

6. 135 – 24.7 =

7. 39.6 – 12 =

8. 53 – 43.8 =

9. 130.64 – 15.9 =

10. 17.2 – 14 =

11. 60.03 – 5.69 =

12. 42 – 15.89 =

13. 32 – 12.11 =

14. 1.8 – .97 =

15. .765 – .349 =

16. .6 – .489 =

17. 5.6 – .89 =

18. .4 – .398 =

19. .97 – .499 =

20. .3 – .296 =

21. 7 – .334 =

22. 11 – 3.67 =

23. .5 – .0012 =

24. 45 – 3.8765 =

25. .71 – .3334 =

26. 3 – .177 =

27. 19.766 – .3 =

28. 97.5 – 12 =

29. 51 – .2344 =

30. 4.111 – .99 =

11-5 Using Inverse Operations to Find Missing Decimals

We used inverse operations to find missing numbers in Chapter 5. We can also use inverse operations to find missing decimals.

Example:

_____ – 3.5 = .67

We use the inverse operation (addition).

.67 + 3.5 = 4.17

Answer: 4.17 – 3.5 = .67

Example:

2.34 + _____ = 7.5

We use the inverse operation (subtraction).

7.5 – 2.34 = 5.16

Answer: 2.34 + 5.16 = 7.5

On a separate sheet of paper, use the inverse operation to find the missing numbers.

1. $3.45 + \underline{} = 4.33$

2. $\underline{} + .224 = 2.33$

3. $\underline{} - 4.5 = 10.6$

4. $.345 + \underline{} = 1.99$

5. $\underline{} - .39 = 5.67$

6. $\underline{} - .23 = 12.44$

7. $8.76 + \underline{} = 19.7$

8. $\underline{} - .87 = 8$

9. $\underline{} - 1.22 = .99$

10. $6 + \underline{} = 23.86$

11. $\underline{} + 23.445 = 67.5$

12. $\underline{} - 3.89 = 5$

13. $\underline{} - 6 = 8.67$

14. $.54 + \underline{} = 3.666$

15. $.234 + \underline{} = 7$

16. $\underline{} - .233 = .112$

17. $\underline{} - 7.66 = 2.389$

18. $\underline{} - .293 = 1.245$

19. $1.23 + \underline{} = 3.44$

20. $\underline{} + .334 = 198.3$

21. $\underline{} - .983 = 2.12$

22. $\underline{} + .231 = 4.55$

23. $\underline{} + .345 = .67$

24. $\underline{} - 13.2 = 2.56$

25. $\underline{} - 8 = 2.33$

26. $\underline{} + .12 = .34$

27. $45 + \underline{} = 65.00$

28. $\underline{} - .243 = 5$

29. $\underline{} - 8.34 = 0$

30. $.191 + \underline{} = .191$

The members of The Get Fit Health Club want to lose weight. Look at the chart on the next page with their weights for three weeks. Then answer the questions. Show your work on a separate sheet of paper. Write your answers on the lines.

Name	Week 1	Week 2	Week 3
Emilio Rivera	184.34 pounds	180.26 pounds	176.24 pounds
Leon Jackson	219.26 pounds	217.16 pounds	216.32 pounds
Amanda Wright	148.29 pounds	147.64 pounds	146.26 pounds
Michael Carpenter	174.55 pounds	171.24 pounds	170.06 pounds
Teresa López	139.65 pounds	134.21 pounds	132.19 pounds

1. Look at Amanda Wright's weights. How much did she lose from Week 1 to Week 2? _____

2. Look at Teresa López's weights. How much did she lose from Week 1 to Week 2? _____

3. Look at Emilio Rivera's weights. How much did he lose from Week 1 to Week 3? _____

4. How much weight did Leon Jackson lose from Week 1 to Week 3? _____

5. How much weight did Michael Carpenter lose from Week 1 to Week 3? _____

11-6 Rounding Off Decimals

We learned how to round off numbers in Chapter 3. We can round off decimals in the same way.

Example:

We can round off 1.38 to the nearest tenths place.

1. First, we underline the tenths place digit and look at the number to the right.

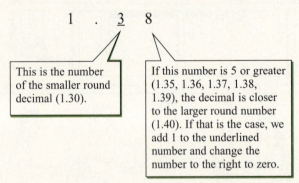

1 . <u>3</u> 8

This is the number of the smaller round decimal (1.30).

If this number is 5 or greater (1.35, 1.36, 1.37, 1.38, 1.39), the decimal is closer to the larger round number (1.40). If that is the case, we add 1 to the underlined number and change the number to the right to zero.

1.38 → 1.40

2. Since we are rounding to the nearest tenths place, we want the decimal to end in the tenths place. We then drop all the numbers after the tenths digit.

$$1.4\cancel{0} \longrightarrow 1.4$$

Answer: $1.38 \longrightarrow 1.4$

Example:

We can round off 5.0132 to the nearest hundredths place.

5 . 0 <u>1</u> 3 2

> Since this number is less than 5:
> **1.** We keep the underlined number (1).
> **2.** We then drop all numbers to the right of the underlined number.

5 . 0 1 $\cancel{3}$ $\cancel{2}$

> We keep this number.

> We drop these numbers.

Answer: $5.0132 \longrightarrow 5.01$

Example:

We can round off 5.978 to the nearest tenths place.

5 . <u>9</u> 7 8

> Since this number is greater than 5:
> **1.** We add 1 to the underlined number (9 + 1 = 10). We write the 0 in the tenths column. We carry the 1 to the ones column.
> **2.** We then drop the numbers to the right.

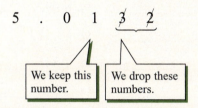

Answer: $5.978 \longrightarrow 6.0$

Example:

We can round 3.6 to the nearest whole number.

We underline the ones place digit.

<u>3</u> . 6

Since this number is greater than 5:
1. We add 1 to the underlined number.
2. We then drop the numbers to the right.

Answer: 3.6 ⟶ 4

Exercise 10

A. Round the decimals off to the nearest tenths place.

1. 6.12 _____6.1_____

2. 24.35 _____

3. 19.87 _____

4. 2.317 _____

5. 1.96 _____

6. 7.613 _____

7. 2.188 _____

8. 49.54 _____

9. 3.96 _____

10. 4.773 _____

11. 6.692 _____

12. 49.573 _____

13. 1.845 _____

14. 3.788 _____

15. 2.556 _____

B. Round the decimals off to the nearest hundredths place.

1. 34.723 _____34.72_____

2. 3.677 _____

3. 4.782 _____

4. 11.941 _____

5. 2.6971 _____

6. 1.339 _____

7. 243.5921 _____

8. 36.995 _____

9. 7.9421 _____

10. 42.641 _____

11. 3.5643 _____

12. 11.432 _____

13. 45.009 _____

14. 33.999 _____

15. 1.2388 _____

A. Round the decimals off to the nearest whole number.

1. 7.34 _____7_____
2. 9.58 _____
3. 2.98 _____
4. 9.21 _____
5. 1.80 _____

6. 21.44 _____
7. 8.34 _____
8. 7.66 _____
9. 2.554 _____
10. 9.05 _____

11. 7.256 _____
12. 9.827 _____
13. 9.82 _____
14. 30.78 _____
15. 21.80 _____

B. Round the decimals off to the nearest thousandths place.

1. 4.3987 _____4.399_____
2. 32.51223 _____
3. 7.4998 _____
4. 21.92336 _____
5. 5.45788 _____

6. 165.92655 _____
7. 1.22344 _____
8. 2.00833 _____
9. 12.38054 _____
10. 29.6744 _____

11. 8.21098 _____
12. 11.40032 _____
13. .29384 _____
14. .11354 _____
15. .289939 _____

 Have I Learned? (✓)

Work with a partner. Check what you have learned. Review what you need help with.

1. money ☐
2. bills ☐
3. dollars ☐
4. coins ☐
5. cents ☐

6. penny ☐
7. nickel ☐
8. dime ☐
9. quarter ☐
10. half-dollar ☐

Exercise 1

On a separate sheet of paper, rewrite the decimals and add them.

1. .45 + 5 + 12.2 =
2. 10.33 + 2.4 + 2 =
3. 45 + 4.5 + .45 =
4. 193.4 + 2.77 + .5 =
5. 261.3 + 4.62 + .3 =

6. 98.33 + 75 + 23.3 =
7. 15.33 + 567 + .002 =
8. 25 + 334 + .544 =
9. 205.35 + .677 + 49 =
10. 609.28 + .532 + 76 =

Exercise 2

On a separate sheet of paper, rewrite the decimals and subtract them.

1. 3.56 − 2.44 =
2. 5.67 − 4.8 =
3. .334 − .23 =
4. 2.4 − .33 =
5. 5.2 − .66 =

6. 86 − 3.67 =
7. 12 − .005 =
8. 3 − 2.56 =
9. 265.34 − 9.445 =
10. 243.12 − 8.776 =

Exercise 3

On a separate sheet of paper, use the inverse operation to find the missing numbers.

1. 94.3 + _____ = 122.67
2. _____ − .334 = 12.3
3. _____ − 1.76 = 1.76

4. _____ + .867 = 1.223
5. _____ + .645 = 2.204

Exercise 4

Round the decimals off to the nearest tenths, hundredths, and thousandths places.

	tenths	hundredths	thousandths
1. 27.3512	_27.4_	_27.35_	_27.351_
2. 3.7597	_____	_____	_____
3. 10.8321	_____	_____	_____
4. 1.7867	_____	_____	_____
5. 37.9999	_____	_____	_____

CHAPTER 12 Multiplying and Dividing Decimals

12-1 Multiplying Decimals

Look at the following three problems.

(a) $\begin{array}{r} 25 \\ \times\ 4 \\ \hline \end{array}$ (b) $\begin{array}{r} 2.5 \\ \times\ 4 \\ \hline \end{array}$ (c) $\begin{array}{r} .25 \\ \times\ 4 \\ \hline \end{array}$

The numbers in all three problems are the same, but in (b) there is a decimal point between the 2 and 5, and in (c) there is a decimal point before the 2. Will the answers be different for all three problems?

In problem (a): $\begin{array}{r} 25 \\ \times\ 4 \\ \hline 100 \end{array}$

We are multiplying 25 by 4. There are no decimal points in (a). The answer is 100.

In problem (b): $\begin{array}{r} 2.5 \\ \times\ 4 \\ \hline \end{array}$

We are multiplying the decimal 2.5 by 4. The decimal 2.5 is greater than 2 and less than 3, since 2.5 is between 2 and 3.

$\left.\begin{array}{l} 4 \times 2 = 8 \\ \\ 4 \times 3 = 12 \end{array}\right\}$ The answer should be between 8 and 12.

$\begin{array}{r} 2.5 \\ \times\ 4 \\ \hline 10.0 \end{array}$ The answer is 10.

In problem (c): $\begin{array}{r} .25 \\ \times\ 4 \\ \hline \end{array}$

We are multiplying the decimal .25 by 4. The decimal .25 is less than 1. The answer should be less than 4.

$\begin{array}{r} .25 \\ \times\ 4 \\ \hline 1.00 \end{array}$ The answer is 1.

In problems (a), (b), and (c) the numbers were the same, but the decimal points changed the value of the numbers and the answers:

(a) $\begin{array}{r} 25 \\ \times\ 4 \\ \hline 100 \end{array}$ **(b)** $\begin{array}{r} 2.5 \\ \times\ 4 \\ \hline 10.0 \end{array}$ **(c)** $\begin{array}{r} .25 \\ \times\ 4 \\ \hline 1.00 \end{array}$

When multiplying with decimals, always remember to include the decimal point in the answers.

In problem (b): $\begin{array}{r} 2.5 \\ \times\ 4 \\ \hline 10.0 \end{array}$ ← There is one number (5) to the right of the decimal point.

← The answer also shows one number to the right of the decimal point.

In problem (c): $\begin{array}{r} .25 \\ \times\ 4 \\ \hline 1.00 \end{array}$ ← There are two numbers to the right of the decimal point.

← The answer also shows two numbers to the right of the decimal point.

How do we multiply with decimals?

1. First, we multiply the numbers together.

2. Then we count the number of numbers to the right of the decimal point in each factor.

3. Last, we place the decimal point in the answer so that there is the same number of numbers to the right of the decimal point as in the factors.

Example:

$\begin{array}{r} 12.3 \\ \times\ \ 3 \\ \hline 36.9 \end{array}$ ← one number to the right of the point

← one number to the right of the point

$\begin{array}{r} 1.23 \\ \times\ \ 3 \\ \hline 3.69 \end{array}$ ← two numbers to the right

← two numbers to the right (Count two places to the left ← and write the decimal point.)

$\begin{array}{r} 1.23 \\ \times\ \ .3 \\ \hline .369 \end{array}$ ← two numbers
← + one number

← three numbers (Count three places to the left ← and write the decimal point.)

Sometimes we need to add zeros.

Example:

$$
\begin{array}{r}
.123 \\
\times \quad .3 \\
\hline
.0369 \\
\end{array}
$$

.123 ← three numbers
× .3 ← + one number
.0369 ← four numbers (Count four places to the left. Then write in a zero and write the decimal point.)

.0123 ← four numbers
× .03 ← + two numbers
.000369 ← six numbers (Count six places to the left. Then write in three zeros and write the decimal point.)

Example:

Count how many numbers are to the right of the decimal point in each factor. Then place the decimal point in the correct place in the answers.

(a)	**(b)**	**(c)**
.45	.45	.045
× .4	× .04	× .004
180	180	180

Answers: (a) .180   (b) .0180   (c) .000180

Exercise 1

Place the decimal point in the correct place in each answer. (For some answers, you will need to add zeros before you place the decimal point.)

1. 3.4 × 4 13.6	**5.** .0034 × .004 136	**9.** .2456 × .004 9824	**13.** 16.30 × .02 3260
2. .34 × 4 136	**6.** 245.6 × 4 9824	**10.** .2456 × .0004 9824	**14.** .63 × .23 1449
3. .034 × .4 136	**7.** 24.56 × .04 9824	**11.** 1630 × .2 3260	**15.** 100 × .3 300
4. .034 × .04 136	**8.** 2.456 × .04 9824	**12.** 163.0 × .2 3260	**16.** 1.00 × .03 300

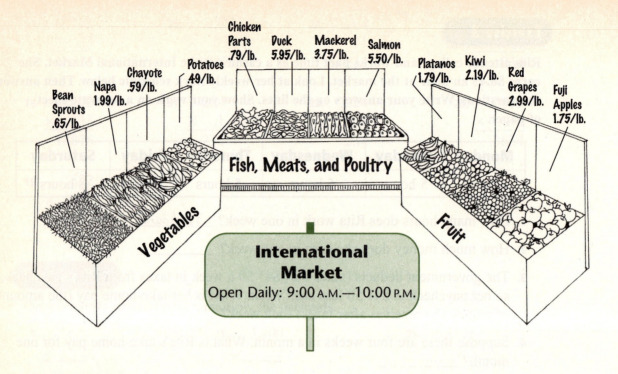

Bean Sprouts .65/lb.
Napa 1.99/lb.
Chayote .59/lb.
Potatoes .49/lb.

Chicken Parts .79/lb.
Duck 5.95/lb.
Mackerel 3.75/lb.
Salmon 5.50/lb.

Platanos 1.79/lb.
Kiwi 2.19/lb.
Red Grapes 2.99/lb.
Fuji Apples 1.75/lb.

Fish, Meats, and Poultry

Vegetables

Fruit

International Market
Open Daily: 9:00 A.M.—10:00 P.M.

The next week, all the prices at the International Market changed. Some prices *increased*, while other prices *decreased*. Look at the chart below.

Increase per Pound		Decrease per Pound	
kiwi	+ $.25	platanos	− $.73
Fuji apples	+ $.39	napa	− $.74
bean sprouts	+ $.15	duck	− $1.19
chayote	+ $.08	mackerel	− $.93
potatoes	+ $.13	red grapes	− $.10
chicken parts	+ $.27		
salmon	+ $1.27		

Mrs. Li bought the following items. Complete the list with the new information. Round off to the nearest cent (hundredths place). Show your work on a separate sheet of paper.

Item	New Price	Amount	Total Cost
1. potatoes	$.49 + .13 = $.62	3.24 lb	3.24 × .62 = $2.0088 = $2.01
2. chayote	_____	4.13 lb	_____
3. chicken parts	_____	6.74 lb	_____
4. duck	_____	1.25 lb	_____
5. mackerel	_____	1.5 lb	_____

Item	New Price	Amount	Total Cost
6. kiwi	_____	.90 lb	_____
7. platanos	_____	3.82 lb	_____
8. bean sprouts	_____	1.55 lb	_____
9. napa	_____	2.33 lb	_____
10. red grapes	_____	1.16 lb	_____

12-2 Multiplying Decimals by Multiples of Ten

In Chapter 6, we learned how to multiply numbers by multiples of ten quickly. We wrote zeros at the end of the number:

$34 \times 100 = 3{,}400$

$75 \times 10^4 = 750{,}000$

When we multiply decimals by multiples of ten quickly, we move the decimal point to the right $\longrightarrow$.

Example:

$2.765 \times 100 = 276.5$

[2 zeros]

Move the point two places to the right $\longrightarrow$.

$.87554 \times 10^4 = 8{,}755.4$

[4 zeros]

Move the point four places to the right $\longrightarrow$.

Example:

$4.35 \times 10{,}000 = 43{,}500$

[4 zeros]

Move the point four places to the right $\longrightarrow$.
Since there are only two numbers to the right, we have to write in two more zeros.

Multiply the decimals by moving the decimal point.

1. $1.23 \times 100 = $ _____ *123* _____   11. $2.389 \times 100,000 = $ _____

2. $.445 \times 10 = $ _____   12. $3.4 \times 100,000 = $ _____

3. $.54 \times 1,000 = $ _____   13. $29.876 \times 10 = $ _____

4. $23.456 \times 10,000 = $ _____   14. $19.4 \times 10,000 = $ _____

5. $19 \times 100 = $ _____   15. $123.678 \times 1,000,000 = $ _____

6. $2.387 \times 100 = $ _____   16. $123.678 \times 10 = $ _____

7. $.45 \times 100,000 = $ _____   17. $9.2 \times 1,000,000 = $ _____

8. $198.1 \times 100 = $ _____   18. $745.30 \times 1,000 = $ _____

9. $23.4 \times 10 = $ _____   19. $.33948 \times 100 = $ _____

10. $.755 \times 10,000 = $ _____   20. $.00002 \times 10 = $ _____

Multiply the decimals by moving the decimal point.

1. $17.3 \times 10^1 = $ _____ *173* _____   11. $67.1432 \times 10^4 = $ _____

2. $14.345 \times 10^3 = $ _____   12. $14.21 \times 10^3 = $ _____

3. $6.114 \times 10^2 = $ _____   13. $1.21 \times 10^5 = $ _____

4. $.1134 \times 10^3 = $ _____   14. $.666 \times 10^2 = $ _____

5. $.01145 \times 10^4 = $ _____   15. $.666 \times 10^6 = $ _____

6. $67.392 \times 10^5 = $ _____   16. $.49238 \times 10^2 = $ _____

7. $42.3 \times 10^3 = $ _____   17. $2345.3 \times 10^4 = $ _____

8. $.413 \times 10^5 = $ _____   18. $34.596 \times 10^1 = $ _____

9. $.413 \times 10^6 = $ _____   19. $3.456 \times 10^0 = $ _____

10. $.413 \times 10^1 = $ _____   20. $2938.4 \times 10^4 = $ _____

12-3   Dividing with Decimals

How do we divide with decimals? Look at the following three problems.

(a) $2\overline{)184}$ **(b)** $2\overline{)18.4}$ **(c)** $.2\overline{)184}$

The numbers in all three problems are the same, but in (a) there are no decimal points, in (b) there is a decimal point in the dividend, and in (c) there is a decimal point in the divisor. Will the answer be different for all three problems?

In problem (a): $\dfrac{92}{2\overline{)184}}$

We are dividing 184 by 2. There are no decimal points. The answer is 92.

In problem (b): $2\overline{)18.4}$

We are dividing 18.4 (a decimal between 18 and 19) by 2. The answer should be about 9 or a little greater than 9.

$\dfrac{9.2}{2\overline{)18.4}}$ The answer is 9.2.

In problem (c): $.2\overline{)184}$

We are dividing 184 by a decimal much less than 1 (.2 < 1). Therefore, the answer should be much greater than 184, since 184 divided by 1 equals 184.

$\dfrac{920}{.2\overline{)184}}$ The answer is 920.

In problems (a), (b), and (c) the numbers were the same, but the decimal points changed the value of the numbers and the answers.

(a) $\dfrac{92}{2\overline{)184}}$ **(b)** $\dfrac{9.2}{2\overline{)18.4}}$ **(c)** $\dfrac{920}{.2\overline{)184}}$

When dividing with decimals, we need to remember the decimal points.

12-4 If the Dividend Is a Decimal ·····································

How do we divide when the dividend is a decimal? Look at the following problem.

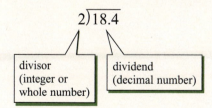

divisor
(integer or
whole number)

dividend
(decimal number)

When the dividend is a decimal number, the quotient will also be a decimal number. Therefore, we first rewrite the decimal point above ↑ to the quotient.

$$2 \overline{)18.4}$$

Next, we divide.

$$
\begin{array}{r}
9.2 \\
2 \overline{)18.4} \\
-18 \\
\hline
0\,4 \\
-4 \\
\hline
0
\end{array}
$$

Answer: 9.2

Example:

$$5 \overline{).1305}$$

First, we rewrite the decimal point above ↑ to the quotient. Next, we divide.

$$
\begin{array}{r}
.0261 \\
5 \overline{).1305} \\
-10 \\
\hline
30 \\
-30 \\
\hline
05 \\
-5 \\
\hline
0
\end{array}
$$

Answer: .0261

Remember, in examples like the one above, we must write in a zero after the decimal point in the quotient.

$$
\begin{array}{cc}
\begin{array}{r}
.0261 \\
5 \overline{).1305}
\end{array}
&
\begin{array}{r}
.\ 261 \\
5 \overline{).1305}
\end{array}
\\
\text{correct} & \text{not correct} \\
.0261 \ \neq & .261
\end{array}
$$

Exercise 8

On a separate sheet of paper, divide the decimals.

1. $1.24 \div 2 =$ 5. $23.4 \div 6 =$ 9. $106.4 \div 4 =$

2. $64.2 \div 2 =$ 6. $2.008 \div 2 =$ 10. $.40085 \div 5 =$

3. $95.5 \div 5 =$ 7. $1.988 \div 2 =$ 11. $698.36 \div 4 =$

4. $.168 \div 8 =$ 8. $84.7 \div 7 =$ 12. $.18720 \div 9 =$

13. 1,201.2 ÷ 6 =

14. 24.064 ÷ 8 =

15. 727.8 ÷ 6 =

16. .9891 ÷ 7 =

17. 2.124 ÷ 3 =

18. .2124 ÷ 3 =

19. 212.4 ÷ 3 =

20. 4.788 ÷ 4 =

21. 416.06 ÷ 71 =

22. .00518 ÷ 37 =

23. 5,198.7 ÷ 43 =

24. .56400 ÷ 50 =

25. 7.5600 ÷ 16 =

26. .01095 ÷ 15 =

27. 43.550 ÷ 25 =

28. 10.490 ÷ 10 =

29. .03045 ÷ 15 =

30. 147.960 ÷ 30 =

31. 152.685 ÷ 65 =

32. 9.725 ÷ 25 =

33. 28.226 ÷ 22 =

34. .702 ÷ 18 =

35. 479.550 ÷ 75 =

12-5 If the Divisor Is a Decimal

How do we divide when the divisor is a decimal? Look at the following problem.

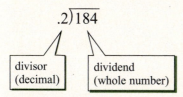

divisor (decimal)   dividend (whole number)

It would be easier if we could divide by a whole number instead of by a decimal number. But we cannot just erase the decimal point in the divisor. We *can* move the point to the right one place (remember, this is the same as multiplying by 10).

2.

But if we multiply the divisor by 10, we must also multiply the dividend by 10 (remember, this is the same as writing in one zero at the end of the number).

1840

.2)184 → 2.)1840

Now we can divide.

$$
\begin{array}{r}
920 \\
2.\overline{)1840} \\
-18 \\
\hline
04 \\
-4 \\
\hline
00 \\
-0 \\
\hline
0
\end{array}
$$

Answer: 920

Example:

$$.04\overline{)8}$$

1. First, we move the decimal point to the right two places (multiplying by 100).

04.
◡

2. Next, we multiply the dividend by 100 also. (We write in two zeros.)
8 × 100 = 800

$$.04\overline{)8} \longrightarrow 04.\overline{)800}$$

3. Then we divide.

$$
\begin{array}{r}
200 \\
04.\overline{)800} \\
-8 \\
\hline
00 \\
-0 \\
\hline
00 \\
-0 \\
\hline
0
\end{array}
$$

Exercise 9

On a separate sheet of paper, divide the following numbers.

1. 15 ÷ .3 =

2. 35 ÷ .5 =

3. 21 ÷ .07 =

4. 40 ÷ .8 =

5. 66 ÷ .2 =

6. 13 ÷ .01 =

7. 4 ÷ .05 =

8. 1,506 ÷ .3 =

9. 920 ÷ .04 =

10. 15 ÷ .10 =

11. 5 ÷ .25 =

12. 81 ÷ .9 =

13. 45 ÷ .5 =

14. 42 ÷ .6 =

15. 348 ÷ .02 =

16. 28 ÷ .04 =

17. 150 ÷ .30 =

18. 10 ÷ .20 =

19. 2 ÷ .1 =

20. 6 ÷ .12 =

21. 21 ÷ .7 =

22. 54 ÷ .90 =

23. 720 ÷ .008 =

24. 25 ÷ .20 =

25. 26 ÷ .004 =

26. 261 ÷ .3 =

27. 4 ÷ .005 =

28. 42 ÷ .60 =

29. 35 ÷ .050 =

30. 385 ÷ .07 =

31. 12 ÷ .0004 =

32. 364 ÷ .04 =

33. 2,970 ÷ .090 =

34. 1,260 ÷ .30 =

35. 322 ÷ .0002 =

How do we divide when the dividend and divisor are decimals? Look at the following problem.

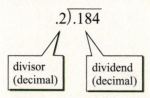

divisor (decimal) dividend (decimal)

Again, it would be easier if we could divide by a whole number instead of by a decimal number. To change .2 to a whole number, we move the decimal point to the right one place (which is the same as multiplying .2 by 10). Then we multiply the dividend .184 by 10 also (we move the decimal point to the right one place).

$$2.\overline{)1.84}$$

Next, we rewrite the decimal point above ↑ to the quotient and divide.

```
     .92
2.)1↑84
   -1 8
   ----
     04
     -4
     --
      0
```

Answer: .92

Example:

$$.12\overline{)\,.6}$$

1. We write .12 as a whole number (we move the decimal point to the right two places).

$$12.\overline{)60.}$$

2. Then we move the decimal point of the dividend two places to the right. The dividend .6 has only one digit, so we must write in one zero.

3. Next, we rewrite the decimal point in the dividend above ↑ to the quotient and divide.

```
       5.
12.)60↑
    -60
    ---
      0
```

Answer: 5

On a separate sheet of paper, divide the following numbers.

1. 21.6 ÷ .6 =

2. .117 ÷ .9 =

3. 40.56 ÷ .8 =

4. 7.2 ÷ .8 =

5. .1506 ÷ .3 =

6. .0384 ÷ .4 =

7. 3505.6 ÷ .7 =

8. .144 ÷ .08 =

9. 244.2 ÷ .03 =

10. 56.98 ÷ .07 =

11. .03752 ÷ .07 =

12. .42 ÷ .0006 =

13. 175.6 ÷ .004 =

14. 1.5 ÷ .25 =

15. 1.2 ÷ .30 =

16. 6.0 ÷ .10 =

17. 3.0 ÷ 1.5 =

18. 14.4 ÷ .12 =

19. 30.020 ÷ .05 =

20. 119.7 ÷ .21 =

21. 3.888 ÷ .9 =

22. .014580 ÷ .04 =

23. 307.7580 ÷ .33 =

24. .09872 ÷ .002 =

25. 145.920 ÷ .60 =

26. 2.8864 ÷ .04 =

27. .325260 ÷ .006 =

28. 3.544 ÷ .02 =

29. 11.5025 ÷ 4.3 =

30. 72.390 ÷ 1.5 =

31. .03015 ÷ .09 =

32. .00175 ÷ .35 =

33. .1896 ÷ .003 =

34. .24 ÷ .0002 =

35. 11.2 ÷ .007 =

12-7 If the Divisor Is Greater Than the Dividend

How do we divide when the divisor is greater than the dividend? Look at the following problem.

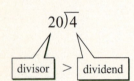

$$20\overline{)4}$$

We cannot divide 4 by 20. However, if we use decimals, we can. Remember, we can write any integer or whole number as a decimal. We just write a decimal point to the right of the integer or whole number and as many zeros as we need.

4 = 4.0 = 4.00 = 4.000 . . .
24 = 24.0 = 24.00 = 24.000 = 24.0000 . . .

Here's how we can solve our problem: $20\overline{)4}$

1. First, we write 4 as a decimal: 4 = 4.0

   We then have: $20\overline{)4.0}$

2. Now we can divide:

$$\begin{array}{r} .2 \\ 20\overline{)4\overset{\cdot}{|}0} \\ -4\,0 \\ \hline 0 \end{array}$$

Example:

$$40\overline{)2}$$

1. First, we write the dividend as a decimal. We can write it as 2.0 or 2.00. Let's try by writing it as 2.0 (by adding one zero).

$$40\overline{)2\overset{\cdot}{|}0}$$

We still cannot divide because 40 is greater than 20.

Now let's try by writing it as 2.00 (by adding two zeros).

$$\begin{array}{r} .05 \\ 40\overline{)2\overset{\cdot}{|}00} \\ -2\,00 \\ \hline 0 \end{array}$$

We *can* divide 200 by 40. The answer is .05.

Remember, if the divisor is much larger than the dividend, we may need to write in more than one zero.

Example:

$$300\overline{).36}$$

1. First, we rewrite the decimal point above ↑ to the quotient.

$$300\ \overline{)\overset{\cdot}{|}36}$$

We cannot divide 36 by 300.

2. Since .36 = .360, we can write one zero to the right of 6. Now we can divide.

$$\begin{array}{r} .001 \\ 300\overline{)\overset{\cdot}{|}360} \\ -300 \\ \hline 60 \end{array}$$

↑

There is a remainder of 60.

3. We write in one more zero in the dividend and continue to divide.

$$
\begin{array}{r}
.0012 \\
300\overline{)\,.3600} \\
-300 \\
\hline
600 \\
-600 \\
\hline
0
\end{array}
$$

Remember, when there is a remainder, we need to write in more zeros in the dividend and continue to divide and write in more zeros until there is no remainder.

Remember, in examples like the one above, we must write in zeros after the decimal point in the quotient.

$$
\begin{array}{cc}
.0012 & .\quad 12 \\
300\overline{)\,.3600} & \quad 300\overline{)\,.3600}
\end{array}
$$

correct   not correct

.0012 $\neq$. 12

Exercise 11

On a separate sheet of paper, divide the following numbers.

1. $4 \div 20 =$	**13.** $1 \div 8 =$	**25.** $3.445 \div 65 =$
2. $6 \div 8 =$	**14.** $10.5 \div 700 =$	**26.** $.209 \div 11 =$
3. $3 \div 4 =$	**15.** $22.95 \div 850 =$	**27.** $.5456 \div 62 =$
4. $3 \div 6 =$	**16.** $1.6 \div 20 =$	**28.** $.66 \div 200 =$
5. $3 \div 5 =$	**17.** $.3 \div 25 =$	**29.** $2 \div 5 =$
6. $7 \div 8 =$	**18.** $.475 \div 50 =$	**30.** $1 \div 25 =$
7. $2 \div 8 =$	**19.** $4.5 \div 60 =$	**31.** $.1 \div 8 =$
8. $.12 \div 8 =$	**20.** $1.64 \div 20 =$	**32.** $.1 \div 25 =$
9. $.2 \div 5 =$	**21.** $4 \div 50 =$	**33.** $3 \div 400 =$
10. $10 \div 50 =$	**22.** $1.4 \div 400 =$	**34.** $1 \div 250 =$
11. $4.8 \div 800 =$	**23.** $22.5 \div 45 =$	**35.** $.4 \div 20 =$
12. $.3 \div 4 =$	**24.** $.054 \div 30 =$	

Exercise 12

On a separate sheet of paper, divide the following numbers.

1. $6.39 \div 3 =$
2. $72.4 \div .2 =$
3. $75.85 \div 5 =$
4. $33 \div .11 =$
5. $.3 \div 5 =$
6. $2 \div .005 =$
7. $86.48 \div 8 =$
8. $.5266 \div 4 =$
9. $3 \div 4,000 =$
10. $.665 \div .025 =$

11. $943.06 \div 4 =$
12. $.1 \div 80 =$
13. $.00350 \div .50 =$
14. $672.5 \div .05 =$
15. $2.8 \div 800 =$
16. $20 \div 100 =$
17. $2.8 \div .14 =$
18. $6,493 \div .004 =$
19. $1 \div 40 =$
20. $9.0 \div 120 =$

21. $7 \div 8 =$
22. $9.9456 \div 56 =$
23. $.675 \div 30 =$
24. $24 \div .0008 =$
25. $.02916 \div .08 =$
26. $7.776 \div .18 =$
27. $12 \div 16 =$
28. $.418 \div 22 =$
29. $1.32 \div 400 =$
30. $84 \div 1.20 =$

12-8 Problem Solving with Decimals

How do we solve problems with decimals? Look at the following problem.

Joel bought 6 pounds of chicken for $7.50. David bought 4 pounds of turkey for $5.20. Which is the better buy?

First, we need to find the cost per pound (for 1 pound) of both the chicken and the turkey. Then we need to compare the prices. To find the cost per pound, we divide the price by the total pounds.

chicken:
$$\begin{array}{r} 1.25 \\ 6\overline{)7.50} \\ -6 \\ \hline 15 \\ -12 \\ \hline 30 \\ -30 \\ \hline 0 \end{array}$$

turkey:
$$\begin{array}{r} 1.30 \\ 4\overline{)5.20} \\ -4 \\ \hline 12 \\ -12 \\ \hline 00 \\ -0 \\ \hline 0 \end{array}$$

The better buy is the chicken, at $1.25 a pound.

179

Marta and Yuri need to go shopping for their Math Club party. They also need to decide which items are the better buys. First, read the problems below. Then write the answers on the lines. Show all your work on a separate sheet of paper.

1. Super Cooler sodas are eight cans for $3.36. Just Right sodas are six cans for $2.46.

   a. How much are Super Cooler sodas per can? _____ *$.42* _____

   b. How much are Just Right sodas per can? _____

   c. Which is the better buy? _____

2. Blue Star potato chips are three bags for $2.67. Red Star potato chips are five bags for $4.55.

   a. How much are Blue Star potato chips per bag? _____

   b. How much are Red Star potato chips per bag?_____

   c. Which is the better buy? _____

3. Chocolate chip cookies are $2.88 a dozen. Peanut butter cookies are $1.92 for eight.

   a. How much is one chocolate chip cookie? _____

   b. How much is one peanut butter cookie? _____

   c. Which is the better buy? _____

4. Health bars cost $.40 each. How many bars can Marta and Yuri buy for $8?

   _____

5. There are twenty students in the Math Club. Marta and Yuri will buy three pounds of grapes. How many pounds will each student get to eat?

   _____

12-9 Average, or Mean ···

How do we find the **average**, or **mean**, in a group of numbers? Look at the following problem.

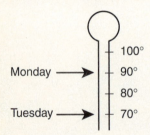

Monday → 100°
90°
80°
Tuesday → 70°

On Monday, the temperature was 90 degrees. On Tuesday, the temperature was 70 degrees. What was the average, or mean, temperature for both days?

To find the average, or mean:

1. We add the numbers together.

2. Then we divide the sum by the number of addends.

$$\underbrace{70° + 90°}_{\text{2 addends}} = 160°$$

$160° \div 2 = 80°$

Answer: 80° is the average, or mean, temperature for the two days.

Example:

Here are the math test scores for five students:

Becky   85
Jaimie   90
Wilson   80
Hanh   85
Henry   95

What is the average, or mean, score of the five students?

$$\underbrace{85 + 90 + 80 + 85 + 95}_{\text{5 addends}} = 435$$

$435 \div 5 = 87$

Answer: 87 is the average, or mean, score of the five students.

Exercise 14

Read the problems below. Then find the average, or mean, for each problem. Write your answers on the lines. Show all your work on a separate sheet of paper.

1. Mark weighs 135.7 pounds, Teresa weighs 105.73 pounds, Violet weighs 127.33 pounds, and Harry weighs 119 pounds. What is the mean weight of the four friends? _121.94 lb_

2. In May, apples were $.79 per pound. In June, apples were $1.23 per pound, and in July, apples cost $1.19 per pound. What was the average cost of apples for the three months? _____

3. Look at Mr. Contini's telephone bills below for the year. What was his average bill for the year? Round your answer to the nearest cent (hundredths place). _____

January	$23.19		July	$32.95
February	$16.45		August	$45.16
March	$30.20		September	$24.59
April	$22.74		October	$27.33
May	$19.50		November	$21.00
June	$18.48		December	$25.47

4. In the Radar Corporation, four employees earn $35,000 a year, two employees earn $53,000 a year, and seventeen employees earn $28,000 a year. What is the mean salary of the employees? Round your answer to the nearest whole number (ones place).

_____

5. Julie and ten friends went on a walking tour through an old neighborhood. For lunch, they stopped at a Japanese restaurant. Five friends each ordered lunch for $10.99; four friends each ordered lunch for $15.00; and Julie and one friend each ordered lunch for $12.50. What was the average price for lunch? Round your answer to the nearest ten cents (the hundredths place). _____

Exercise 15

On a separate sheet of paper, use inverse operations to find the missing numbers.

1. _33_ × .3 = 9.9

2. _____ ÷ 4.5 = 12.6

3. .9 × _____ = .81

4. _____ ÷ .98 = 8.54

5. _____ ÷ .8 = 12.34

6. _____ × .10 = 3.0

7. _____ ÷ .87 = 54.4

8. _____ ÷ .91 = 12.4

9. .7 × _____ = .42

10. .002 × _____ = 26

11. _____ ÷ .65 = 90

12. .004 × _____ = .56

13. 1.2 × _____ = .36

14. .005 × _____ = 3.5

15. _____ ÷ 6.55 = .12

12-10 Dividing Decimals by Multiples of Ten

We learned that to multiply decimals by multiples of ten quickly, we move the decimal point to the right.

To divide decimals by multiples of ten quickly, we move the decimal point to the left. Look at the following problems.

436.2 ÷ 100 = 4.362

2 zeros

We move the point two places to the left ←.

$25,467.1 ÷ 10^5 = .254671$

5 zeros

We move the point five places to the left ←.

Example:

34.587 ÷ 10,000 = .0034587

4 zeros

We move the point four places to the left ←.
Since there are only two numbers to the left, we need to write in two more zeros.

Divide the decimals by moving the decimal point.

1. $14.2 \div 10 =$ _____ 1.42 _____

2. $7.11 \div 100 =$ _____

3. $.673 \div 1,000 =$ _____

4. $143.22 \div 100 =$ _____

5. $7 \div 1,000 =$ _____

6. $19 \div 10 =$ _____

7. $376 \div 100 =$ _____

8. $44.4 \div 10 =$ _____

9. $444 \div 100 =$ _____

10. $.444 \div 10 =$ _____

11. $3,294.11 \div 10,000 =$ _____

12. $7,463.4 \div 10 =$ _____

13. $2.1 \div 1,000 =$ _____

14. $111.4 \div 100 =$ _____

15. $14.31 \div 10,000 =$ _____

16. $5,342 \div 1,000 =$ _____

17. $1.433 \div 100 =$ _____

18. $9 \div 10,000 =$ _____

19. $3 \div 100 =$ _____

20. $2 \div 10,000 =$ _____

Divide the decimals by moving the decimal point.

1. $43.5 \div 10^2 =$ _____ .435 _____

2. $.1254 \div 10^3 =$ _____

3. $365.66 \div 10^3 =$ _____

4. $354.99 \div 10^4 =$ _____

5. $.12938 \div 10^3 =$ _____

6. $1,543.66 \div 10^5 =$ _____

7. $3,546 \div 10^3 =$ _____

8. $2,435.1 \div 10^7 =$ _____

9. $34.445 \div 10^2 =$ _____

10. $34.777 \div 10^1 =$ _____

11. $9,887.1 \div 10^0 =$ _____

12. $9,857 \div 10^4 =$ _____

13. $.88675 \div 10^7 =$ _____

14. $.12 \div 10^5 =$ _____

15. $95,744.32 \div 10^3 =$ _____

16. $.7756 \div 10^0 =$ _____

17. $34.44 \div 10^2 =$ _____

18. $2,300 \div 10^2 =$ _____

19. $1,000 \div 10^3 =$ _____

20. $10,000 \div 10^4 =$ _____

Have I Learned? (✓)

Work with a partner. Check what you have learned. Review what you need help with.

1. increase ☐
2. decrease ☐
3. average ☐
4. mean ☐

CHAPTER REVIEW

Exercise 1

On a separate sheet of paper, multiply the following decimals.

1. $5.46 \times 4 =$
2. $.457 \times 32 =$
3. $7.22 \times .01 =$
4. $.001 \times .45 =$
5. $854.3 \times 2.3 =$
6. $1.26 \times .34 =$
7. $.945 \times .12 =$
8. $487.44 \times .002 =$
9. $54.667 \times 12.3 =$
10. $67.228 \times 23.1 =$

Exercise 2

On a separate sheet of paper, divide the following decimals.

1. $4.24 \div 2 =$
2. $12.4 \div .2 =$
3. $15.50 \div .05 =$
4. $4 \div .002 =$
5. $2 \div 2,000 =$
6. $.4032 \div .336 =$
7. $.3 \div 50 =$
8. $30 \div 600 =$
9. $.00856 \div .214 =$
10. $.02172 \div .724 =$

Exercise 3

On a separate sheet of paper, multiply or divide the following decimals.

1. $3.21 \times 10^1 =$
2. $5.48 \times 10^2 =$
3. $6.334 \times 10^4 =$
4. $7,834.3 \div 10^3 =$
5. $.1255 \div 10^2 =$
6. $.3665 \times 10^6 =$
7. $1,543.2 \times 10^4 =$
8. $9.567 \div 10^3 =$
9. $.213 \div 10^0 =$
10. $34.992 \times 10^5 =$

Exercise 4

Solve the following problems. Write your answers on the lines. Show your work on a separate sheet of paper.

1. Raul spends $11.70 on gasoline each month. How much does he spend in one year?
   $140.40

2. Maggie bought 1.75 pounds of chocolate. The chocolate cost $1.20 a pound. How much did she pay for the chocolate? _____

3. Casey went shopping. She bought 2.5 pounds of apples for $1.25. How much did she pay per pound? _____

4. Maurice received $279.27 for 32.5 hours of work last month. How much does he earn per hour? Round to the nearest cent (hundredths place).

   _____

5. For the month of January, Chan received four paychecks—Week 1: $100.00; Week 2: $93.75; Week 3: $112.50; and Week 4: $106.25. What was the average weekly pay? Round to the nearest cent (hundredths place). _____

Operations with Fractions

In this unit, you will learn . . .

- reading and saying fractions
- fractions less than, equal to, and greater than a whole
- changing improper fractions and mixed numbers
- equivalent fractions
- comparing fractions
- simplifying fractions
- multiplying fractions
- simplifying by canceling
- solving word problems
- dividing fractions
- adding fractions
- finding the lowest common denominator (LCD)
- subtracting fractions

CHAPTER 13 Fractions

13-1 Naming Fractions ···

We can cut a pie into three equal pieces.

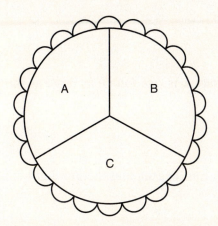

Compare piece A to the whole pie (three pieces). Piece A is *one third* as large as the whole pie.

$$\frac{1}{3}$$ ← piece A
← whole pie

Piece B is also *one third* as large as the whole pie.

$$\frac{1}{3}$$ ← piece B
← whole pie

Piece C is also *one third* as large as the whole pie.

$$\frac{1}{3}$$ ← piece C
← whole pie

Each piece is a **fraction** of the pie. Piece A = piece B = piece C. If we compare the whole pie to one piece, the pie is 3 times as large as one piece.

$$\frac{3}{1}$$ ← whole pie
← one piece

So we can think of fractions as comparing one thing with another thing.

Example:

Pour colored water into a glass.

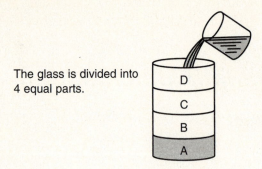

The glass is divided into
4 equal parts.

Part A is 1 part.

If we compare part A to the whole glass, part A is *one fourth* as large as the whole glass.

$$\frac{1}{4} \quad \leftarrow \text{part A} \\ \quad \leftarrow \text{the whole glass}$$

In all fractions, the number above is called the **numerator** and the number below is called the **denominator**.

$$\text{numerator} \longrightarrow \frac{1}{4} \longleftarrow \text{denominator}$$

Usually, fractions are comparisons of smaller parts to larger parts:

$$\frac{1}{3}, \frac{2}{5}, \frac{7}{9}$$

but they can also be comparisons of equal parts:

$$\frac{2}{2}, \frac{4}{4}, \frac{3}{3}$$

or they can be comparisons of larger parts to smaller parts:

$$\frac{3}{2}, \frac{8}{3}, \frac{4}{1}$$

Example:

The circle below is divided into four equal parts. There are three shaded parts and one unshaded part.

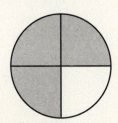

If we compare the shaded parts to the unshaded parts, we have the fraction $\frac{3}{1}$.

If we compare the shaded parts to the whole circle, we have the fraction $\frac{3}{4}$.

If we compare the unshaded parts to the shaded parts, we have the fraction $\frac{1}{3}$.

13-2 Reading and Saying Fractions

We use cardinal and ordinal numbers to read and say fractions.

$\frac{1}{4} = one \qquad fourth$

↑ cardinal number
↑ ordinal number

$\frac{3}{4} = three\ fourths$

The "s" tells us "more than 1 part."

Some fractions have special names.

$\frac{1}{2} = one\ half$

$\frac{2}{2} = two\ halves$ (*halves* is the plural of *half*)

$\frac{3}{1} = three\ wholes$ (when the denominator = 1)

Exercise 1

Write the fractions with words. Then work with a partner. Practice saying them aloud.

1. $\frac{6}{7}$ _____six sevenths_____

2. $\frac{1}{3}$ _____

3. $\frac{7}{11}$ _____

4. $\frac{3}{4}$ _____

5. $\frac{2}{2}$ _____

6. $\frac{3}{9}$ _____

7. $\frac{4}{1}$ _____

8. $\frac{9}{10}$ _____

9. $\frac{7}{2}$ _____

10. $\frac{1}{7}$ _____

11. $\frac{8}{8}$ _____

12. $\frac{10}{1}$ _____

13. $\frac{1}{1}$ _____

14. $\frac{9}{20}$ _____

15. $\frac{11}{15}$ _____

16. $\frac{3}{3}$ _____

17. $\frac{12}{12}$ _____

18. $\frac{1}{12}$ _____

19. $\frac{19}{1}$ _____

20. $\frac{3}{6}$ _____

21. $\frac{6}{6}$ _____

22. $\frac{6}{2}$ _____

23. $\frac{1}{8}$ _____

24. $\frac{3}{30}$ _____

25. $\frac{8}{1}$ _____

Exercise 2

Read the following words. Write them as fractions.

1. one fourth ___$\frac{1}{4}$___
2. three sixths _____
3. seventeen tenths _____
4. five wholes _____
5. eleven fiftieths _____
6. twenty-five fifths _____
7. six halves _____
8. eight thirteenths _____
9. five fifths _____
10. one third _____

11. seventy sixteenths _____
12. ninety wholes _____
13. two halves _____
14. eight forty-fifths _____
15. thirty thirtieths _____
16. forty eighths _____
17. sixty nineteenths _____
18. two wholes _____
19. twelve twenty-seconds _____
20. eighteen twentieths _____

Exercise 3

Look at the figures below. Compare the shaded parts to the whole figure.
Write the fraction.

1. 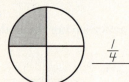 $\frac{1}{4}$

5. 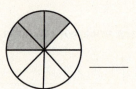 _____

8. 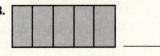 _____

2. 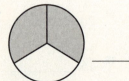 _____

6. 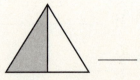 _____

9. 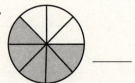 _____

3.  _____

7.  _____

10. 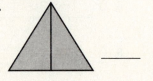 _____

4.  _____

Look at the figures and the fractions below each one. Shade the figures to equal the fractions.

1.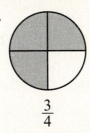

$$\frac{3}{4}$$

5.

$$\frac{4}{4}$$

8.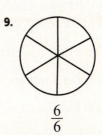

$$\frac{3}{9}$$

2.

$$\frac{1}{5}$$

6.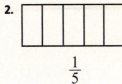

$$\frac{1}{3}$$

9.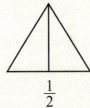

$$\frac{6}{6}$$

3.

$$\frac{1}{2}$$

7.

$$\frac{8}{16}$$

10.

$$\frac{1}{2}$$

4.

$$\frac{2}{3}$$

We can use fractions to compare numbers of people.

Example:

There are 5 girls at a party. Of the girls, 3 have black hair and 2 have brown hair. What fraction of the 5 girls have black hair?

Number of girls with black hair = 3
Total number of girls = 5

Fraction of girls with black hair = $\frac{3}{5}$

What fraction of the girls have brown hair?

Number of girls with brown hair = 2
Total number of girls = 5

Fraction of girls with brown hair = $\frac{2}{5}$

Read the following problems. Write a fraction for each one.

1. There are 6 people in Grady's family. Two people are under 10 years old. What fraction of the family is under 10 years old? $\frac{2}{6}$

2. In Mrs. Garcia's classroom, 15 students buy lunch. There are 28 students in her class. What fraction of the students buy lunch? _____

3. In Dodge City, 2 out of every 3 women have blond hair. What fraction of the women have blond hair? _____

4. At Hanover High School, 4 out of every 5 students go to college after graduation. What fraction of the students go to college? _____

5. On Stratford Avenue, 7 out of 10 families own two cars.

   a. What fraction of the families own two cars? _____

   b. What fraction of the families *don't* own two cars? _____

6. In Mrs. Doyle's Math Club, 15 out of a total of 18 students speak two languages.

   a. What fraction of the students speak two languages? _____

   b. What fraction of the students *don't* speak two languages? _____

7. In the United States, 96 out of 100 people watch television at home. What fraction of the people watch television at home? _____

8. In the Spirit Shopping Mall, 10 out of every 50 shoppers buy shoes. What fraction of the shoppers *don't* buy shoes? _____

9. There are 27 families in the Villa Park Apartments. Twelve of the families have pets. What fraction of the families *don't* have pets? _____

10. The Central School basketball team played 11 games. They won 4 games. What fraction of their games did they win? _____

13-3 Fractions Less Than, Equal to, and Greater Than a Whole ••••

Fractions can be **less than a whole**.

Example:

These fractions are less than a whole:

$$\frac{2}{5}, \quad \frac{1}{3}, \quad \frac{3}{8}, \quad \frac{3}{4}$$

Their numerators are less than their denominators.

Write ten fractions that are less than a whole.

1. $\dfrac{2}{3}$ 3. _____   5. _____   7. _____   9. _____

2. _____   4. _____   6. _____   8. _____   10. _____

Fractions can be **equal to a whole**.

Example:

These fractions are equal to a whole:

$$\frac{3}{3}, \quad \frac{2}{2}, \quad \frac{4}{4}, \quad \frac{8}{8}$$

Their numerators are equal to their denominators.

Write ten fractions that are equal to a whole.

1. $\dfrac{6}{6}$ 3. _____   5. _____   7. _____   9. _____

2. _____   4. _____   6. _____   8. _____   10. _____

Fractions can be **greater than a whole**.

Example:

These fractions are greater than a whole:

$$\frac{3}{2}, \quad \frac{6}{3}, \quad \frac{7}{4}, \quad \frac{9}{1}$$

Their numerators are greater than their denominators.

When a fraction is greater than a whole, it is called an **improper fraction**.

Write ten improper fractions.

1. $\dfrac{7}{4}$ 3. _____   5. _____   7. _____   9. _____

2. _____   4. _____   6. _____   8. _____   10. _____

Look at the fractions below. For each one, write L if it is less than a whole, E if it is equal to a whole, or G if it is greater than a whole.

1. $\dfrac{1}{2}$ $\underline{\quad A \quad}$ 6. $\dfrac{3}{11}$ _____   11. $\dfrac{15}{15}$ _____   16. $\dfrac{9}{2}$ _____

2. $\dfrac{3}{8}$ _____   7. $\dfrac{6}{10}$ _____   12. $\dfrac{19}{20}$ _____   17. $\dfrac{12}{11}$ _____

3. $\dfrac{6}{6}$ _____   8. $\dfrac{10}{6}$ _____   13. $\dfrac{1}{1}$ _____   18. $\dfrac{30}{100}$ _____

4. $\dfrac{8}{7}$ _____   9. $\dfrac{1}{5}$ _____   14. $\dfrac{2}{1}$ _____   19. $\dfrac{100}{100}$ _____

5. $\dfrac{4}{4}$ _____   10. $\dfrac{8}{4}$ _____   15. $\dfrac{3}{10}$ _____   20. $\dfrac{7}{9}$ _____

13-4 Whole Numbers as Fractions

We can write fractions that are equal to the whole numbers 1, 2, 3, 4, . . .

Example:

$$\frac{1}{1} = 1 \qquad\qquad \frac{3}{1} = 3 \qquad\qquad \frac{5}{1} = 5$$

$$\frac{2}{1} = 2 \qquad\qquad \frac{4}{1} = 4 \qquad\qquad \frac{6}{1} = 6$$

When the denominator of a fraction is equal to 1, the fraction is equal to a whole number.

A. Write a fraction for each whole number.

1. $5 = \dfrac{5}{1}$

2. $2 = \underline{\hspace{1.5cm}}$

3. $6 = \underline{\hspace{1.5cm}}$

4. $10 = \underline{\hspace{1.5cm}}$

5. $8 = \underline{\hspace{1.5cm}}$

6. $12 = \underline{\hspace{1.5cm}}$

7. $7 = \underline{\hspace{1.5cm}}$

8. $3 = \underline{\hspace{1.5cm}}$

9. $1 = \underline{\hspace{1.5cm}}$

10. $100 = \underline{\hspace{1.5cm}}$

B. Write a whole number for each fraction.

1. $\dfrac{5}{1} = \underline{\hspace{1cm}} 5$

2. $\dfrac{3}{1} = \underline{\hspace{1cm}}$

3. $\dfrac{1}{1} = \underline{\hspace{1cm}}$

4. $\dfrac{8}{1} = \underline{\hspace{1cm}}$

5. $\dfrac{2}{1} = \underline{\hspace{1cm}}$

6. $\dfrac{100}{1} = \underline{\hspace{1cm}}$

7. $\dfrac{36}{1} = \underline{\hspace{1cm}}$

8. $\dfrac{15}{1} = \underline{\hspace{1cm}}$

9. $\dfrac{7}{1} = \underline{\hspace{1cm}}$

10. $\dfrac{12}{1} = \underline{\hspace{1cm}}$

13-5 Changing Improper Fractions to Mixed Numbers

In Section 13-3, we learned that in an improper fraction, the numerator is greater than the denominator.

$\dfrac{5}{3}$ is an improper fraction.

A **mixed number** is a whole number written together with a fraction.

$1\dfrac{2}{3}$ is a mixed number $\left(1 + \dfrac{2}{3}\right)$.

We say, "One and two thirds."

For every improper fraction, we can write an equivalent mixed number. In all fractions, the bar between the numerator and the denominator means *divided by*.

$\dfrac{4}{3}$ ← This bar means *divided by.*

We say, "Four divided by three."

Example:

We can write $\frac{4}{3}$ as a mixed number. If we divide the numerator by the denominator, we get an equivalent mixed number.

> Write the remainder 1 as a fraction over the divisor 3.

$$\frac{4}{3} = 4 \div 3 = 3\overline{)4} \quad \begin{array}{r} 1\frac{1}{3} \\ \end{array}$$
$$\frac{-3}{1}$$

$$\frac{4}{3} = 1\frac{1}{3}$$

Example:

We can change $\frac{12}{5}$ to a mixed number.

$$\frac{12}{5} = 12 \div 5 = 5\overline{)12} \quad \begin{array}{r} 2\frac{2}{5} \end{array} \leftarrow \text{remainder} \atop \leftarrow \text{divisor}$$
$$\frac{-10}{2}$$

$$\frac{12}{5} = 2\frac{2}{5}$$

Example:

We can change $\frac{8}{4}$.

$$\frac{8}{4} = 8 \div 4 = 4\overline{)8} \quad \begin{array}{r} 2 \end{array}$$
$$\frac{-8}{0}$$

$$\frac{8}{4} = 2$$

There is no remainder, so the answer is 2, a whole number, not a mixed number.

Change the improper fractions below to the equivalent mixed numbers. Show your work on a separate sheet of paper. Write your answers on the lines.

1. $\frac{6}{5}$ = $1\frac{1}{5}$

2. $\frac{9}{7}$ = _____

3. $\frac{11}{3}$ = _____

4. $\frac{3}{2}$ = _____

5. $\frac{17}{5}$ = _____

6. $\frac{20}{9}$ = _____

7. $\frac{11}{10}$ = _____

8. $\frac{15}{7}$ = _____

9. $\frac{25}{24}$ = _____

10. $\frac{18}{5}$ = _____

11. $\frac{12}{9}$ = _____

12. $\frac{7}{3}$ = _____

13. $\frac{19}{6}$ = _____

14. $\frac{10}{5}$ = _____

15. $\frac{9}{8}$ = _____

16. $\frac{24}{9}$ = _____

17. $\frac{87}{10}$ = _____

18. $\frac{19}{12}$ = _____

19. $\frac{37}{18}$ = _____

20. $\frac{20}{10}$ = _____

13-6 Changing Mixed Numbers to Improper Fractions

We learned how to change improper fractions to equivalent mixed numbers. We can also change mixed numbers to equivalent improper fractions.

Example:

How do we change $4\frac{2}{3}$ to an equivalent improper fraction?

1. We multiply the whole number by the denominator.

   $3 \times 4 = 12$

2. We add the product to the numerator.

   $12 + 2 = 14$

3. We write the sum over the original denominator.

   $\frac{14}{3}$

   $4\frac{2}{3} = \frac{14}{3}$

Example:

We can change $3\frac{1}{2}$ to an equivalent improper fraction.

1. $2 \times 3 = 6$

2. $6 + 1 = 7$

3. $\frac{7}{2}$

$3\frac{1}{2} = \frac{7}{2}$

Exercise 12

Change the mixed numbers below to the equivalent improper fractions. Show your work on a separate sheet of paper. Write your answers on the lines.

1. $1\frac{1}{3} = \frac{4}{3}$

2. $3\frac{1}{2} = $ _____

3. $6\frac{1}{3} = $ _____

4. $9\frac{2}{5} = $ _____

5. $7\frac{3}{5} = $ _____

6. $4\frac{1}{3} = $ _____

7. $10\frac{1}{2} = $ _____

8. $5\frac{2}{3} = $ _____

9. $7\frac{5}{6} = $ _____

10. $19\frac{1}{3} = $ _____

11. $3\frac{7}{8} = $ _____

12. $4\frac{3}{4} = $ _____

13. $5\frac{9}{17} = $ _____

14. $2\frac{3}{4} = $ _____

15. $10\frac{1}{5} = $ _____

16. $14\frac{1}{7} = $ _____

17. $3\frac{7}{11} = $ _____

18. $14\frac{3}{4} = $ _____

19. $35\frac{4}{5} = $ _____

20. $100\frac{2}{7} = $ _____

LISTENING

Your teacher will say fractions aloud. Listen. Circle the letter next to the correct fraction.

1. a. $\frac{3}{1}$ b. $\frac{3}{4}$ c. $3\frac{1}{4}$

2. a. $2\frac{1}{2}$ b. $\frac{21}{2}$ c. $2\frac{1}{4}$

3. a. $\frac{4}{1}$ b. $\frac{3}{4}$ c. $\frac{4}{3}$

4. a. $\frac{17}{10}$ b. $\frac{7}{10}$ c. $7\frac{1}{10}$

5. a. $\frac{5}{2}$ b. $\frac{5}{1}$ c. $5\frac{1}{2}$

6. a. $\frac{42}{3}$ b. $\frac{4}{3}$ c. $4\frac{2}{3}$

7. a. $\frac{9}{2}$ b. $\frac{9}{1}$ c. $\frac{90}{1}$

8. a. $11\frac{1}{7}$ b. $\frac{11}{7}$ c. $\frac{11}{11}$

9. a. $3\frac{1}{5}$ b. $\frac{31}{5}$ c. $\frac{3}{5}$

10. a. $\frac{40}{6}$ b. $\frac{4}{6}$ c. $\frac{46}{1}$

Write the fractions below using words. Then work with a partner. Practice saying them aloud.

1. $1\frac{3}{4}$ _one and three fourths_

2. $3\frac{1}{2}$ _____

3. $\frac{7}{2}$ _____

4. $9\frac{2}{3}$ _____

5. $6\frac{1}{5}$ _____

6. $\frac{17}{3}$ _____

7. $\frac{4}{4}$ _____

8. $17\frac{2}{3}$ _____

9. $4\frac{7}{12}$ _____

10. $7\frac{1}{9}$ _____

11. $6\frac{5}{8}$ _____

12. $\frac{8}{1}$ _____

13. $\frac{19}{5}$ _____

14. $4\frac{1}{3}$ _____

15. $5\frac{4}{5}$ _____

16. $\frac{5}{2}$ _____

17. $\frac{2}{1}$ _____

18. $11\frac{4}{7}$ _____

19. $2\frac{1}{10}$ _____

20. $8\frac{3}{4}$ _____

Read the following words. Write them as fractions.

1. four and seven eighths $4\frac{7}{8}$

2. nine and one third _____

3. fifteen halves _____

4. nine and two tenths _____

5. twenty-five wholes _____

6. thirteen and three fourths _____

7. forty-two and a half _____

8. eleven wholes _____

9. twelve and five twelfths _____

10. six and seventy eightieths _____

11. six hundredths _____

12. nine and two fifths _____

13. seven and one twenty-fifth _____

17. sixty and one ninth _____

14. seventy-nine and five eighths _____

18. sixty-one ninths _____

15. three and twelve fifteenths _____

19. sixty-one and nine tenths _____

16. forty-nine halves _____

20. sixty-one nineteenths _____

13-7 Equivalent Fractions

Here are three circles of equal size. Let's compare the shaded parts to the whole figure.

We see that the shaded parts in all three circles are equal, so $\frac{1}{2}$, $\frac{2}{4}$, and $\frac{4}{8}$ are **equivalent fractions** (that is, they have the same value).

$$\frac{1}{2} = \frac{2}{4} = \frac{4}{8}$$

Example:

The two rectangles below are of equal size. The shaded parts are equal, so the fractions that name the shaded parts are also equal.

$\frac{1}{3}$ →

$\frac{2}{6}$ →

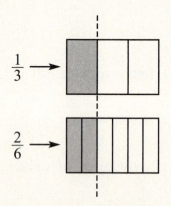

In the two rectangles above, $\frac{1}{3} = \frac{2}{6}$. They are equivalent fractions.

Compare the shaded parts to the whole figure. Write the equivalent fractions.

1.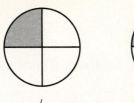

$$\frac{1}{4} = \frac{2}{8}$$

6.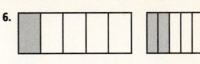

_____ = _____

2.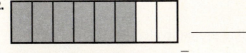

_____ = _____

7.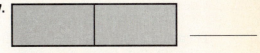

_____ = _____

3.

_____ = _____

8.

_____ = _____

4.

_____ = _____

9.

_____ = _____

5.

_____ = _____

10.

_____ = _____

In Chapter 6, we learned the Multiplicative Identity Property. That property says that if we multiply any number by 1, the value of that number does not change.

$$3 \times 1 = 3$$
$$100 \times 1 = 100$$

We can also multiply any fraction by 1, and the value of that fraction does not change.

$$\frac{1}{2} \times 1 = \frac{1}{2}$$

$$\frac{2}{3} \times 1 = \frac{2}{3}$$

There are an infinite number of fractions that are equivalent to 1. Here are some examples:

$$\frac{1}{1} = 1 \qquad \frac{2}{2} = 1 \qquad \frac{3}{3} = 1 \qquad \frac{10}{10} = 1$$

$$\frac{50}{50} = 1 \qquad \frac{65}{65} = 1 \qquad \frac{80}{80} = 1 \qquad \frac{100}{100} = 1$$

Remember, when the numerator of a fraction equals the denominator, the fraction is equal to one whole.

If we multiply a fraction by a fraction equivalent to 1, the value of the fraction will not change.

$$\left. \frac{1}{2} \times \frac{3}{3} = \frac{3}{6} \right\} \text{ a product equivalent to } \frac{1}{2}$$

↑

a fraction equivalent to 1

How do we multiply fractions by fractions equivalent to 1?

1. We multiply the numerators together.

2. We multiply the denominators together.

$$\frac{1}{2} \times \frac{3}{3} = \frac{1 \times 3}{2 \times 3} = \frac{3}{6}$$

↑   ↑

These fractions are equivalent.

We can multiply $\frac{1}{2}$ by another fraction equivalent to 1.

$$\frac{1}{2} \times \frac{4}{4} = \frac{1 \times 4}{2 \times 4} = \frac{4}{8}$$

So, $\frac{1}{2} = \frac{3}{6} = \frac{4}{8}$.

The three fractions are all equivalent fractions.

To find equivalent fractions, we multiply the original fraction by fractions equivalent to 1.

$$\frac{1}{2} \times \frac{2}{2} = \frac{2}{4}$$

$$\frac{1}{2} \times \frac{5}{5} = \frac{5}{10}$$ These products are all fractions equivalent to $\frac{1}{2}$.

$$\frac{1}{2} \times \frac{6}{6} = \frac{6}{12}$$

These fractions are all equivalent to 1.

Example:

Find two fractions equivalent to $\frac{3}{7}$.

$$\frac{3}{7} \times \frac{6}{6} = \frac{18}{42} \qquad\qquad \frac{3}{7} \times \frac{4}{4} = \frac{12}{28}$$

So, $\frac{3}{7} = \frac{18}{42} = \frac{12}{28}$

Exercise 16

Look at the following fractions. Write two equivalent fractions for each one. Show your work on a separate sheet of paper.

1. $\frac{5}{6} = \frac{10}{12} = \frac{15}{18}$ 4. $\frac{1}{7} = $ _____ = _____   7. $\frac{10}{20} = $ _____ = _____

2. $\frac{2}{3} = $ _____ = _____   5. $\frac{8}{10} = $ _____ = _____   8. $\frac{1}{9} = $ _____ = _____

3. $\frac{4}{8} = $ _____ = _____   6. $\frac{12}{15} = $ _____ = _____   9. $\frac{6}{15} = $ _____ = _____

10. $\dfrac{2}{5} = $ _____ = _____

11. $\dfrac{9}{10} = $ _____ = _____

12. $\dfrac{5}{7} = $ _____ = _____

13. $\dfrac{6}{6} = $ _____ = _____

14. $\dfrac{25}{1} = $ _____ = _____

15. $\dfrac{9}{15} = $ _____ = _____

16. $\dfrac{11}{20} = $ _____ = _____

17. $\dfrac{2}{1} = $ _____ = _____

18. $\dfrac{5}{5} = $ _____ = _____

19. $\dfrac{16}{4} = $ _____ = _____

20. $\dfrac{1}{4} = $ _____ = _____

Sometimes, we need to change a fraction to an equivalent fraction with a different numerator or denominator.

Example:

Find a fraction equivalent to $\dfrac{1}{2}$ with a denominator of 6.

If we multiply the denominator of $\dfrac{1}{2}$ by 3, the product will be 6.

$$\dfrac{1}{2} \times \dfrac{}{3} = \dfrac{}{6}$$

We must also multiply the numerator by 3 to get a fraction equivalent to $\dfrac{1}{2}$.

$$\dfrac{1 \times 3}{2 \times 3} = \dfrac{3}{6}$$

The fraction $\dfrac{3}{6}$ has a denominator of 6 and is equivalent to $\dfrac{1}{2}$.

Exercise 17

Write the missing numerator or denominator to make equivalent fractions.

1. $\dfrac{2}{3} = \dfrac{8}{12}$

2. $\dfrac{1}{5} = \dfrac{}{10}$

3. $\dfrac{3}{9} = \dfrac{9}{}$

4. $\dfrac{4}{10} = \dfrac{}{30}$

5. $\dfrac{2}{4} = \dfrac{6}{}$

6. $\dfrac{4}{6} = \dfrac{}{18}$

7. $\dfrac{2}{5} = \dfrac{}{15}$

8. $\dfrac{7}{10} = \dfrac{70}{}$

9. $\dfrac{3}{15} = \dfrac{}{30}$

10. $\dfrac{1}{7} = \dfrac{}{21}$

11. $\dfrac{3}{6} = \dfrac{12}{}$

12. $\dfrac{1}{6} = \dfrac{}{36}$

13. $\dfrac{3}{3} = \dfrac{}{12}$

14. $\dfrac{3}{5} = \dfrac{12}{}$

15. $\dfrac{2}{12} = \dfrac{6}{}$

16. $\dfrac{4}{7} = \dfrac{}{28}$

17. $\dfrac{1}{4} = \dfrac{4}{}$

18. $\dfrac{9}{18} = \dfrac{36}{}$

19. $\dfrac{3}{8} = \dfrac{6}{}$

20. $\dfrac{4}{4} = \dfrac{}{20}$

21. $\dfrac{5}{10} = \dfrac{25}{}$

22. $\dfrac{3}{11} = \dfrac{}{33}$

23. $\dfrac{4}{5} = \dfrac{20}{}$

24. $\dfrac{4}{18} = \dfrac{16}{}$

25. $\dfrac{7}{12} = \dfrac{42}{}$

Have I Learned? (✓)

Work with a partner. Check what you have learned. Review what you need help with.

1. fraction ☐
2. numerator ☐
3. denominator ☐
4. fractions less than a whole ☐
5. fractions equal to a whole ☐
6. fractions greater than a whole ☐
7. improper fractions ☐
8. mixed number ☐
9. equivalent fractions ☐

Exercise 1

A. Write the words for the fractions below.

1. $\frac{1}{2}$ = _____one half_____

2. $\frac{3}{4}$ = _____

3. $\frac{2}{1}$ = _____

4. $\frac{6}{2}$ = _____

5. $6\frac{1}{3}$ = _____

B. Write the fractions for the words below.

1. eleven fifteenths $\frac{11}{15}$

2. thirteen wholes _____

3. six ninths _____

4. three thirds _____

5. four and two eighths _____

Exercise 2

A. Change the improper fractions to mixed numbers.

1. $\frac{17}{3}$ = $5\frac{2}{3}$ 2. $\frac{9}{2}$ = _____   3. $\frac{25}{6}$ = _____   4. $\frac{20}{9}$ = _____   5. $\frac{11}{10}$ = _____

B. Change the mixed numbers to improper fractions.

1. $3\frac{2}{6}$ = $\frac{20}{6}$ 2. $1\frac{1}{3}$ = _____   3. $5\frac{5}{8}$ = _____   4. $7\frac{2}{5}$ = _____   5. $10\frac{1}{2}$ = _____

Exercise 3

Write <, >, or =.

1. $\frac{3}{1}$ __>__ 1   2. $\frac{2}{5}$ _____ 1   3. $\frac{5}{2}$ _____ 1   4. $\frac{12}{12}$ _____ 1   5. $\frac{9}{8}$ _____ 1

Exercise 4

Write an equivalent fraction for each of the fractions below.

1. $\frac{1}{2}$ = $\frac{2}{4}$ 2. $\frac{3}{4}$ = _____   3. $\frac{7}{7}$ = _____   4. $\frac{8}{3}$ = _____   5. $\frac{6}{1}$ = _____

Exercise 5

Write the missing numerator or denominator to make equivalent fractions.

1. $\frac{9}{27}$ = $\frac{27}{81}$ 2. $\frac{3}{5}$ = $\frac{}{20}$ 3. $\frac{4}{7}$ = $\frac{24}{}$ 4. $\frac{3}{6}$ = $\frac{}{48}$ 5. $\frac{8}{9}$ = $\frac{}{99}$

More Work with Fractions

14-1 Comparing Fractions

Sometimes we need to find out if a fraction is greater than, equal to, or less than another fraction. We do this by comparing fractions. We can compare two fractions with the same numerator.

Example:

Compare $\frac{1}{3}$ and $\frac{1}{8}$.

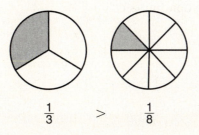

$$\frac{1}{3} \quad > \quad \frac{1}{8}$$

The two circles are equal in size. The circle on the left is divided into 3 equal parts. The circle on the right is divided into 8 equal parts. We can see that the more we divide a whole, the smaller each part becomes. So, 1 part of 3 is greater than 1 part of 8, that is, $\frac{1}{3}$ is greater than $\frac{1}{8}$.

Example:

Compare $\frac{3}{12}$ and $\frac{3}{5}$.

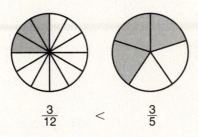

$$\frac{3}{12} \quad < \quad \frac{3}{5}$$

In the two circles above, we can see that 3 parts of 12 is less than 3 parts of 5. That is, $\frac{3}{12}$ is less than $\frac{3}{5}$.

When we compare fractions with equal numerators and different denominators, the fraction with the greater denominator is always the lesser fraction.

Compare the fractions. Write < or >.

1. $\dfrac{1}{6}$ ___<___ $\dfrac{1}{2}$

2. $\dfrac{2}{3}$ _____ $\dfrac{2}{5}$

3. $\dfrac{1}{7}$ _____ $\dfrac{1}{9}$

4. $\dfrac{4}{15}$ _____ $\dfrac{4}{10}$

5. $\dfrac{3}{4}$ _____ $\dfrac{3}{5}$

6. $\dfrac{5}{12}$ _____ $\dfrac{5}{9}$

7. $\dfrac{1}{3}$ _____ $\dfrac{1}{8}$

8. $\dfrac{2}{5}$ _____ $\dfrac{2}{2}$

9. $\dfrac{3}{6}$ _____ $\dfrac{3}{10}$

10. $\dfrac{6}{8}$ _____ $\dfrac{6}{9}$

11. $\dfrac{1}{15}$ _____ $\dfrac{1}{12}$

12. $\dfrac{5}{20}$ _____ $\dfrac{5}{10}$

13. $\dfrac{5}{7}$ _____ $\dfrac{5}{8}$

14. $\dfrac{8}{12}$ _____ $\dfrac{8}{16}$

15. $\dfrac{6}{11}$ _____ $\dfrac{6}{10}$

We can compare two fractions with the same denominator.

Example:

Compare $\dfrac{3}{8}$ and $\dfrac{2}{8}$.

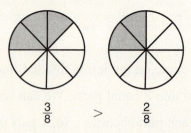

$\dfrac{3}{8}$ > $\dfrac{2}{8}$

The circle on the left is divided into 8 parts. The circle on the right is also divided into 8 parts. Each part in the left circle is equal to each part in the right circle. Therefore, 3 parts are greater than 2 parts.

When we compare fractions with equal denominators, the fraction with the greater numerator is always the greater fraction.

Compare the fractions. Write < or >.

1. $\dfrac{7}{10}$ ___>___ $\dfrac{6}{10}$

2. $\dfrac{4}{7}$ _____ $\dfrac{2}{7}$

3. $\dfrac{3}{3}$ _____ $\dfrac{1}{3}$

4. $\dfrac{5}{6}$ _____ $\dfrac{6}{6}$

5. $\dfrac{9}{15}$ _____ $\dfrac{10}{15}$

6. $\dfrac{2}{3}$ _____ $\dfrac{1}{3}$

7. $\dfrac{1}{4}$ _____ $\dfrac{3}{4}$

8. $\dfrac{6}{16}$ _____ $\dfrac{8}{16}$

9. $\dfrac{4}{4}$ _____ $\dfrac{3}{4}$

10. $\dfrac{2}{2}$ _____ $\dfrac{3}{2}$

11. $\dfrac{12}{16}$ _____ $\dfrac{10}{16}$

12. $\dfrac{1}{9}$ _____ $\dfrac{7}{9}$

13. $\dfrac{6}{7}$ _____ $\dfrac{5}{7}$

14. $\dfrac{19}{20}$ _____ $\dfrac{20}{20}$

15. $\dfrac{4}{5}$ _____ $\dfrac{2}{5}$

We know how to compare fractions with equal denominators or equal numerators. How do we compare fractions with different denominators and different numerators? Before we can compare these fractions, we need to make their denominators equal.

Sometimes, we only need to change one fraction.

Example:

Compare $\frac{2}{4}$ and $\frac{3}{8}$.

To compare these two fractions, we need to find a fraction equivalent to $\frac{2}{4}$ with a denominator of 8.

$$\frac{2}{4} \times \frac{2}{2} = \frac{4}{8}$$

Now we can compare the two fractions.

These are equivalent fractions.

$$\frac{2}{4} \quad \frac{3}{8}$$

$$\frac{4}{8} > \frac{3}{8}$$

$$\text{So, } \frac{2}{4} > \frac{3}{8}.$$

Sometimes, we need to change both fractions.

Example:

Compare $\frac{1}{3}$ and $\frac{2}{5}$.

We need to change both fractions to equivalent fractions with equal denominators. The denominators are 3 and 5. What numbers can we multiply 3 and 5 by to make them equal?

$$3 \times 5 = 15 \qquad\qquad 5 \times 3 = 15$$

$$\frac{1}{3} \times \frac{5}{5} = \frac{5}{15} \qquad\qquad \frac{2}{5} \times \frac{3}{3} = \frac{6}{15}$$

$$\frac{5}{15} < \frac{6}{15} \text{, so } \frac{1}{3} < \frac{2}{5}.$$

Compare the fractions. Write <, >, or =. Show your work on a separate sheet of paper.

1. $\dfrac{2}{6}$ _____<_____ $\dfrac{3}{3}$

2. $\dfrac{4}{5}$ _____ $\dfrac{2}{10}$

3. $\dfrac{3}{4}$ _____ $\dfrac{2}{3}$

4. $\dfrac{1}{2}$ _____ $\dfrac{2}{4}$

5. $\dfrac{4}{6}$ _____ $\dfrac{3}{4}$

6. $\dfrac{4}{5}$ _____ $\dfrac{3}{3}$

7. $\dfrac{9}{12}$ _____ $\dfrac{3}{4}$

8. $\dfrac{1}{6}$ _____ $\dfrac{3}{10}$

9. $\dfrac{4}{5}$ _____ $\dfrac{2}{7}$

10. $\dfrac{2}{3}$ _____ $\dfrac{4}{6}$

11. $\dfrac{10}{15}$ _____ $\dfrac{4}{5}$

12. $\dfrac{3}{3}$ _____ $\dfrac{9}{9}$

13. $\dfrac{6}{10}$ _____ $\dfrac{4}{5}$

14. $\dfrac{5}{9}$ _____ $\dfrac{7}{8}$

15. $\dfrac{8}{15}$ _____ $\dfrac{3}{5}$

Exercise 4

A. The circle graph below shows the ingredients in a pancake. There are five ingredients: sugar, water, milk, egg, and flour.

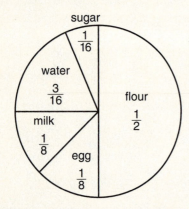

1. Of the five ingredients, which ingredient is the greatest fraction of the pancake? _____*flour*_____

2. Which ingredient is equal in amount to egg? _____

3. Is there more sugar or water in the pancake? _____

4. Is there more milk or sugar in the pancake? _____

5. Of the five ingredients, which ingredient is the smallest fraction of the pancake? _____

B. The circle graph below shows the ingredients in a cookie.

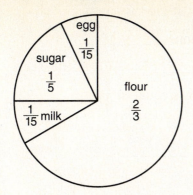

1. How many ingredients are there in the cookie? _____

2. What fraction of the cookie is sugar? _____

3. Which ingredient is the greatest fraction of the cookie? _____

4. Which ingredients are in equal amounts in the cookie? _____

5. Is there more sugar or egg in the cookie? _____

C. Compare the two circle graphs.

1. Which has a greater fraction of flour, the pancake or the cookie? _____

2. Which has a greater fraction of egg, the pancake or the cookie? _____

3. Which has a lesser fraction of milk, the pancake or the cookie? _____

4. Which has a lesser fraction of sugar, the pancake or the cookie? _____

5. Which has more ingredients, the pancake or the cookie? _____

Exercise 5

Read each statement. Write *True* if the statement is correct. Write *False* if the statement is not correct.

1. The numerator of $\frac{3}{4}$ is 3. _____*True*_____

2. The fraction $\frac{2}{3}$ is a part of a whole. _____

3. An improper fraction is less than 1. _____

4. A fraction always has a numerator and a denominator. _____

5. A mixed number is always greater than 1. _____

6. When the numerator of a fraction is equal to the denominator, the fraction is equal to zero. _____

7. The denominator of $\frac{3}{4}$ is 3. _____

8. We read denominators as ordinal numbers. _____

9. If we compare fractions with equal numerators, the fraction with the greater denominator is smaller. _____

10. A mixed number is a whole number and a fraction. _____

11. We read numerators as ordinal numbers. _____

12. If we divide a circle into 2 equal parts, each part is equal to $\frac{2}{1}$.

13. > means *greater than*. _____

14. If two fractions are equal, they are equivalent. _____

15. < means *greater than*. _____

14-2 Simplifying Fractions

In Chapter 13, we learned that if we multiply a fraction by a fraction equal to 1, we will get an equivalent fraction.

$$\frac{1}{3} \times \frac{2}{2} = \frac{2}{6}.$$

↑
equal to 1

We can also divide a fraction by a fraction equal to 1. When we do, we get an equivalent fraction.

$$\frac{2}{4} \div \frac{2}{2} = \frac{1}{2}$$

↑
equal to 1

We call this **simplifying a fraction**. The fraction $\frac{1}{2}$ is in its **simplest form**, because we cannot divide the numerator 1 and the denominator 2 evenly by a common number.

Example:

Is the fraction $\frac{4}{16}$ in its simplest form?

No, it isn't, because we can divide $\frac{4}{16}$ by $\frac{2}{2}$ or $\frac{4}{4}$. When we simplify, we always divide by the fraction with the larger numbers, so we will use $\frac{4}{4}$ rather than $\frac{2}{2}$.

$$\frac{4}{16} \div \frac{4}{4} = \frac{1}{4}$$

We cannot divide the numerator 1 and the denominator 4 evenly by a common number, so $\frac{1}{4}$ is in its simplest form.

What if we use the fraction with the smaller numbers $\left(\dfrac{2}{2}\right)$?

$$\dfrac{4}{16} \div \dfrac{2}{2} = \dfrac{2}{8}$$

Now we must divide again to get the simplest form.

$$\dfrac{2}{8} \div \dfrac{2}{2} = \dfrac{1}{4}$$

It is always better to divide by the fraction with the larger numbers.

Exercise 6

Simplify the fractions below. Show your work on a separate sheet of paper. Write the simplest forms on the lines.

1. $\dfrac{4}{6} =$ _____ $\dfrac{2}{3}$ _____

11. $\dfrac{8}{16} =$ _____

21. $\dfrac{7}{21} =$ _____

2. $\dfrac{3}{9} =$ _____

12. $\dfrac{10}{12} =$ _____

22. $\dfrac{3}{18} =$ _____

3. $\dfrac{5}{10} =$ _____

13. $\dfrac{9}{18} =$ _____

23. $\dfrac{9}{12} =$ _____

4. $\dfrac{10}{20} =$ _____

14. $\dfrac{10}{14} =$ _____

24. $\dfrac{10}{30} =$ _____

5. $\dfrac{3}{15} =$ _____

15. $\dfrac{5}{25} =$ _____

25. $\dfrac{16}{18} =$ _____

6. $\dfrac{6}{18} =$ _____

16. $\dfrac{8}{12} =$ _____

26. $\dfrac{14}{21} =$ _____

7. $\dfrac{12}{14} =$ _____

17. $\dfrac{25}{35} =$ _____

27. $\dfrac{10}{25} =$ _____

8. $\dfrac{6}{8} =$ _____

18. $\dfrac{15}{18} =$ _____

28. $\dfrac{15}{30} =$ _____

9. $\dfrac{6}{10} =$ _____

19. $\dfrac{12}{36} =$ _____

29. $\dfrac{12}{20} =$ _____

10. $\dfrac{15}{20} =$ _____

20. $\dfrac{4}{20} =$ _____

30. $\dfrac{8}{32} =$ _____

Sometimes we need to simplify an improper fraction.

Example:

We can simplify $\frac{15}{8}$.

To simplify an improper fraction, we change it to a mixed number.

$$\frac{15}{8} = 1\frac{7}{8}$$

The fraction $1\frac{7}{8}$ is in its simplest form.

Example:

We can simplify $\frac{20}{18}$.

$$\frac{20}{18} = 1\frac{2}{18}$$

The fraction $1\frac{2}{18}$ is not in simplest form, because we can simplify $\frac{2}{18}$.

$$\frac{2}{18} \div \frac{2}{2} = \frac{1}{9}$$

$$\frac{20}{18} = 1\frac{2}{18} = 1\frac{1}{9}$$

The fraction $1\frac{1}{9}$ is in its simplest form.

Exercise 7

Simplify the fractions below. Show your work on a separate sheet of paper. Then write the simplest forms on the lines.

1. $\frac{15}{2} = \underline{7\frac{1}{2}}$

2. $\frac{12}{4} = \underline{\hspace{1cm}}$

3. $\frac{25}{18} = \underline{\hspace{1cm}}$

4. $\frac{30}{24} = \underline{\hspace{1cm}}$

5. $\frac{40}{36} = \underline{\hspace{1cm}}$

6. $\frac{16}{6} = \underline{\hspace{1cm}}$

7. $\frac{33}{5} = \underline{\hspace{1cm}}$

8. $\frac{100}{1} = \underline{\hspace{1cm}}$

9. $\frac{65}{20} = \underline{\hspace{1cm}}$

10. $\frac{14}{8} = \underline{\hspace{1cm}}$

11. $\frac{19}{3} = \underline{\hspace{1cm}}$

12. $\frac{160}{160} = \underline{\hspace{1cm}}$

13. $\dfrac{9}{7}$ = _____

14. $\dfrac{22}{20}$ = _____

15. $\dfrac{18}{16}$ = _____

16. $\dfrac{25}{20}$ = _____

17. $\dfrac{8}{1}$ = _____

18. $\dfrac{17}{3}$ = _____

19. $\dfrac{50}{3}$ = _____

20. $\dfrac{75}{60}$ = _____

21. $\dfrac{5}{1}$ = _____

22. $\dfrac{22}{11}$ = _____

23. $\dfrac{60}{20}$ = _____

24. $\dfrac{49}{14}$ = _____

25. $\dfrac{38}{19}$ = _____

Have I Learned? (✓)

Work with a partner. Check what you have learned. Review what you need help with.

1. comparing fractions ☐
2. fractions with equal numerators and different denominators ☐
3. fractions with equal denominators ☐
4. greater denominator ☐
5. greater numerator ☐
6. greater fraction ☐
7. lesser fraction ☐
8. simplifying fractions ☐
9. simplest form ☐

Exercise 1

Compare the fractions. Write <, >, or =. Show your work on a separate sheet of paper. Write your answers on the lines.

1. $\frac{1}{4}$ __>__ $\frac{1}{6}$

2. $\frac{3}{5}$ ___ $\frac{2}{5}$

3. $\frac{1}{7}$ ___ $\frac{1}{6}$

4. $\frac{8}{10}$ ___ $\frac{5}{10}$

5. $\frac{4}{6}$ ___ $\frac{2}{3}$

6. $\frac{7}{9}$ ___ $\frac{1}{3}$

7. $\frac{6}{8}$ ___ $\frac{6}{9}$

8. $\frac{4}{16}$ ___ $\frac{6}{32}$

9. $\frac{3}{20}$ ___ $\frac{1}{5}$

10. $\frac{5}{10}$ ___ $\frac{3}{10}$

11. $\frac{3}{5}$ ___ $\frac{8}{20}$

12. $\frac{7}{12}$ ___ $\frac{7}{10}$

13. $\frac{9}{15}$ ___ $\frac{18}{30}$

14. $\frac{6}{24}$ ___ $\frac{2}{12}$

15. $\frac{9}{15}$ ___ $\frac{25}{45}$

16. $\frac{11}{33}$ ___ $\frac{1}{3}$

17. $\frac{16}{30}$ ___ $\frac{12}{30}$

18. $\frac{16}{25}$ ___ $\frac{16}{20}$

19. $\frac{3}{5}$ ___ $\frac{4}{6}$

20. $\frac{8}{16}$ ___ $\frac{25}{50}$

Exercise 2

Simplify the fractions. Show your work on a separate sheet of paper. Write your answers on the lines.

1. $\frac{4}{6}$ = $\frac{2}{3}$

2. $\frac{10}{12}$ = ___

3. $\frac{15}{25}$ = ___

4. $\frac{18}{36}$ = ___

5. $\frac{20}{50}$ = ___

6. $\frac{14}{21}$ = ___

7. $\frac{6}{18}$ = ___

8. $\frac{8}{56}$ = ___

9. $\frac{11}{44}$ = ___

10. $\frac{35}{70}$ = ___

11. $\frac{15}{7}$ = ___

12. $\frac{26}{8}$ = ___

13. $\frac{36}{5}$ = ___

14. $\frac{40}{36}$ = ___

15. $\frac{45}{18}$ = ___

16. $\frac{60}{20}$ = ___

17. $\frac{55}{75}$ = ___

18. $\frac{125}{150}$ = ___

19. $\frac{150}{125}$ = ___

20. $\frac{66}{4}$ = ___

CHAPTER 15 Multiplying and Dividing Fractions

15-1 Multiplying Fractions

What does it mean to multiply fractions by fractions?

Example:

$\dfrac{1}{2} \times \dfrac{1}{2}$

This means *one half of one half*.

one half
of a circle =

What is one half of this?

Divide $\frac{1}{2}$ into
2 equal parts.

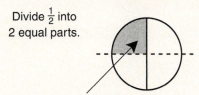

The shaded part is one half of one half, or one fourth.

One half of one half equals one fourth. (*Of* means to *multiply*.)

$\dfrac{1}{2} \times \dfrac{1}{2} = \dfrac{1}{4}$

Example:

$\dfrac{1}{2} \times 3$

This means *one half of three*.

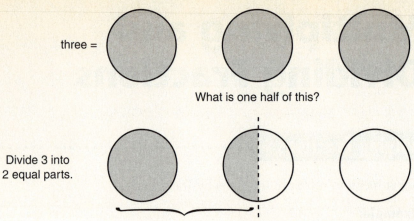

three =

What is one half of this?

Divide 3 into
2 equal parts.

The shaded part is one half of three, or one and one half.

$$\frac{1}{2} \times 3 = 1\frac{1}{2}$$

Example:

$$\frac{1}{4} \times \frac{1}{2}$$

This means *one fourth of one half*.

one half =

What is one fourth of this?

Divide $\frac{1}{2}$ into
4 equal parts.

The shaded part is one fourth of one half, or one eighth.

$$\frac{1}{4} \times \frac{1}{2} = \frac{1}{8}$$

How do we multiply fractions?

1. We change all mixed numbers to improper fractions.

$$\left(1\frac{2}{3} = \frac{5}{3}\right)$$

2. We change all whole numbers to improper fractions.

$$\left(3 = \frac{3}{1}\right)$$

3. We multiply numerator with numerator.

4. We multiply denominator with denominator.

5. We simplify, if possible.

Example:

$$\frac{1}{2} \times 1\frac{2}{3} = \frac{1}{2} \times \frac{5}{3} = \frac{1 \times 5}{2 \times 3} = \frac{5}{6}$$

Example:

$$\frac{1}{2} \times 3 = \frac{1}{2} \times \frac{3}{1} = \frac{1 \times 3}{2 \times 1} = \frac{3}{2} = 1\frac{1}{2}$$

Exercise 1

Multiply the fractions and simplify, if possible. Show your work on a separate sheet of paper. Write your answers on the lines.

1. $\frac{1}{2} \times \frac{1}{4} =$ $\frac{1}{8}$

2. $\frac{3}{6} \times \frac{1}{3} =$ $\frac{3}{18}$

3. $\frac{2}{7} \times \frac{2}{7} =$ $\frac{4}{19}$

4. $\frac{9}{10} \times \frac{1}{3} =$ $\frac{9}{30}$

5. $\frac{3}{6} \times \frac{2}{5} =$ $\frac{6}{30}$

6. $\frac{4}{5} \times \frac{5}{4} =$ $\frac{20}{20}$

7. $\frac{3}{10} \times \frac{2}{2} =$ $\frac{6}{20}$

8. $\frac{9}{18} \times \frac{1}{2} =$ $\frac{9}{36}$

9. $\frac{3}{4} \times \frac{3}{5} =$ $\frac{5}{20}$

10. $\frac{6}{7} \times \frac{1}{3} =$ $\frac{6}{21}$

11. $\frac{5}{10} \times \frac{3}{4} =$ _____

12. $\frac{6}{12} \times \frac{3}{5} =$ _____

13. $\frac{5}{15} \times \frac{5}{6} =$ _____

14. $\frac{9}{12} \times \frac{1}{3} =$ _____

15. $\frac{2}{4} \times \frac{2}{4} =$ _____

16. $\dfrac{1}{6} \times \dfrac{7}{10} =$ _____

17. $\dfrac{11}{22} \times \dfrac{1}{2} =$ _____

18. $\dfrac{10}{30} \times \dfrac{1}{4} =$ _____

19. $\dfrac{15}{45} \times \dfrac{2}{5} =$ _____

20. $\dfrac{2}{5} \times \dfrac{1}{2} =$ _____

21. $\dfrac{8}{24} \times \dfrac{3}{30} =$ _____

22. $\dfrac{6}{11} \times \dfrac{11}{6} =$ _____

23. $\dfrac{12}{15} \times \dfrac{2}{4} =$ _____

24. $\dfrac{9}{20} \times \dfrac{3}{3} =$ _____

25. $\dfrac{18}{36} \times \dfrac{1}{2} =$ _____

26. $\dfrac{13}{15} \times \dfrac{2}{5} =$ _____

27. $\dfrac{10}{25} \times \dfrac{2}{4} =$ _____

28. $\dfrac{7}{11} \times \dfrac{11}{7} =$ _____

29. $\dfrac{8}{64} \times \dfrac{1}{8} =$ _____

30. $\dfrac{14}{21} \times \dfrac{7}{14} =$ _____

Exercise 2

Multiply the fractions and simplify, if possible. Show your work on a separate sheet of paper. Write your answers on the lines.

1. $3\dfrac{1}{2} \times \dfrac{4}{5} = \underline{2\dfrac{4}{5}}$

2. $1\dfrac{1}{3} \times 1\dfrac{1}{2} =$ _____

3. $\dfrac{9}{10} \times 4 =$ _____

4. $6\dfrac{2}{3} \times \dfrac{1}{2} =$ _____

5. $4\dfrac{1}{3} \times 1\dfrac{1}{2} =$ _____

6. $\dfrac{1}{2} \times 4\dfrac{2}{7} =$ _____

7. $1\dfrac{1}{3} \times 3 =$ _____

8. $\dfrac{3}{4} \times 6 =$ _____

9. $\dfrac{14}{15} \times \dfrac{1}{2} =$ _____

10. $\dfrac{6}{20} \times 5 =$ _____

11. $2\dfrac{1}{2} \times 1\dfrac{1}{4} =$ _____

12. $3 \times \dfrac{7}{15} =$ _____

13. $\dfrac{11}{15} \times 2 =$ _____

14. $6\dfrac{2}{4} \times 4 =$ _____

15. $1\dfrac{1}{8} \times 3 =$ _____

16. $\dfrac{4}{16} \times 1\dfrac{1}{2} =$ _____

17. $5 \times \dfrac{3}{9} =$ _____

18. $6 \times 4\dfrac{1}{2} =$ _____

19. $\dfrac{1}{2} \times \dfrac{3}{4} \times \dfrac{3}{5} =$ _____

20. $1\dfrac{1}{2} \times 3 \times 2 =$ _____

21. $\dfrac{5}{20} \times 2\dfrac{1}{5} =$ _____

22. $\dfrac{1}{2} \times \dfrac{3}{4} \times 4 =$ _____

23. $2\dfrac{1}{3} \times 3 \times \dfrac{2}{7} =$ _____

24. $11\dfrac{1}{3} \times 3 =$ _____

25. $9\dfrac{1}{3} \times 2 \times \dfrac{1}{2} =$ _____

26. $\dfrac{13}{15} \times 3 =$ _____

27. $\dfrac{3}{4} \times 4\dfrac{2}{3} \times 2 =$ _____

28. $\dfrac{6}{10} \times 5 =$ _____

29. $2\dfrac{1}{2} \times 3 \times \dfrac{1}{4} =$ _____

30. $2\dfrac{1}{4} \times \dfrac{3}{6} =$ _____

Before we multiply fractions, we can simplify by **canceling**.

Example:

$$\frac{2}{4} \times \frac{4}{6}$$

We divide the numerator 2 and the denominator 6 by 2.

$$\frac{\overset{1}{2}}{4} \times \frac{4}{\underset{3}{6}}$$

We divide the denominator 4 and the numerator 4 by 4.

$$\frac{\overset{1}{2}}{\underset{1}{4}} \times \frac{\overset{1}{4}}{\underset{3}{6}}$$

We multiply.

$$\frac{\overset{1}{2}}{\underset{1}{4}} \times \frac{\overset{1}{4}}{\underset{3}{6}} = \frac{1 \times 1}{1 \times 3} = \frac{1}{3}$$

Example:

$$\frac{15}{12} \times \frac{6}{30}$$

We can divide the numerator 15 and the denominator 30 by 3, 5, or 15. We always divide by the largest number, so we divide by 15.

$$\frac{\overset{1}{15}}{12} \times \frac{6}{\underset{2}{30}}$$

We can divide the denominator 12 and the numerator 6 by 2, 3, or 6. We always divide by the largest number, so we divide by 6.

$$\frac{\overset{1}{15}}{\underset{2}{12}} \times \frac{\overset{1}{6}}{\underset{2}{30}} = \frac{1 \times 1}{2 \times 2} = \frac{1}{4}$$

Simplify the fractions. Then multiply them. Show your work on a separate sheet of paper. Write your answers on the lines.

1. $\dfrac{6}{15} \times \dfrac{9}{12} = \underline{\dfrac{3}{10}}$

2. $\dfrac{14}{21} \times \dfrac{7}{28} = \underline{\hspace{1cm}}$

3. $\dfrac{3}{8} \times \dfrac{6}{9} = \underline{\hspace{1cm}}$

4. $\dfrac{4}{7} \times \dfrac{14}{16} = \underline{\hspace{1cm}}$

5. $\dfrac{40}{100} \times \dfrac{10}{80} = \underline{\hspace{1cm}}$

6. $\dfrac{5}{25} \times \dfrac{15}{30} = \underline{\hspace{1cm}}$

7. $\dfrac{8}{16} \times \dfrac{32}{40} = \underline{\hspace{1cm}}$

8. $4\dfrac{1}{2} \times \dfrac{2}{9} = \underline{\hspace{1cm}}$

9. $3\dfrac{2}{3} \times \dfrac{9}{22} = \underline{\hspace{1cm}}$

10. $4 \times 2\dfrac{1}{2} = \underline{\hspace{1cm}}$

11. $\dfrac{8}{20} \times \dfrac{10}{16} = \underline{\hspace{1cm}}$

12. $7 \times \dfrac{9}{21} = \underline{\hspace{1cm}}$

13. $\dfrac{9}{24} \times \dfrac{8}{45} = \underline{\hspace{1cm}}$

14. $\dfrac{9}{27} \times \dfrac{9}{36} = \underline{\hspace{1cm}}$

15. $4\dfrac{3}{4} \times \dfrac{16}{19} = \underline{\hspace{1cm}}$

16. $\dfrac{9}{36} \times \dfrac{18}{30} = \underline{\hspace{1cm}}$

17. $5 \times \dfrac{42}{5} = \underline{\hspace{1cm}}$

18. $\dfrac{55}{80} \times \dfrac{20}{11} = \underline{\hspace{1cm}}$

19. $\dfrac{6}{48} \times \dfrac{8}{9} = \underline{\hspace{1cm}}$

20. $14 \times 2\dfrac{1}{4} = \underline{\hspace{1cm}}$

21. $2\dfrac{2}{5} \times 25 = \underline{\hspace{1cm}}$

22. $7\dfrac{1}{2} \times \dfrac{8}{15} = \underline{\hspace{1cm}}$

23. $2\dfrac{2}{3} \times 4\dfrac{1}{8} = \underline{\hspace{1cm}}$

24. $\dfrac{12}{64} \times \dfrac{8}{24} = \underline{\hspace{1cm}}$

25. $\dfrac{5}{7} \times 1\dfrac{1}{6} = \underline{\hspace{1cm}}$

15-3 Solving Word Problems

Some problems require us to multiply fractions.

Example:

Sara is making chicken soup. She needs to add $\dfrac{1}{2}$ teaspoon of salt for 1 chicken. How much salt does she need for $2\dfrac{1}{2}$ chickens?

$$\dfrac{1}{2} \times 2\dfrac{1}{2} = \dfrac{1}{2} \times \dfrac{5}{2} = \dfrac{5}{4} = 1\dfrac{1}{4} \text{ teaspoons salt}$$

Connie had a party for her classmates. Her grandmother helped her make the food. They made pizza, tacos, chocolate cake, and cookies. Read the word problems. Then answer the questions. Write your answers on the lines.

1. A recipe for chocolate cake uses $\frac{3}{4}$ cup of milk and $4\frac{1}{2}$ cups of flour. Connie's grandmother made 2 cakes.

   a. How much milk did she use for the cakes? ___$1\frac{1}{2}$ cups___

   b. How much flour did she use for the cakes? _____

2. One cookie recipe uses $\frac{1}{2}$ tsp salt, $3\frac{1}{4}$ cups flour, $\frac{1}{3}$ lb butter, and $\frac{1}{3}$ cup oil.
   How much of each ingredient did Connie use to make $2\frac{1}{2}$ recipes of cookies?

   a. salt _____   b. flour _____   c. butter _____   d. oil _____

3. Connie also made 3 big pizza crusts. For 1 crust, she needed $5\frac{1}{3}$ cups flour, $\frac{1}{2}$ tsp salt, $3\frac{1}{2}$ oz yeast, and $\frac{2}{3}$ cup water. How much of each ingredient did she need for 3 crusts?

   a. flour _____   b. salt _____   c. yeast _____   d. water _____

4. There were 24 guests at Connie's party. $\frac{1}{4}$ of the guests ate tacos and $\frac{3}{4}$ of the guests ate pizza.

   a. How many guests ate tacos? _____

   b. How many guests ate pizza? _____

5. $\frac{1}{3}$ of the 24 guests at the party drank soda.

   a. How many guests drank soda? _____

   b. $\frac{1}{4}$ of the guests who drank soda wanted ice. How many guests wanted ice? _____

223

Sometimes, we need to find the **reciprocal** of a fraction.

Examples:

The reciprocal of $\frac{3}{4}$ is $\frac{4}{3}$.

The reciprocal of $\frac{1}{5}$ is $\frac{5}{1}$.

The reciprocal of 7, or $\frac{7}{1}$, is $\frac{1}{7}$.

To write the reciprocal of a fraction, write the denominator as the numerator and the numerator as the denominator.

We can also find the reciprocal of a mixed number.

Example:

What is the reciprocal of $1\frac{1}{3}$?

We change the mixed number to an improper fraction.

$$1\frac{1}{3} = \frac{4}{3}$$

The reciprocal of $\frac{4}{3}$ is $\frac{3}{4}$, so the reciprocal of $1\frac{1}{3}$ is $\frac{3}{4}$.

If we multiply a fraction by its reciprocal, the product is always equal to 1.

Example:

$$\frac{4}{3} \times \frac{3}{4} = \frac{12}{12} = 1$$

Write the reciprocal for each of the following fractions.

1. $\frac{2}{3}$ $\frac{3}{2}$ _____

2. $\frac{1}{2}$ _____

3. $\frac{6}{5}$ _____

4. 9 _____

5. $4\frac{1}{4}$ _____

6. $2\frac{1}{3}$ _____

7. 3 _____

8. $\frac{1}{10}$ _____

9. $\frac{6}{7}$ _____

10. $5\frac{2}{5}$ _____

11. $\frac{17}{1}$ _____

12. 1 _____

13. $\frac{4}{4}$ _____

14. $\frac{7}{8}$ _____

15. 12 _____

15-5 Dividing Fractions

Dividing two numbers is the same as comparing two numbers.

Example:

$8 \div 4$ means *compare* 8 with 4.

8 is 2 times greater than 4 ($4 \times 2 = 8$).

So, $8 \div 4 = 2$.

Example:

$10 \div 2$

Compare 10 with 2.

10 is 5 times greater than 2 ($5 \times 2 = 10$).

So, $10 \div 2 = 5$.

Dividing two fractions is the same as comparing two fractions.

Example:

$\frac{1}{2} \div \frac{1}{4}$ means *compare* $\frac{1}{2}$ with $\frac{1}{4}$.

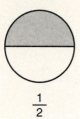 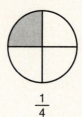

$\frac{1}{2}$ $\frac{1}{4}$

$\frac{1}{2}$ is 2 times greater than $\frac{1}{4}$.

So, $\frac{1}{2} \div \frac{1}{4} = 2$.

Example:

$2 \div \frac{1}{2}$

Compare 2 with $\frac{1}{2}$.

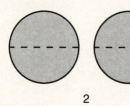 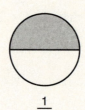

2                    $\frac{1}{2}$

2 is 4 times greater than $\frac{1}{2}$.

So, $2 \div \frac{1}{2} = 4$.

Example:

$\frac{1}{4} \div \frac{1}{2}$

Compare $\frac{1}{4}$ with $\frac{1}{2}$.

$\frac{1}{4}$

$\frac{1}{2}$

$\frac{1}{4}$ is $\frac{1}{2}$ as great as $\frac{1}{2}$.

So, $\frac{1}{4} \div \frac{1}{2} = \frac{1}{2}$.

Example:

$1\frac{1}{2} \div \frac{1}{4}$

Compare $1\frac{1}{2}$ with $\frac{1}{4}$.

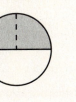

$1\frac{1}{2}$

$\frac{1}{4}$

$1\frac{1}{2}$ is 6 times greater than $\frac{1}{4}$.

So, $1\frac{1}{2} \div \frac{1}{4} = 6$.

How do we divide fractions?

1. We find the reciprocal of the divisor.

2. We simplify the fractions, if possible.

3. We multiply the reciprocal by the dividend.

4. We simplify again, if necessary.

Example:

$$\frac{1}{2} \div \frac{1}{4}$$

The reciprocal of $\frac{1}{4} = \frac{4}{1}$.

$$\frac{1}{\overset{2}{\underset{1}{2}}} \times \frac{\overset{2}{4}}{1} = \frac{2}{1} = 2$$

Note: When a number or fraction is divided by a fraction less than one, the result is always larger than the dividend.

Example:

$$1\frac{1}{4} \div 3$$

Write as an improper fraction.   Write as a fraction.

$$\frac{5}{4} \div \frac{3}{1} = \frac{5}{4} \times \frac{1}{3} = \frac{5}{12}$$

Note: When a number or fraction is divided by a whole number or fraction greater than one, the result is always smaller than the dividend.

Exercise 6

Divide the fractions. Simplify, if possible. Show your work on a separate sheet of paper. Write your answers on the lines.

1. $\frac{2}{3} \div \frac{3}{4} = \underline{\frac{8}{9}}$

2. $\frac{4}{5} \div \frac{1}{2} = \underline{\quad}$

3. $3 \div \frac{1}{2} = \underline{\quad}$

4. $\frac{7}{8} \div 2 = \underline{\quad}$

5. $\frac{3}{4} \div \frac{3}{4} = \underline{\quad}$

6. $\frac{1}{9} \div 9 = \underline{\quad}$

7. $\frac{4}{8} \div \frac{1}{2} = \underline{\quad}$

8. $6 \div \frac{2}{3} = \underline{\quad}$

9. $\frac{15}{16} \div \frac{1}{2} = \underline{\quad}$

10. $30 \div \frac{3}{4} = \underline{\quad}$

11. $\frac{12}{15} \div 2 = \underline{\quad}$

12. $\frac{9}{16} \div 45 = \underline{\quad}$

13. $\frac{7}{11} \div \frac{7}{11} =$ _____

14. $45 \div \frac{5}{6} =$ _____

15. $\frac{19}{20} \div 2 =$ _____

16. $\frac{5}{6} \div \frac{5}{6} =$ _____

17. $\frac{11}{2} \div 5 =$ _____

18. $\frac{6}{30} \div 5 =$ _____

19. $\frac{5}{9} \div \frac{7}{8} =$ _____

20. $\frac{3}{6} \div \frac{1}{2} =$ _____

21. $\frac{6}{8} \div \frac{3}{4} =$ _____

22. $3 \div \frac{1}{3} =$ _____

23. $\frac{1}{2} \div 3 =$ _____

24. $\frac{3}{6} \div \frac{2}{4} =$ _____

25. $\frac{5}{8} \div \frac{3}{8} =$ _____

Exercise 7

Divide the fractions. Simplify, if possible. Show your work on a separate sheet of paper. Write your answers on the lines.

1. $1\frac{1}{2} \div \frac{3}{4} = \underline{\quad 2 \quad}$

2. $\frac{4}{5} \div \frac{2}{3} =$ _____

3. $\frac{5}{6} \div 1\frac{2}{4} =$ _____

4. $3\frac{1}{2} \div 2\frac{4}{5} =$ _____

5. $6\frac{2}{3} \div 1\frac{1}{2} =$ _____

6. $\frac{2}{3} \div 1\frac{2}{3} =$ _____

7. $5 \div 1\frac{1}{2} =$ _____

8. $4\frac{5}{6} \div 6 =$ _____

9. $3\frac{7}{8} \div \frac{1}{8} =$ _____

10. $7\frac{1}{2} \div 3\frac{1}{4} =$ _____

11. $5\frac{1}{4} \div 2\frac{1}{4} =$ _____

12. $\frac{4}{5} \div \frac{5}{4} =$ _____

13. $3\frac{1}{2} \div 3\frac{1}{2} =$ _____

14. $\frac{20}{30} \div \frac{2}{3} =$ _____

15. $6\frac{1}{3} \div 2\frac{1}{3} =$ _____

16. $\frac{40}{5} \div 2\frac{1}{2} =$ _____

17. $\frac{9}{10} \div \frac{1}{10} =$ _____

18. $1\frac{2}{3} \div 2\frac{1}{6} =$ _____

19. $2\frac{2}{8} \div 1\frac{1}{8} =$ _____

20. $2\frac{1}{5} \div 2\frac{1}{2} =$ _____

21. $8\frac{1}{10} \div 9 =$ _____

22. $9 \div 3\frac{3}{5} =$ _____

23. $\frac{1}{5} \div 3\frac{4}{5} =$ _____

24. $2\frac{4}{8} \div 1\frac{1}{4} =$ _____

25. $3 \div 2\frac{2}{8} =$ _____

Some problems require us to divide fractions.

Example:

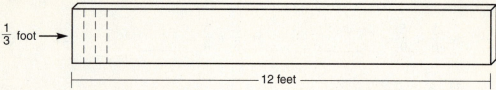

$\frac{1}{3}$ foot ⟶

|←——————————— 12 feet ———————————→|

Marcos wants to cut a board 12 feet long into pieces that are $\frac{1}{3}$ foot each.

How many pieces will he have?

Divide: $12 \div \frac{1}{3}$

$$\frac{12}{1} \times \frac{3}{1} = \frac{36}{1} = 36 \text{ pieces}$$

Exercise 8

Ivan is going to build bookcases for his room. Right now, he's shopping for the materials. Read the word problems. Then answer the questions. Write your answers on the lines.

1. Ivan needs to buy lumber for his bookcases. Each piece weighs $2\frac{1}{4}$ pounds. He's going to buy a total of $49\frac{1}{2}$ pounds of lumber. How many pieces is he going to buy? _22 pieces_

2. One bag of nails weighs 12 ounces. Each nail weighs $\frac{1}{8}$ ounce. How many nails are in one bag? _____

3. The bookcases will be $5\frac{1}{3}$ feet long. How many bookcases can Ivan put into a space $10\frac{2}{3}$ feet long? _____

4. Ivan is going to carry all of his books upstairs to his room. He can carry $32\frac{1}{2}$ pounds at one time. If each book weighs $1\frac{1}{4}$ pounds, how many books can he carry at one time? _____

5. Ivan needs $25\frac{3}{4}$ feet of lumber to make 1 bookcase. He's going to buy 78 feet of lumber altogether.

a. Can he make 4 bookcases? _____

b. How many bookcases can he make? _____

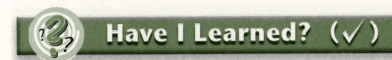

Have I Learned? (✓)

Work with a partner. Check what you have learned. Review what you need help with.

1. multiplying fractions ☐

2. canceling ☐

3. reciprocal ☐

4. dividing fractions ☐

CHAPTER REVIEW

Exercise 1

Multiply the fractions. Simplify, if possible. Show your work on a separate sheet of paper.

1. $\dfrac{3}{4} \times \dfrac{2}{3} =$

2. $\dfrac{1}{8} \times \dfrac{1}{10} =$

3. $2\dfrac{3}{6} \times \dfrac{4}{5} =$

4. $\dfrac{10}{15} \times \dfrac{5}{20} =$

5. $6 \times \dfrac{9}{11} =$

6. $\dfrac{2}{3} \times 1\dfrac{1}{2} =$

7. $7\dfrac{1}{2} \times 5 =$

8. $2\dfrac{1}{4} \times 1\dfrac{1}{3} =$

9. $1\dfrac{1}{7} \times 1\dfrac{1}{4} =$

10. $3\dfrac{6}{8} \times 2 \times \dfrac{4}{6} =$

Exercise 2

Divide the fractions. Simplify, if possible. Show your work on a separate sheet of paper.

1. $\dfrac{1}{5} \div \dfrac{1}{2} =$

2. $\dfrac{3}{6} \div \dfrac{1}{4} =$

3. $30 \div \dfrac{2}{3} =$

4. $4\dfrac{2}{8} \div 1\dfrac{1}{2} =$

5. $7\dfrac{4}{5} \div 3 =$

6. $\dfrac{4}{5} \div \dfrac{1}{8} =$

7. $2\dfrac{2}{9} \div 1\dfrac{2}{3} =$

8. $\dfrac{9}{11} \div \dfrac{1}{11} =$

9. $1 \div \dfrac{5}{7} =$

10. $\dfrac{18}{36} \div \dfrac{18}{36} =$

Exercise 3

Solve the following problems. Show your work on a separate sheet of paper. Write your answers on the lines.

1. There are 40 students in Mrs. Lin's class. $\dfrac{3}{4}$ of the students use red books and $\dfrac{1}{4}$ of the students use blue books.

   a. How many students use red books? ___*30 students*___

   b. How many students use blue books? _____

2. Joshua has $\dfrac{2}{3}$ of a pizza left. He's going to give $\dfrac{1}{4}$ of the leftover pizza to Alex.

   How much of a whole pizza will Alex get? _____

3. Norma has $3\dfrac{1}{4}$ cups of oil. She is going to use $\dfrac{1}{4}$ cup of oil for each cake that she makes.

   How many cakes can she make? _____

4. Timothy has $6\dfrac{2}{5}$ pounds of grapes. He wants to give equal amounts to 16 children. How

   many pounds of grapes will each child get? _____

5. Danny ate $3\dfrac{1}{2}$ cookies. Each cookie weighed $\dfrac{4}{5}$ ounce. How many ounces of cookies did

   he eat? _____

CHAPTER 16 Adding and Subtracting Fractions

16-1 Adding Fractions with Like Denominators ················

Sometimes we need to add fractions with **like denominators**. (*Like denominators* means *equal* or *same* denominators.)

Example:

$$\frac{1}{4} + \frac{1}{4}$$

 + =

$$\frac{1}{4} + \frac{1}{4} = \frac{1+1}{4} = \frac{2}{4} = \frac{1}{2}$$

How do we add fractions with like (or same) denominators?

1. We add the numerators.

2. We write the sum of the numerators over the denominator.

Example:

$$\frac{1}{3} + \frac{2}{3}$$

$$\frac{1}{3} + \frac{2}{3} = \frac{1+2}{3} = \frac{3}{3} = 1$$

Exercise 1

Add the fractions and simplify, if possible. Write your answers on the lines.

1. $\frac{1}{5} + \frac{3}{5} = \underline{\frac{4}{5}}$

2. $\frac{2}{4} + \frac{1}{4} = \underline{\quad}$

3. $\frac{1}{3} + \frac{1}{3} = \underline{\quad}$

4. $\frac{3}{7} + \frac{5}{7} = \underline{\quad}$

5. $\frac{6}{8} + \frac{6}{8} = \underline{\quad}$

6. $\frac{1}{9} + \frac{5}{9} = \underline{\quad}$

7. $\frac{10}{20} + \frac{5}{20} = \underline{\quad}$

8. $\frac{6}{12} + \frac{9}{12} = \underline{\quad}$

233

9. $\frac{4}{11} + \frac{7}{11} =$ _____

10. $\frac{5}{12} + \frac{11}{12} =$ _____

11. $\frac{6}{8} + \frac{16}{8} =$ _____

12. $\frac{10}{10} + \frac{10}{10} =$ _____

13. $\frac{5}{12} + \frac{11}{12} =$ _____

14. $\frac{1}{7} + \frac{6}{7} =$ _____

15. $\frac{8}{5} + \frac{1}{5} =$ _____

16. $\frac{14}{30} + \frac{15}{30} =$ _____

17. $\frac{9}{11} + \frac{4}{11} =$ _____

18. $\frac{5}{8} + \frac{8}{8} =$ _____

19. $\frac{6}{6} + \frac{6}{6} =$ _____

20. $\frac{12}{24} + \frac{12}{24} =$ _____

How do we add mixed numbers with like denominators?

1. We add the whole numbers together.

2. We add the numerators of the fractions and write the sum over the denominator.

3. We simplify, if possible.

Example:

$$1\frac{2}{5} + 1\frac{1}{5}$$

$$1\frac{2}{5} + 1\frac{1}{5} = 2\frac{2+1}{5} = 2\frac{3}{5}$$

Example:

$$2\frac{3}{5} + 3\frac{2}{5}$$

$$2\frac{3}{5} + 3\frac{2}{5} = 5\frac{3+2}{5} = 5\frac{5}{5}$$

Since $\frac{5}{5} = 1$, $5\frac{5}{5} = 5 + 1 = 6$.

Example:

$$4\frac{2}{3} + 2\frac{2}{3}$$

$$4\frac{2}{3} + 2\frac{2}{3} = 6\frac{2+2}{3} = 6\frac{4}{3}$$

Since $\frac{4}{3} = 1\frac{1}{3}$, $6\frac{4}{3} = 6 + 1\frac{1}{3} = 7\frac{1}{3}$.

Add the fractions and simplify, if possible. Show your work on a separate sheet of paper. Write your answers on the lines.

1. $1\frac{1}{4} + 2\frac{1}{4} =$ ___$3\frac{1}{2}$___

2. $6\frac{3}{8} + 4\frac{1}{8} =$ _____

3. $2\frac{3}{5} + 1\frac{2}{5} =$ _____

4. $1\frac{1}{2} + 3\frac{1}{2} =$ _____

5. $3\frac{4}{10} + 4\frac{7}{10} =$ _____

6. $1\frac{2}{3} + 2\frac{1}{3} =$ _____

7. $9\frac{4}{5} + 6\frac{4}{5} =$ _____

8. $1\frac{2}{10} + 2\frac{4}{10} =$ _____

9. $3\frac{4}{6} + 1\frac{2}{6} =$ _____

10. $2\frac{3}{15} + 2\frac{2}{15} =$ _____

11. $6\frac{12}{20} + 3\frac{10}{20} =$ _____

12. $1\frac{2}{8} + 2\frac{7}{8} =$ _____

13. $3\frac{4}{9} + 1\frac{5}{9} =$ _____

14. $\frac{7}{6} + 1\frac{1}{6} =$ _____

15. $3\frac{2}{9} + \frac{7}{9} =$ _____

16. $6\frac{20}{25} + 1\frac{10}{25} =$ _____

17. $4\frac{14}{18} + 3\frac{7}{18} =$ _____

18. $2\frac{6}{7} + \frac{7}{7} =$ _____

19. $19\frac{2}{10} + \frac{9}{10} =$ _____

20. $5\frac{2}{4} + 1\frac{3}{4} =$ _____

21. $2\frac{10}{16} + 1\frac{1}{16} + 3\frac{6}{16} =$ _____

22. $6\frac{1}{2} + 3\frac{1}{2} + 1\frac{1}{2} =$ _____

23. $5\frac{2}{6} + 1\frac{1}{6} + \frac{5}{6} =$ _____

24. $7\frac{2}{8} + \frac{2}{8} + 1\frac{2}{8} =$ _____

25. $\frac{1}{7} + 2\frac{2}{7} + 4\frac{4}{7} =$ _____

Fractions with different denominators are called **unlike fractions**. For example, $\frac{5}{8}$ and $\frac{3}{4}$ are unlike fractions.

To add unlike fractions, we must first find a **common denominator** for both fractions. A common denominator is a denominator, or number, that both denonimators can divide into evenly.

Example:

What is the common denominator of $\frac{5}{8}$ and $\frac{3}{4}$?

That is, what number can both 8 and 4 divide into evenly?

Answer: 8, 16, 24, 32, 40, . . . There is more than one number. We always choose the lowest number, so the answer is 8. The **lowest common denominator**, or **LCD**, of $\frac{5}{8}$ and $\frac{3}{4}$ is 8.

When fractions have large, unlike denominators, like those in $\frac{3}{24}$ and $\frac{2}{36}$, it is not so easy to find the LCD. Here is a simple method for finding the lowest (or least) common denominator (LCD) for all fractions.

1. If the smaller denominator can divide evenly into the larger denominator, the larger denominator is the LCD.

   Example:

   $\frac{1}{15}$ and $\frac{1}{30}$

   We can divide 30 by 15 evenly ($30 \div 15 = 2$).
   So, the LCD = 30.

2. If the smaller denominator cannot divide evenly into the larger denominator, multiply the larger denominator by 2. Can the smaller denominator divide evenly into that product? If yes, that is the LCD.

   Example:

   $\frac{1}{4}$ and $\frac{1}{10}$

   $$\begin{array}{r} 10 \\ \times\ 2 \\ \hline 20 \end{array} \longrightarrow \text{4 divides evenly into 20.}$$

   LCD = 20

If no, multiply the same denominator by 3. Continue to multiply until you get a number that the smaller denominator divides evenly into.

Example:

$\frac{2}{4}$ and $\frac{6}{9}$

$$\begin{array}{r} 9 \\ \times\ 2 \\ \hline 18 \end{array}$$ 4 does not divide into 18.

$$\begin{array}{r} 9 \\ \times\ 3 \\ \hline 27 \end{array}$$ 4 does not divide into 27.

$$\begin{array}{r} 9 \\ \times\ 4 \\ \hline 36 \end{array}$$ 4 divides evenly into 36 (36 ÷ 4 = 9).

LCD = 36

Exercise 3

Find the LCD of the following fractions. Show your work on a separate sheet of paper. Write your answers on the lines.

1. $\frac{1}{5}$ and $\frac{5}{20}$ ___20___

2. $\frac{4}{28}$ and $\frac{2}{7}$ _____

3. $\frac{1}{8}$ and $\frac{2}{12}$ _____

4. $\frac{2}{10}$ and $\frac{3}{4}$ _____

5. $\frac{1}{3}$ and $\frac{3}{9}$ _____

6. $\frac{1}{8}$ and $\frac{3}{16}$ _____

7. $\frac{2}{18}$ and $\frac{6}{24}$ _____

8. $\frac{1}{3}$ and $\frac{2}{5}$ _____

9. $\frac{4}{9}$ and $\frac{3}{12}$ _____

10. $\frac{3}{7}$ and $\frac{5}{9}$ _____

11. $\frac{3}{11}$ and $\frac{4}{7}$ _____

12. $\frac{2}{9}$ and $\frac{4}{36}$ _____

13. $\frac{3}{15}$ and $\frac{2}{10}$ _____

14. $\frac{2}{24}$ and $\frac{3}{36}$ _____

15. $\frac{3}{12}$ and $\frac{4}{15}$ _____

16. $\frac{3}{25}$ and $\frac{2}{10}$ _____

17. $\frac{1}{15}$ and $\frac{2}{30}$ _____

18. $\frac{1}{30}$ and $\frac{3}{20}$ _____

19. $\frac{3}{10}$ and $\frac{2}{16}$ _____

20. $\frac{2}{24}$ and $\frac{1}{32}$ _____

21. $\frac{3}{13}$ and $\frac{2}{26}$ _____

22. $\frac{2}{8}$ and $\frac{3}{9}$ _____

23. $\frac{5}{7}$ and $\frac{6}{49}$ _____

24. $\frac{1}{8}$ and $\frac{5}{36}$ _____

25. $\frac{7}{9}$ and $\frac{7}{8}$ _____

We have learned to find the LCD of two fractions. Now we can add unlike fractions.

How do we add unlike fractions?

1. We find the LCD of the fractions.

2. We change each fraction to an equivalent fraction with a denominator equal to the LCD.

3. We add the numerators of the fractions and write the sum over the LCD.

4. We simplify, if possible.

Example:

$$\frac{1}{4} + \frac{4}{8}$$

The LCD of 4 and 8 is 8. We will use 8 as the common denominator. The fraction $\frac{4}{8}$ already has a denominator of 8. We need to change $\frac{1}{4}$ to an equivalent fraction with a denominator equal to 8.

$$\frac{1}{4} \times \frac{2}{2} = \frac{2}{8}$$

$$\frac{2}{8} + \frac{4}{8} = \frac{2+4}{8} = \frac{6}{8} = \frac{3}{4}$$

Example:

$$\frac{3}{5} + \frac{4}{7}$$

The LCD of 5 and 7 is 35. We change $\frac{3}{5}$ and $\frac{4}{7}$ to equivalent fractions with denominators equal to 35.

$$\frac{3}{5} \times \frac{7}{7} = \frac{21}{35} \qquad \frac{4}{7} \times \frac{5}{5} = \frac{20}{35}$$

$$\frac{21}{35} + \frac{20}{35} = \frac{21+20}{35} = \frac{41}{35} = 1\frac{6}{35}$$

Example:

$1\frac{1}{2} + 3\frac{1}{5}$

We change mixed numbers to improper fractions.

$1\frac{1}{2} = \frac{3}{2}$ $3\frac{1}{5} = \frac{16}{5}$

The LCD of 2 and 5 is 10. We change $\frac{3}{2}$ and $\frac{16}{5}$ to equivalent fractions with denominators equal to 10.

$\frac{3 \times 5}{2 \times 5} = \frac{15}{10}$ $\frac{16 \times 2}{5 \times 2} = \frac{32}{10}$

$\frac{15}{10} + \frac{32}{10} = \frac{15 + 32}{10} = \frac{47}{10} = 4\frac{7}{10}$

Exercise 4

Find the LCD and add the fractions. Simplify, if possible. Show your work on a separate sheet of paper. Write your answers on the lines.

1. $\frac{1}{4} + \frac{1}{12} = \underline{\frac{1}{3}}$

2. $\frac{1}{6} + \frac{1}{18} = \underline{\hphantom{xxx}}$

3. $\frac{2}{3} + \frac{3}{4} = \underline{\hphantom{xxx}}$

4. $\frac{6}{9} + \frac{2}{18} = \underline{\hphantom{xxx}}$

5. $\frac{4}{7} + \frac{3}{35} = \underline{\hphantom{xxx}}$

6. $\frac{4}{8} + \frac{3}{24} = \underline{\hphantom{xxx}}$

7. $\frac{9}{12} + \frac{3}{8} = \underline{\hphantom{xxx}}$

8. $\frac{6}{6} + \frac{9}{4} = \underline{\hphantom{xxx}}$

9. $\frac{8}{9} + \frac{1}{3} = \underline{\hphantom{xxx}}$

10. $\frac{11}{15} + \frac{2}{30} = \underline{\hphantom{xxx}}$

11. $\frac{6}{21} + \frac{3}{14} = \underline{\hphantom{xxx}}$

12. $\frac{7}{20} + \frac{4}{15} = \underline{\hphantom{xxx}}$

13. $\frac{2}{15} + \frac{1}{5} = \underline{\hphantom{xxx}}$

14. $\frac{14}{15} + \frac{2}{5} = \underline{\hphantom{xxx}}$

15. $\frac{7}{30} + \frac{3}{20} = \underline{\hphantom{xxx}}$

16. $\frac{4}{11} + \frac{6}{22} = \underline{\hphantom{xxx}}$

17. $\frac{9}{18} + \frac{3}{36} = \underline{\hphantom{xxx}}$

18. $\frac{2}{6} + \frac{7}{8} = \underline{\hphantom{xxx}}$

19. $\frac{10}{20} + \frac{3}{40} = \underline{\hphantom{xxx}}$

20. $\frac{7}{25} + \frac{3}{5} = \underline{\hphantom{xxx}}$

21. $\frac{7}{10} + \frac{2}{25} = \underline{\hphantom{xxx}}$

22. $\frac{9}{12} + \frac{3}{30} = \underline{\hphantom{xxx}}$

23. $\frac{2}{7} + \frac{1}{9} = \underline{\hphantom{xxx}}$

24. $\frac{2}{22} + \frac{2}{11} = \underline{\hphantom{xxx}}$

25. $\frac{1}{3} + \frac{2}{8} = \underline{\hphantom{xxx}}$

Find the LCD and add the fractions. Simplify, if possible. Show your work on a separate sheet of paper. Write your answers on the lines.

1. $6\frac{2}{3} + 1\frac{1}{10} =$ _7$\frac{23}{30}$_

2. $2\frac{1}{2} + 1\frac{2}{8} =$ _____

3. $\frac{3}{5} + 1\frac{3}{6} =$ _____

4. $1\frac{2}{4} + 1\frac{2}{5} =$ _____

5. $1\frac{1}{12} + \frac{1}{9} =$ _____

6. $2\frac{1}{3} + 1\frac{2}{5} =$ _____

7. $\frac{2}{7} + 1\frac{2}{35} =$ _____

8. $\frac{3}{9} + 1\frac{1}{18} =$ _____

9. $2\frac{1}{8} + \frac{3}{24} =$ _____

10. $1\frac{1}{7} + \frac{3}{28} =$ _____

11. $2\frac{1}{10} + 1\frac{2}{5} =$ _____

12. $2\frac{1}{9} + 3\frac{1}{3} =$ _____

13. $\frac{2}{7} + 1\frac{1}{4} =$ _____

14. $1\frac{2}{4} + 2\frac{2}{3} =$ _____

15. $\frac{2}{5} + \frac{3}{9} =$ _____

16. $2\frac{1}{8} + \frac{3}{6} =$ _____

17. $1\frac{1}{7} + 2\frac{1}{3} =$ _____

18. $\frac{2}{12} + 1\frac{1}{6} =$ _____

19. $2\frac{1}{10} + 2\frac{2}{4} =$ _____

20. $\frac{9}{6} + \frac{3}{4} =$ _____

21. $\frac{4}{7} + 1\frac{1}{5} =$ _____

22. $1\frac{1}{12} + 1\frac{1}{30} =$ _____

23. $1\frac{1}{5} + \frac{6}{25} =$ _____

24. $1\frac{1}{18} + 1\frac{3}{36} =$ _____

25. $1\frac{2}{21} + 1\frac{1}{7} =$ _____

Complete the sentences with the following words.

wholes	one	greater than
halves	like	~~ordinal~~
mixed	divide	LCD
denominator		

1. When we read fractions, we read the numerators as cardinal numbers and the denominators as _____*ordinal*_____ numbers.

2. In an improper fraction, the numerator is _____ _____ the denominator.

3. The plural of half is _____.

4. Fractions with different denominators are called unlike fractions, and fractions with same denominators are called _____ fractions.

5. A _____ number is a whole number and a fraction.

6. When the numerator of a fraction is equal to its denominator, the fraction is equal to

_____.

7. When the denominator of a fraction is 1, as in $\frac{7}{1}$, we read the denominator as

_____.

8. A fraction is equal to a whole number if the _____ is equal to 1.

9. Before we add fractions with different denominators, we must find

the _____.

10. We use reciprocals when we need to _____ fractions.

16-4 Solving Word Problems

Some problems require us to add fractions.

Example:

Marlon studied for $3\frac{1}{2}$ hours on Saturday and $4\frac{1}{2}$ hours on Sunday. How many hours did he study altogether?

$3\frac{1}{2} + 4\frac{1}{2} =$

$\frac{7}{2} + \frac{9}{2} = \frac{16}{2} = 8$ hours

Exercise 7

Wendy works at Cloth Craft after school and on Saturdays. She helps customers, and she cuts material. Solve the word problems on the next page. Write your answers on the lines. Show your work on a separate sheet of paper.

1. Mrs. Tran wants to make a dress. She needs $2\frac{1}{2}$ yards of green cotton and $3\frac{1}{2}$ yards of white cotton. How much cotton does she need altogether? __6 yards__

2. Laura Mendez bought wool and velvet.

   a. She bought $\frac{1}{5}$ yard of pink wool, $\frac{3}{5}$ yard of white wool, $\frac{4}{5}$ yard of black wool, and $3\frac{2}{5}$ yards of yellow wool. How much wool did she buy? _____

   b. She bought $\frac{3}{4}$ yard of red velvet, $\frac{2}{3}$ yard of green velvet, $\frac{5}{6}$ yard of gold velvet, and $\frac{1}{4}$ yard of black velvet. How much velvet did she buy? _____

3. Mrs. Parry needed $1\frac{5}{6}$ yards of silk, $\frac{2}{3}$ yard of cotton, $3\frac{4}{6}$ yards of denim, and $\frac{1}{6}$ yard of velvet. How much material did Wendy cut for Mrs. Parry altogether? _____

4. Each day Wendy cuts about $56\frac{2}{3}$ yards of material. How much does she cut in 4 days? _____

5. Steve Wu needed brown corduroy to cover a sofa, some pillows, and a chair. There were only $14\frac{3}{4}$ yards of brown corduroy in the store. He asked Wendy to cut $5\frac{3}{4}$ yards for the sofa, $3\frac{1}{2}$ yards for the pillows, and $4\frac{7}{8}$ yards for the chair.

   a. How much brown corduroy did Steve need? _____

   b. Was there enough brown corduroy for him? _____

16-5 Subtracting Fractions with Like Denominators

Sometimes, we need to subtract fractions with like denominators.

Example:

$$\frac{6}{8} - \frac{4}{8}$$

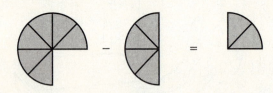

$$\frac{6}{8} - \frac{4}{8} = \frac{6-4}{8} = \frac{2}{8} = \frac{1}{4}$$

How do we subtract fractions with like denominators?

1. We subtract the numerators.

2. We write the difference over the denominator.

Example:

$$2\frac{3}{6} - 1\frac{4}{6}$$

$$\frac{15}{6} - \frac{10}{6} = \frac{15 - 10}{6} = \frac{5}{6}$$

How do we subtract mixed numbers with like denominators?

1. We change the mixed numbers to improper fractions.

2. We subtract the numerators.

3. We write the difference over the denominator.

Exercise 8

Subtract the fractions and simplify, if possible. Write the answers on the lines.

1. $\frac{3}{5} - \frac{2}{5} = \underline{\frac{1}{5}}$

2. $\frac{7}{8} - \frac{3}{8} = \underline{\hspace{1cm}}$

3. $\frac{5}{6} - \frac{1}{6} = \underline{\hspace{1cm}}$

4. $\frac{10}{15} - \frac{3}{15} = \underline{\hspace{1cm}}$

5. $\frac{5}{30} - \frac{1}{30} = \underline{\hspace{1cm}}$

6. $\frac{16}{25} - \frac{3}{25} = \underline{\hspace{1cm}}$

7. $\frac{6}{12} - \frac{4}{12} = \underline{\hspace{1cm}}$

8. $\frac{8}{9} - \frac{4}{9} = \underline{\hspace{1cm}}$

9. $\frac{9}{10} - \frac{1}{10} = \underline{\hspace{1cm}}$

10. $\frac{8}{8} - \frac{2}{8} = \underline{\hspace{1cm}}$

11. $\frac{25}{50} - \frac{25}{50} = \underline{\hspace{1cm}}$

12. $\frac{11}{12} - \frac{5}{12} = \underline{\hspace{1cm}}$

13. $\frac{14}{12} - \frac{1}{12} =$ _____

14. $\frac{3}{5} - \frac{3}{5} =$ _____

15. $\frac{16}{8} - \frac{14}{8} =$ _____

16. $\frac{12}{24} - \frac{8}{24} =$ _____

17. $\frac{25}{50} - \frac{5}{50} =$ _____

18. $\frac{10}{15} - \frac{5}{15} =$ _____

19. $\frac{19}{19} - \frac{1}{19} =$ _____

20. $\frac{14}{15} - \frac{5}{15} =$ _____

Exercise 9

Subtract the fractions and simplify, if possible. Show your work on a separate sheet of paper. Write your answers on the lines.

1. $4\frac{2}{3} - 2\frac{1}{3} =$ _$2\frac{1}{3}$_

2. $9\frac{3}{4} - 4\frac{2}{4} =$ _____

3. $8\frac{1}{3} - \frac{2}{3} =$ _____

4. $10\frac{1}{2} - 4\frac{1}{2} =$ _____

5. $5\frac{6}{7} - \frac{6}{7} =$ _____

6. $3\frac{9}{10} - 1\frac{6}{10} =$ _____

7. $4\frac{5}{9} - 4\frac{4}{9} =$ _____

8. $3\frac{2}{12} - 2\frac{5}{12} =$ _____

9. $6\frac{7}{8} - 4\frac{7}{8} =$ _____

10. $5\frac{4}{5} - 3\frac{3}{5} =$ _____

11. $9\frac{10}{20} - 8\frac{15}{20} =$ _____

12. $9\frac{6}{8} - 7\frac{7}{8} =$ _____

13. $15\frac{4}{5} - 13\frac{4}{5} =$ _____

14. $3\frac{4}{25} - \frac{18}{25} =$ _____

15. $19\frac{7}{10} - \frac{9}{10} =$ _____

16. $8\frac{2}{3} - \frac{2}{3} =$ _____

17. $10\frac{1}{2} - 10\frac{1}{2} =$ _____

18. $5\frac{3}{19} - \frac{18}{19} =$ _____

19. $7\frac{2}{3} - 6\frac{1}{3} =$ _____

20. $6\frac{3}{4} - 2\frac{3}{4} =$ _____

16-6 Writing Whole Numbers as Fractions

In Chapter 13, Section 13-3, we learned how to write fractions as whole numbers equal to 1.

Example:

$$\frac{2}{2} = 1 \qquad \frac{4}{4} = 1 \qquad \frac{10}{10} = 1$$

Remember, when the numerator is equal to the denominator, the fraction is equal to 1.

Example:

Complete the fraction: $1 = \dfrac{}{7}$

Since the fraction is equal to 1, the numerator must be equal to the denominator. The denominator = 7, so the numerator = 7.

$$1 = \dfrac{7}{7}$$

Exercise 10

Complete the following fractions so that they are equal to 1.

1. $1 = \dfrac{8}{8}$

2. $1 = \dfrac{}{10}$

3. $1 = \dfrac{}{45}$

4. $1 = \dfrac{}{18}$

5. $1 = \dfrac{}{11}$

6. $1 = \dfrac{}{1}$

7. $1 = \dfrac{}{25}$

8. $1 = \dfrac{}{15}$

9. $1 = \dfrac{}{4}$

10. $1 = \dfrac{}{8}$

11. $1 = \dfrac{}{12}$

12. $1 = \dfrac{}{16}$

13. $1 = \dfrac{}{30}$

14. $1 = \dfrac{}{100}$

15. $1 = \dfrac{}{150}$

We can write whole numbers as mixed numbers.

Example:

We can write 2 as a mixed number that includes a fraction with a denominator of four.

$$2 = 1 + 1$$

$$= 1 + \dfrac{4}{4}$$

$$= 1\dfrac{4}{4}$$

Complete the fractions. Then write each whole number as a mixed number.

1. $4 = 3 + \dfrac{2}{2} = $ _____

2. $5 = 4 + \dfrac{}{8} = $ _____

3. $10 = 9 + \dfrac{}{6} = $ _____

4. $12 = 11 + \dfrac{}{9} = $ _____

5. $9 = 8 + \dfrac{}{8} = $ _____

6. $6 = 5 + \dfrac{}{20} = $ _____

7. $7 = 6 + \dfrac{}{12} = $ _____

8. $15 = 14 + \dfrac{}{2} = $ _____

9. $8 = 7 + \dfrac{}{3} = $ _____

10. $23 = 22 + \dfrac{}{10} = $ _____

11. $14 = 13 + \dfrac{}{30} = $ _____

12. $13 = 12 + \dfrac{}{5} = $ _____

13. $25 = 24 + \dfrac{}{6} = $ _____

14. $32 = 31 + \dfrac{}{15} = $ _____

15. $18 = 17 + \dfrac{}{16} = $ _____

16-7 Subtracting Fractions from Whole Numbers

Sometimes, we need to subtract a fraction from a whole number.

Example:

$$3 - 1\frac{4}{5}$$

First, we change the whole number (3) to a mixed number with a denominator equal to the denominator of the other fraction or subtrahend ($1\frac{4}{5}$):

$$3 = 2\frac{5}{5}$$

We subtract the whole numbers. Then we subtract the numerators and write the difference over the denominator:

$$2\frac{5}{5} - 1\frac{4}{5} = 1\frac{5-4}{5} = 1\frac{1}{5}$$

Subtract the fractions and simplify, if possible. Show your work on a separate sheet of paper. Write your answer on the lines.

1. $7 - 4\frac{3}{4} =$ ___ $2\frac{1}{4}$ ___

2. $3 - 2\frac{1}{2} =$ _____

3. $15 - 7\frac{5}{6} =$ _____

4. $10 - 4\frac{6}{8} =$ _____

5. $1 - \frac{3}{4} =$ _____

6. $12 - 10\frac{7}{10} =$ ____

7. $4 - 3\frac{1}{3} =$ _____

8. $8 - \frac{5}{6} =$ _____

9. $7 - 5\frac{1}{15} =$ ____

10. $9 - 7\frac{3}{9} =$ ____

11. $2 - 1\frac{3}{4} =$ ____

12. $6 - 5\frac{1}{9} =$ ____

13. $1 - \frac{15}{16} =$ ____

14. $3 - \frac{16}{20} =$ ____

15. $4 - 3\frac{5}{15} =$ _____

16. $13 - 12\frac{9}{10} =$ ____

17. $3 - \frac{45}{50} =$ _____

18. $2 - \frac{6}{16} =$ _____

19. $8 - 2\frac{1}{2} =$ _____

20. $16 - 15\frac{3}{7} =$ _____

16-8 Subtracting Unlike Fractions

Before we subtract fractions with unlike denominators, we need to find the LCD.

Example:

$$\frac{5}{6} - \frac{3}{4}$$

The LCD of 6 and 4 is 12. We find equivalent fractions with denominators equal to 12.

$$\frac{5 \times 2}{6 \times 2} = \frac{10}{12} \qquad \frac{3 \times 3}{4 \times 3} = \frac{9}{12}$$

We subtract the numerators.

$$\frac{10}{12} - \frac{9}{12} = \frac{10 - 9}{12} = \frac{1}{12}$$

Example:

$$2\frac{1}{8} - 1\frac{3}{12}$$

We change mixed numbers to improper fractions.

$$2\frac{1}{8} = \frac{17}{8} \qquad\qquad 1\frac{3}{12} = \frac{15}{12}$$

The LCD of 8 and 12 is 24. We find equivalent fractions with denominators equal to 24.

$$\frac{17}{8} \times \frac{3}{3} = \frac{51}{24} \qquad\qquad \frac{15}{12} \times \frac{2}{2} = \frac{30}{24}$$

We subtract the numerators and then simplify, if possible.

$$\frac{51}{24} - \frac{30}{24} = \frac{51-30}{24} = \frac{21}{24} = \frac{7}{8}$$

Exercise 13

Subtract the fractions and simplify, if possible. Show your work on a separate sheet of paper. Write your answers on the lines.

1. $\frac{7}{8} - \frac{1}{4} = \underline{\frac{5}{8}}$

2. $\frac{3}{5} - \frac{2}{15} = \underline{\hspace{1cm}}$

3. $\frac{6}{8} - \frac{2}{24} = \underline{\hspace{1cm}}$

4. $\frac{9}{10} - \frac{2}{5} = \underline{\hspace{1cm}}$

5. $\frac{4}{7} - \frac{2}{21} = \underline{\hspace{1cm}}$

6. $\frac{5}{6} - \frac{1}{5} = \underline{\hspace{1cm}}$

7. $\frac{10}{20} - \frac{2}{8} = \underline{\hspace{1cm}}$

8. $\frac{10}{15} - \frac{3}{9} = \underline{\hspace{1cm}}$

9. $\frac{9}{12} - \frac{2}{8} = \underline{\hspace{1cm}}$

10. $\frac{5}{7} - \frac{3}{35} = \underline{\hspace{1cm}}$

11. $\frac{8}{12} - \frac{2}{8} = \underline{\hspace{1cm}}$

12. $\frac{15}{18} - \frac{2}{12} = \underline{\hspace{1cm}}$

13. $\frac{8}{10} - \frac{2}{6} = \underline{\hspace{1cm}}$

14. $\frac{7}{8} - \frac{3}{6} = \underline{\hspace{1cm}}$

15. $\frac{18}{21} - \frac{4}{14} = \underline{\hspace{1cm}}$

16. $\frac{9}{15} - \frac{6}{30} = \underline{\hspace{1cm}}$

17. $\frac{9}{10} - \frac{4}{25} = \underline{\hspace{1cm}}$

18. $\frac{5}{6} - \frac{1}{9} = \underline{\hspace{1cm}}$

19. $\frac{2}{3} - \frac{1}{6} = \underline{\hspace{1cm}}$

20. $\frac{8}{12} - \frac{3}{6} = \underline{\hspace{1cm}}$

21. $\frac{3}{15} - \frac{1}{5} = \underline{\hspace{1cm}}$

22. $\frac{1}{7} - \frac{1}{9} = \underline{\hspace{1cm}}$

23. $\frac{10}{20} - \frac{3}{40} = \underline{\hspace{1cm}}$

24. $\frac{20}{25} - \frac{3}{10} = \underline{\hspace{1cm}}$

25. $\frac{7}{8} - \frac{5}{7} = \underline{\hspace{1cm}}$

Find and circle the words listed below. The words are written horizontally (left to right →), horizontally (right to left ←), vertically (top to bottom ↓), and vertically (bottom to top ↑). There are also words written diagonally (↗).

B	F	R	E	P	O	R	P	M	I	V
R	A	R	P	F	A	P	E	U	E	M
D	C	L	A	X	E	U	T	R	S	R
E	D	M	R	C	A	N	C	E	L	O
N	P	R	T	Q	T	L	K	I	G	T
O	S	I	M	P	L	I	F	Y	H	A
M	I	X	E	D	L	K	O	J	I	R
I	K	L	A	U	Q	E	F	N	T	E
N	M	O	C	O	M	M	O	N	L	M
A	P	S	A	E	D	F	G	O	R	U
T	P	T	L	F	L	A	H	T	S	N
O	M	S	U	L	O	W	E	S	T	G
R	E	C	I	P	R	O	C	A	L	O
P	R	Q	S	J	T	O	C	A	R	T

CANCEL	SIMPLIFY	NUMERATOR	MIXED
UNLIKE	COMMON	IMPROPER	DENOMINATOR
LIKE	PART	FRACTION	WHOLE
EQUAL	LOWEST	RECIPROCAL	HALF

Have I Learned? (✓)

Work with a partner. Check what you have learned. Review what you need help with.

1. adding fractions ☐
2. like denominators ☐
3. unlike fractions ☐
4. common denominator ☐
5. lowest common denominator (LCD) ☐
6. subtracting fractions ☐

Exercise 1

Add the fractions. Simplify, if possible. Show your work on a separate sheet of paper.

1. $\dfrac{1}{5} + \dfrac{2}{5} =$

2. $3\dfrac{1}{3} + 1\dfrac{2}{3} =$

3. $\dfrac{6}{10} + \dfrac{3}{20} =$

4. $1\dfrac{3}{15} + 2\dfrac{4}{30} =$

5. $2\dfrac{4}{8} + 1\dfrac{1}{12} =$

6. $\dfrac{13}{25} + \dfrac{2}{100} =$

7. $3\dfrac{2}{8} + 1\dfrac{1}{6} =$

8. $6\dfrac{5}{25} + 2\dfrac{9}{10} =$

9. $\dfrac{2}{6} + \dfrac{4}{5} =$

10. $5 + 4\dfrac{1}{4} =$

Exercise 2

Subtract the fractions. Simplify, if possible. Show your work on a separate sheet of paper.

1. $\dfrac{7}{12} - \dfrac{3}{12} =$

2. $1\dfrac{12}{18} - \dfrac{3}{18} =$

3. $6 - \dfrac{4}{5} =$

4. $\dfrac{13}{18} - \dfrac{6}{12} =$

5. $\dfrac{7}{10} - \dfrac{1}{30} =$

6. $\dfrac{6}{7} - \dfrac{2}{3} =$

7. $3\dfrac{1}{2} - 1\dfrac{1}{5} =$

8. $17 - 4\dfrac{2}{3} =$

9. $1\dfrac{1}{8} - \dfrac{1}{5} =$

10. $\dfrac{8}{15} - \dfrac{4}{9} =$

Exercise 3

Solve the following problems. Show your work on a separate sheet of paper. Write your answers on the lines.

1. Willie bought $5\dfrac{1}{2}$ pounds of apples and $3\dfrac{1}{3}$ pounds of oranges. How many pounds of fruit did he buy in all? _____ $8\dfrac{5}{6} \text{ pounds}$ _____

2. It rained $4\dfrac{1}{2}$ inches in April and $2\dfrac{3}{4}$ inches in May. How many inches did it rain in the two months altogether? _____

3. Marta can carry 16 pounds of books in her backpack. She has $12\dfrac{1}{3}$ pounds in her backpack now. How many more pounds can she carry? _____

4. Barbara is $5\dfrac{1}{8}$ feet tall. Her sister is $\dfrac{1}{4}$ foot taller than she is. How tall is Barbara's sister?

_____

5. Barbara's brother is $\dfrac{1}{2}$ foot shorter than she is. How tall is Barbara's brother?

_____

Ratios and Percents

In this unit, you will learn . . .

- ratios

- proportions

- solving proportions using inverse operations

- using proportions in problem solving

- percents

- writing percents as decimals and decimals as percents

- writing percents as fractions

- writing fractions as decimals and as percents

- solving percent problems

- using percents with discounts

CHAPTER 17

Ratios and Proportions

17-1 Ratios

We can use a **ratio** to compare two amounts.

Example:

There are 2 trees and 7 birds altogether. The ratio of trees to birds is 2 to 7.

In a ratio, we compare two numbers. We can write the ratio of 2 trees to 7 birds in three different ways: 2 to 7 or 2:7 or $\frac{2}{7}$.

What is the ratio of birds to trees? There are 7 birds and 2 trees. The ratio of birds to trees is 7 to 2 or 7:2 or $\frac{7}{2}$.

Example:

We can write the ratio 7 to 9 as a fraction.

Answer: $\frac{7}{9}$

Example:

We can write the ratio $\frac{4}{8}$ in words.

Answer: four to eight

Exercise 1

Write the ratios. Use words and fractions.

		Words	**Fraction**
1. 6:9		*six to nine*	$\frac{6}{9}$
2. 4:5			
3. 6:6			
4. 9:1			
5. 1:10			
6. 20:100			
7. 5:15			
8. 8:24			
9. 100:1			
10. 7:20			
11. 2:2			
12. 3:6			
13. 10:1			
14. 50:100			
15. 1:1,000			

Wheels4U.com has 15 vehicles for sale on its Web site. There are cars, pickup trucks, vans, and motorcycles. Look at the pictures. Then answer the questions below.

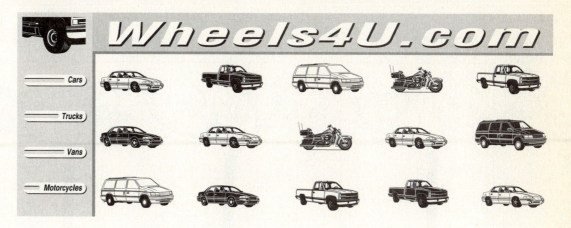

1. What is the ratio of cars to the total number of vehicles? ___6:15___

2. What is the ratio of motorcycles to the total number of vehicles? _____

3. What is the ratio of pickup trucks and vans to the total number of vehicles?
   _____

4. What is the ratio of motorcycles to cars? _____

5. What is the ratio of cars to motorcycles? _____

6. What is the ratio of pickup trucks to vans? _____

7. What is the ratio of cars to pickup trucks and vans? _____

8. What is the ratio of white vehicles to black vehicles? _____

9. What is the ratio of black cars to black pickup trucks? _____

10. What is the ratio of white motorcycles to black motorcycles? _____

A **proportion** states that two ratios are equal.

Example:

Ratio of tree to birds:

1:2 or $\frac{1}{2}$

Ratio of trees to birds:

2:4 or $\frac{2}{4}$

$\frac{1}{2} = \frac{2}{4}$, so the ratios 1:2 and 2:4 are equivalent.

When two ratios are equivalent, we have a proportion. Therefore, $\frac{1}{2} = \frac{2}{4}$ is a proportion. The two fractions, or ratios, are proportional. To check if two fractions are equivalent, we **cross-multiply**. If the two products are equal, then the two fractions are equivalent and proportional.

Example:

Is $\frac{1}{3} = \frac{2}{6}$ a proportion?

If the fractions are equivalent, we have a proportion. We check by cross-multiplying.

$1 \times 6 = 6$ $\qquad$ $3 \times 2 = 6$

$6 = 6$

The products are equal, so $\frac{1}{3} = \frac{2}{6}$ is a proportion.

How do we cross-multiply?

1. We multiply the denominator of the right fraction by the numerator of the left fraction.

2. We multiply the numerator of the right fraction by the denominator of the left fraction.

3. If both products are equal, the fractions are equivalent, and we have a proportion.

Exercise 3

Check each of the following items. If it is a proportion, write *yes*. If it is not a proportion, write *no*. Show your work on a separate sheet of paper.

1. $\dfrac{2}{4} = \dfrac{1}{2}$ _____*yes*_____

2. $\dfrac{3}{5} = \dfrac{12}{20}$ _____

3. $\dfrac{2}{7} = \dfrac{4}{15}$ _____

4. $\dfrac{5}{9} = \dfrac{15}{27}$ _____

5. $\dfrac{6}{10} = \dfrac{60}{90}$ _____

6. $\dfrac{7}{8} = \dfrac{14}{16}$ _____

7. $\dfrac{4}{5} = \dfrac{24}{25}$ _____

8. $\dfrac{11}{22} = \dfrac{1}{3}$ _____

9. $\dfrac{12}{15} = \dfrac{3}{5}$ _____

10. $\dfrac{30}{45} = \dfrac{120}{180}$ _____

11. $\dfrac{25}{100} = \dfrac{2}{8}$ _____

12. $\dfrac{8}{9} = \dfrac{64}{72}$ _____

13. $\dfrac{80}{100} = \dfrac{8}{12}$ _____

14. $\dfrac{13}{26} = \dfrac{4}{8}$ _____

15. $\dfrac{14}{30} = \dfrac{7}{14}$ _____

17-3 Solving Proportions Using Inverse Operations

We have already learned how to use inverse operations to find missing numbers.

Example:

$6 \times \underline{?} = 24$

We use the inverse operation. $? = 24 \div 6$

$? = 4$

We can use inverse operations to solve proportions, too.

Example:

$\dfrac{3}{4} = \dfrac{6}{?}$

First, we cross-multiply. $3 \times ? = 4 \times 6$

$3 \times \underline{?} = 24$

Then we use the inverse operation. $? = 24 \div 3$

$? = 8$

So, $\dfrac{3}{4} = \dfrac{6}{8}$.

Exercise 4

Complete the proportions using inverse operations. Check by cross-multiplying. Show your work on a separate sheet of paper.

1. $\dfrac{3}{4} = \dfrac{9}{12}$

2. $\dfrac{}{8} = \dfrac{3}{24}$

3. $\dfrac{7}{10} = \dfrac{70}{}$

4. $\dfrac{6}{18} = \dfrac{}{36}$

5. $\dfrac{9}{18} = \dfrac{36}{}$

6. $\dfrac{11}{} = \dfrac{44}{44}$

7. $\dfrac{6}{10} = \dfrac{}{60}$

8. $\dfrac{25}{100} = \dfrac{30}{}$

9. $\dfrac{5}{225} = \dfrac{11}{}$

10. $\dfrac{90}{} = \dfrac{360}{200}$

11. $\dfrac{15}{65} = \dfrac{}{260}$

12. $\dfrac{.12}{7.2} = \dfrac{}{3.6}$

13. $\dfrac{33}{} = \dfrac{24}{8}$

14. $\dfrac{120}{3} = \dfrac{80}{}$

15. $\dfrac{75}{300} = \dfrac{60}{}$

17-4 Using Proportions in Problem Solving

Some problems can be solved by using proportions.

Example:

For 2 dollars, Gabriel can buy 5 chocolate candies. How many candies can he buy for 12 dollars?

First, we set up a proportion of dollars to candies.

$$\dfrac{2 \text{ dollars buys}}{5 \text{ candies}} = \dfrac{12 \text{ dollars buys}}{? \text{ candies}}$$

$$\dfrac{2}{5} = \dfrac{12}{?}$$

Next, we cross-multiply. $2 \times ? = 5 \times 12$

$2 \times ? = 60$

Then we use the inverse operation. $? = 60 \div 2$

$? = 30$

Answer: Gabriel can buy 30 candies for 12 dollars.

Example:

Sonia needs 5 cups of apples for 3 pies. How many cups of apples does she need for 4 pies?

We set up a proportion of apples to pies.

$$\frac{5 \text{ cups of apples}}{3 \text{ pies}} = \frac{? \text{ cups of apples}}{4 \text{ pies}}$$

$$\frac{5}{3} = \frac{?}{4}$$

We cross-multiply.

$$3 \times ? = 5 \times 4$$

$$3 \times ? = 20$$

We use the inverse operation.

$$? = 20 \div 3$$

$$? = 6\frac{2}{3}$$

Answer: Sonia needs $6\frac{2}{3}$ cups of apples for 4 pies.

Exercise 5

Read the recipe. Use proportions to solve the problems below. Write your answers on the lines. Show your work on a separate sheet of paper.

Recipe for Spring Garden Spaghetti Sauce

2 cups chicken broth	8 oz peas
3 cups chopped tomatoes	1 tsp salt
12 oz chopped ham	1.5 cups cream
9 oz carrots	4 oz cheese

Serves 4

A. Ellie is inviting 5 friends for dinner. The recipe above serves 4 people, so Ellie needs to increase the amount of each ingredient to serve 6 people.

1. How much chicken broth will she need for 6 people? ___*3 cups*___

2. How many cups of tomatoes will she need? _____

3. How many ounces of ham will she need? _____

4. How many ounces of peas will she need? _____

5. How many cups of cream will she need? _____

B. Dylan is inviting 9 friends for dinner. He's using the same recipe, and he needs to increase the amount of each ingredient to serve 10 people.

1. How much chicken broth will he need for 10 people? _____5 cups_____

2. How many cups of tomatoes will he need? _____

3. How many ounces of carrots will he need? _____

4. How many teaspoons of salt will he need? _____

5. How many ounces of cheese will he need? _____

Exercise 6

In the Design Co-op Clothing Factory, the workers make dresses, blouses, skirts, and shirts. Use proportions to find the answers to the following questions about the workers and their factory. Write your answers on the lines. Show your work on a separate sheet of paper.

1. Ms. Lee can make 6 dresses in 2 hours. She works 7 hours a day. How many dresses can she make in 1 day? _____21_____

2. Ms. Chavez can sew 60 blouses in 5 hours. How many blouses can she sew in 35 hours? _____

3. The factory pays Mr. Johnson $2.25 to cut out 3 dresses. How much does it pay him to cut out 10 dresses? _____

4. It takes 12 weeks for Ms. Oh to design 15 dresses. How many dresses does she design in 4 weeks? _____

5. Each week, the factory makes 1,000 skirts.

a. How many skirts does it make in 1 month? _____

b. How many skirts does it make in 1 year? _____

6. Ms. Park earns $240 in 5 days. How much does she earn in 23 days? _____

7. The factory makes 144,000 shirts in 3 years. How many shirts does it make in 4 months? _____

8. Ms. Leonard earns $30,000 a year. How much does she earn in $1\frac{1}{2}$ months?

_____

9. In the factory, 8 out of 10 workers are women.

    a. Of 100 workers, how many are women? _____

    b. Of 100 workers, how many are men? _____

10. In the factory, 15 out of 20 workers are full-time workers.

    a. Of 60 workers, how many are full-time workers? _____

    b. Of 60 workers, how many are part-time workers? _____

Have I Learned? (✓)

Work with a partner. Check what you have learned. Review what you need help with.

1. ratio   ☐

2. proportion   ☐

3. cross-multiply   ☐

4. inverse operations   ☐

Exercise 1

Write each ratio in two more ways.

1. $\frac{3}{4}$ _3:4_ _three to four_

2. $\frac{5}{9}$ _____ _____

3. $\frac{8}{10}$ _____ _____

4. $\frac{10}{1}$ _____ _____

5. $\frac{100}{3}$ _____ _____

Exercise 2

Look at the figures. There are circles, squares, and triangles. Then answer the questions below.

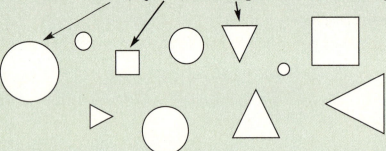

1. What is the ratio of circles to squares? _____5 to 2_____

2. What is the ratio of triangles to circles? _____

3. What is the ratio of squares to triangles? _____

4. What is the ratio of circles to total figures? _____

5. What is the ratio of total figures to squares? _____

Exercise 3

Complete the proportions using inverse operations. Check by cross-multiplying. Show your work on a separate sheet of paper.

1. $\frac{2}{30} = \frac{10}{150}$

2. $\frac{2}{88} = \frac{5}{\underline{}}$

3. $\frac{16}{\underline{}} = \frac{14}{21}$

4. $\frac{8}{\underline{}} = \frac{12}{36}$

5. $\frac{8}{6} = \frac{16}{\underline{}}$

CHAPTER 18 Percents

18-1 Understanding Percents

Percent means *part of a hundred*. Percent is also a *ratio of parts to 100*. The symbol for percent is %. Look at the following examples.

We see: 50%.

We say: "fifty percent."

50% means 50 parts of 100. As a ratio, we write it as 50 to 100, or $\frac{50}{100}$.

We see: 6%.

We say: "six percent."

6% means 6 parts of 100. As a ratio, we write it as 6 to 100, or $\frac{6}{100}$.

Exercise 1

Work with a partner. Practice saying the following percents.

1. 10%
2. 100%
3. 1%
4. 16%
5. 27%

6. 88%
7. 105%
8. 150%
9. 200%
10. 25%

Exercise 2

Write the following expressions with numbers and the % symbol.

1. five percent ___5%___
2. eleven percent _____
3. fourteen percent _____
4. sixty percent _____
5. twelve percent _____

6. fifty-five percent _____
7. eighty percent _____
8. eighteen percent _____
9. ninety-nine percent _____
10. fifteen percent _____

In Chapter 10 we studied decimal numbers. Look at the following example.

.35 = thirty-five hundredths

It means *35 parts of 100.*

Since *percent* means *part of 100,* we can write percents as decimals in hundredths.

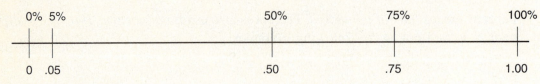

5% = .05
five percent = five hundredths

50% = .50
fifty percent = fifty hundredths

75% = .75
seventy-five percent = seventy-five hundredths

100% = 1.00
one hundred percent = one whole

How do we write percents as decimals? We move the decimal point two places to the left. ←

50% = .50   5% = .05

How do we write decimals as percents? We move the decimal point two places to the right. →

.50 = 50%   .05 = 5%

Exercise 3

A. Write each decimal as a percent.

1. .35 _35%_	**6.** .03 _____	**11.** 1.00 _____
2. .04 _____	**7.** .85 _____	**12.** .72 _____
3. .29 _____	**8.** .19 _____	**13.** .01 _____
4. .99 _____	**9.** .09 _____	**14.** .12 _____
5. .30 _____	**10.** .15 _____	**15.** .49 _____

B. Write each percent as a decimal.

1. 16%   .16
2. 25% _____
3. 95% _____
4. 1% _____
5. 18% _____

6. 6% _____
7. 89% _____
8. 20% _____
9. 8% _____
10. 12% _____

11. 150% _____
12. 33% _____
13. 200% _____
14. 2% _____
15. 44% _____

18-3 Writing Percents as Fractions

We can write percents as fractions.

Example:

We can write 25% as a fraction.

We can write 25% as a ratio of 25 parts to 100. As a fraction, this is $\frac{25}{100}$.

Example:

We can write 110% as a fraction.

As a fraction, it is $\frac{110}{100}$.

Exercise 4

A. Write each percent as a fraction.

1. 35% $\frac{35}{100}$
2. 2% _____
3. 15% _____
4. 91% _____
5. 100% _____

6. 11% _____
7. 50% _____
8. 150% _____
9. 12% _____
10. 51% _____

11. 120% _____
12. 99% _____
13. 75% _____
14. 20% _____
15. 40% _____

B. Write each fraction as a percent.

1. $\frac{10}{100}$ 10%
2. $\frac{9}{100}$ _____
3. $\frac{54}{100}$ _____
4. $\frac{2}{100}$ _____

5. $\frac{100}{100}$ _____
6. $\frac{90}{100}$ _____
7. $\frac{50}{100}$ _____
8. $\frac{19}{100}$ _____

9. $\frac{6}{100}$ _____
10. $\frac{66}{100}$ _____

Fill in the blanks.

	Percent	Decimal	Fraction		Percent	Decimal	Fraction
1.	13%	.13	$\frac{13}{100}$	9.	10%	.10	$\frac{10}{100}$
2.	53%	.53	$\frac{53}{100}$	10.	98%	___	___
3.	3%	.3	$\frac{3}{100}$	11.	___	___	$\frac{180}{100}$
4.	60%	.60	$\frac{60}{100}$	12.	___	___	$\frac{8}{100}$
5.	___	.19	___	13.	___	.89	___
6.	65%	___	___	14.	130%	___	___
7.	___	.04	___	15.	___	1.75	___
8.	___	___	$\frac{100}{100}$				

18-4 Writing Fractions as Decimals and as Percents

We can write fractions as decimals and as percents. For example, we can write $\frac{3}{4}$ as a decimal and as a percent.

The fraction $\frac{3}{4}$ means $3 \div 4$. To divide, we can write:

$$4\overline{)3}$$

Since 3 is less than 4, we need to write a decimal point and one or more zeros.

$$\begin{array}{r} .7 \\ 4\overline{)3.0} \\ -2\,8 \\ \hline 2 \end{array}$$

Since we have a remainder of 2, we need to write in one more zero.

$$
\begin{array}{r}
.75 \\
4\overline{)3.00} \\
-2\ 8 \\
\hline
20 \\
-20 \\
\hline
0
\end{array}
$$

The fraction $\frac{3}{4}$ = .75 or 75%.

We can also write mixed numbers as decimals and as percents.

Example:

We can write $1\frac{1}{2}$ as a decimal and as a percent.

$$1\frac{1}{2} = \frac{3}{2}$$

We divide.

$$
\begin{array}{r}
1.5 \\
2\overline{)3.0} \\
-2 \\
\hline
1\ 0 \\
-1\ 0 \\
\hline
0
\end{array}
$$

$1\frac{1}{2}$ = 1.5 or 150%

Sometimes we need to round off to the nearest hundredths place.

Example:

We can write $\frac{2}{3}$ as a decimal and as a percent.

We divide.

$$
\begin{array}{r}
.666 \\
3\overline{)2.000} \\
-1\ 8 \\
\hline
20 \\
-18 \\
\hline
20
\end{array}
$$

We round .666 to the nearest hundredths place: .666 = .67.

So, $\frac{2}{3}$ = .67 or 67%.

How do we write a fraction as a decimal?

1. We divide the numerator by the denominator. (If the numerator is less than the denominator, we write a decimal point and one or more zeros.)

2. If there is a remainder, we write in one or more zeros.

3. We continue to divide until there is no remainder or we need to round off to the nearest hundredths place.

Exercise 6

Write each fraction as a decimal and as a percent. Show your work on a separate sheet of paper.

1. $\frac{1}{8}$ = _.125_ = _12.5%_

2. $\frac{3}{5}$ = _____ = _____

3. $\frac{4}{10}$ = _____ = _____

4. $\frac{3}{6}$ = _____ = _____

5. $\frac{5}{8}$ = _____ = _____

6. $\frac{1}{2}$ = _____ = _____

7. $\frac{3}{4}$ = _____ = _____

8. $\frac{1}{5}$ = _____ = _____

9. $\frac{2}{20}$ = _____ = _____

10. $\frac{6}{15}$ = _____ = _____

11. $\frac{7}{8}$ = _____ = _____

12. $\frac{1}{3}$ = _____ = _____

13. $\frac{6}{10}$ = _____ = _____

14. $\frac{4}{5}$ = _____ = _____

15. $\frac{9}{25}$ = _____ = _____

16. $\frac{2}{2}$ = _____ = _____

17. $\frac{4}{6}$ = _____ = _____

18. $\frac{5}{25}$ = _____ = _____

19. $\frac{7}{4}$ = _____ = _____

20. $\frac{11}{5}$ = _____ = _____

21. $1\frac{2}{4}$ = _____ = _____

22. $\frac{4}{7}$ = _____ = _____

23. $2\frac{1}{4}$ = _____ = _____

24. $1\frac{1}{10}$ = _____ = _____

25. $4\frac{1}{2}$ = _____ = _____

26. $1\frac{4}{9}$ = _____ = _____

27. $1\frac{7}{8}$ = _____ = _____

28. $\frac{3}{50}$ = _____ = _____

29. $2\frac{2}{3}$ = _____ = _____

30. $1\frac{4}{11}$ = _____ = _____

We can solve problems with percents by using proportions.

Example:

What number is 50% of 20?

or

What number, or what part of 20, is the same as 50 parts of 100?

$50\% = \dfrac{50}{100} = 50$ parts of 100

Look at this problem on a number line.

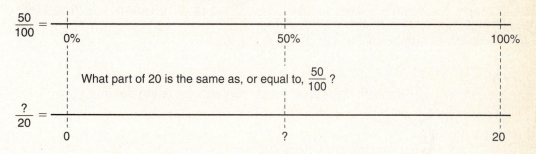

We can solve this problem using proportions.

$$\dfrac{50}{100} = \dfrac{?}{20}$$

We cross-multiply.

$50 \times 20 = 100 \times ?$

$1{,}000 = 100 \times ?$

We use the inverse operation.

$1{,}000 \div 100 = ?$

$10 = ?$

The number is 10. 50 parts of 100 is the same as 10 parts of 20.

Since *of* means *multiply,* we can write 50% of 20 as $\dfrac{50}{100} \times 20 = \dfrac{1{,}000}{100} = 10$.

Use proportions to solve the following problems. Show your work on a separate sheet of paper. Write your answers on the lines.

1. What number is 10% of 50? ___5___   9. What number is 75% of 4? _____

2. What number is 25% of 20? _____   10. What number is 100% of 10? _____

3. What number is 5% of 25? _____   11. What number is 12% of 50? _____

4. What number is 4% of 50? _____   12. What number is 40% of 5? _____

5. What number is 20% of 10? _____   13. What number is 90% of 100? _____

6. What number is 60% of 25? _____   14. What number is 30% of 12? _____

7. What number is 20% of 20? _____   15. What number is 70% of 8? _____

8. What number is 50% of 2? _____

We can also solve problems with percents by using decimals.

Example:

What number is 50% of 20?

We can solve this problem using decimals.

Since *of* means *multiply,* we can rewrite this problem as 50% × 20 = ?

We change 50% to a decimal.

50% = .50

Then we multiply.

.50 × 20 = 10.00 or 10

10 is 50% of 20.

Use decimals to solve the following problems. Show your work on a separate sheet of paper. Write your answers on the lines.

1. What number is 20% of 50? ___10___   6. What number is 100% of 40? _____

2. What number is 25% of 30? _____   7. What number is 12% of 18? _____

3. What number is 5% of 45? _____   8. What number is 40% of 80? _____

4. What number is 60% of 30? _____   9. What number is 80% of 90? _____

5. What number is 3% of 10? _____   10. What number is 35% of 50? _____

11. What number is 65% of 10? _____   **14.** What number is 15% of 30? _____

12. What number is 90% of 90? _____   **15.** What number is 45% of 80? _____

13. What number is 25% of 100? _____

Exercise 9

Use proportions or decimals to solve the following problems. Write your answers on the lines. Show your work on a separate sheet of paper.

In a display at an aquarium, there are 20 tropical fish altogether.

1. 5% of the fish are black. How many are black? (How many is 5% of 20?) __/__

2. 10% of the fish have long tails. How many fish have long tails? _____

3. 50% of the fish are very small. How many fish are very small? _____

4. 25% of the fish are black and white. How many fish are black and white? _____

5. 15% of the fish are very large. How many fish are very large? _____

We can find percents by using proportions.

Example:

5 is what percent of 10?

or

5 parts of 10 is the same as how many parts of 100?

Look at this problem on a number line.

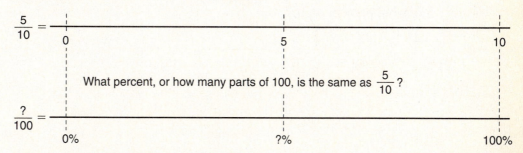

We can solve this problem using proportions.

$$\frac{5}{10} = \frac{?}{100}$$

We cross-multiply.

$5 \times 100 = 10 \times ?$

$500 = 10 \times ?$

We use the inverse operation.

$500 \div 10 = \underline{?}$

$50 = ?$

The answer is 50 parts of 100, or 50%. 5 parts of 10 is equal to 50 parts of 100.

Exercise 10

Use proportions to solve the following problems. Show your work on a separate sheet of paper. Write your answers on the lines.

1. 10 is what percent of 20? ___*50%*___

2. 5 is what percent of 25? _____

3. 2 is what percent of 10? _____

4. 6 is what percent of 50? _____

5. 1 is what percent of 4? _____

6. 90 is what percent of 100? _____

7. 8 is what percent of 10? _____

8. 50 is what percent of 50? _____

9. 15 is what percent of 75?_____

10. 20 is what percent of 80?_____

11. 1 is what percent of 5?_____

12. 7 is what percent of 10?_____

13. 15 is what percent of 25?_____

14. 4 is what percent of 16?_____

15. 8 is what percent of 40?_____

We can also find percents by using decimals.

Example:

5 is what percent of 10?

We can solve this problem using decimals. Since *of* means *multiply* and *is* means *equals*, we have:

5 is what percent of 10?

$\downarrow \downarrow$

$5 = ?\% \times 10$

We can use inverse operations to find the missing percent.

$5 = ?\% \times 10$

We use the inverse operation.

$5 \div 10 = ?\%$

$$10\overline{)5}$$

We need to write in a decimal point and one or more zeros.

$$\begin{array}{r} .5 \\ 10\overline{)5.0} \\ -5\ 0 \\ \hline 0 \end{array}$$

Since we want the answer as a percent, we need to move the decimal point.

$.5 = 50\%$

5 is 50% of 10.

Exercise 11

Use decimals to solve the following problems. Show your work on a separate sheet of paper. Write your answers on the lines.

1. 10 is what percent of 40? ___*25%*___

2. 5 is what percent of 50? _____

3. 2 is what percent of 20? _____

4. 6 is what percent of 100? _____

5. 1 is what percent of 5? _____

6. 90 is what percent of 100? _____

7. 8 is what percent of 16? _____

8. 30 is what percent of 30? _____

9. 15 is what percent of 60? _____

10. 2 is what percent of 10? _____

11. 4 is what percent of 40? _____

12. 8 is what percent of 10? _____

13. 5 is what percent of 40? _____

14. 1 is what percent of 10? _____

15. 75 is what percent of 100? _____

Use proportions or decimals to solve the following problems. Write your answers on the lines. Show your work on a separate sheet of paper.

In the bird section of a zoo, there are 40 parrots altogether. 10 of the parrots are green, 20 are yellow, 2 are red, and 8 are white.

1. What percent of the parrots are green? (10 is what percent of the total?) ___*25%*___

2. What percent of the parrots are red? _____

3. What percent of the parrots are white? _____

4. What percent of the parrots are red and white? _____

5. 50% of the parrots are of one color. Is that color red, green, yellow, or white?

_____

We can find missing numbers by using proportions.

Example:

5 is 25% of what number?

or

5 parts of what number is the same as 25 parts of 100?

Look at this problem on a number line.

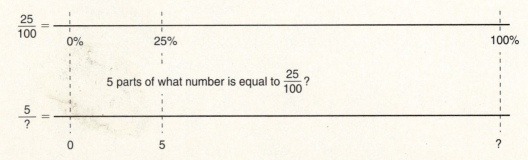

We can solve this problem using proportions.

$$\frac{25}{100} = \frac{5}{?}$$

We cross-multiply.

$$25 \times ? = 100 \times 5$$
$$25 \times ? = 500$$

We use the inverse operation.

$$? = 500 \div 25$$
$$? = 20$$

The number is 20. 25 parts of 100 is equal to 5 parts of 20.

Exercise 13

Solve the following problems using proportions. Show your work on a separate sheet of paper. Write your answers on the lines.

1. 10 is 20% of what number? _____50_____
2. 5 is 50% of what number? _____
3. 2 is 10% of what number? _____
4. 15 is 60% of what number? _____
5. 20 is 2% of what number? _____
6. 30 is 15% of what number? _____
7. 5 is 10% of what number? _____
8. 4 is 20% of what number? _____

9. 3 is 6% of what number? _____
10. 7 is 70% of what number? _____
11. 1 is 20% of what number? _____
12. 15 is 30% of what number? _____
13. 80 is 20% of what number? _____
14. 30 is 2% of what number? _____
15. 10 is 100% of what number? _____

We can also find missing numbers by using decimals.

Example:

5 is 25% of what number?

We can solve this problem using decimals.

5 is 25% of what number?

We change 25% to a decimal.

25% = .25

5 is .25 of what number?

↓   ↓

$$5 = .25 \times ?$$

We use the inverse operation.　　　$5 \div .25 = ?$

$$.25\overline{)5}$$

$$\begin{array}{r} 20. \\ 25.\overline{)500\uparrow} \\ -50 \\ \hline 00 \\ -0 \\ \hline 0 \end{array}$$

5 is 25% of 20.

Exercise 14

Solve the following problems using decimals. Show your work on a separate sheet of paper. Write your answers on the lines.

1. 10 is 40% of what number? ___25___　　**9.** 3 is 50% of what number? _____

2. 5 is 20% of what number? _____　　**10.** 10 is 80% of what number? _____

3. 3 is 10% of what number? _____　　**11.** 2 is 20% of what number? _____

4. 60 is 50% of what number? _____　　**12.** 25 is 5% of what number? _____

5. 2 is 20% of what number? _____　　**13.** 50 is 50% of what number? _____

6. 30 is 25% of what number? _____　　**14.** 9 is 90% of what number? _____

7. 5 is 80% of what number? _____　　**15.** 25 is 25% of what number? _____

8. 4 is 20% of what number? _____

Exercise 15

Use proportions or decimals to solve the following problems. Write your answers on the lines. Show your work on a separate sheet of paper.

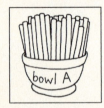    

1. In bowl A, 10 candies are red. That is 50% of the total number of candies in the bowl.

How many candies are there altogether in bowl A? (10 is 50% of how many?) _20_

2. In bowl B, 15 candies are chocolate. That is 75% of the total number of candies in the bowl.

How many candies are there altogether in bowl B? _____

278

3. In bowl C, 2 candies are caramel. That is 20% of the total number of candies in the bowl.

How many candies are there altogether in bowl C? _____

4. In bowl D, 30 candies are yellow. That is 60% of the total number of candies in the bowl.

How many candies are there altogether in bowl D? _____

5. In bowl E, 80 candies are white. That is 80% of the total number of candies in the bowl.

How many candies are there altogether in bowl E? _____

Exercise 16

Lisa's twelfth-grade history class has 50 students in all. Of the total, 5 students speak French and English, 10 students speak Spanish and English, 15 students speak Chinese and English, and 20 students speak English only. Answer the following questions about Lisa's class. Write your answers on the lines. Show all your work on a separate sheet of paper.

1. What percent of the students speak French? (5 is what percent of 50?) _10%_

2. What percent of the students speak Spanish? _____

3. In Lisa's class, 40% of the students work part-time after school. How many students work part-time? (How many is 40% of the total students?) _____

4. 30% of Lisa's class drive cars. How many students drive cars? _____

5. 90% of the students will go to college. How many students will go to college? _____

6. 4 girls want to study math in college. This is 20% of all the girls in Lisa's class. How many girls are there in the class altogether? (4 is 20% of how many?) _____

7. 20 girls want to study business at State College. That is 80% of the students who will go to State College. How many students in the class will go to State College? _____

8. 50% of the students in Lisa's class will travel in the summer. How many will travel? _____

9. What percent of the students speak Chinese? _____

10. 20 students speak English only. Of these students, 15 will study Spanish in college.

What percent of these students will study Spanish? (15 is what percent of 20?) _____

We often see items on sale for less than their original price.

We use percents to find the amount of the discount or the sale price.

Example:

Every item at Century Department Store is discounted 20%. The original price of a shirt is $24.00. What is the sale price?

We want to know the amount of the discount, or 20% of $24.00.

We can find the amount of the discount using decimals.

.20 × $24.00 = $4.80

We subtract to find the sale price.

original price − amount of discount = sale price

$24.00 − $4.80 = $19.20, the sale price

Another way to find the sale price is to find it directly. Since the percent of discount is 20%, the sale price is 100% − 20%, or 80%, of the original price.

.80 × 24.00 = $19.20, the sale price

At North Hills High School, each twelfth-grade student can buy a senior activity card. With that card, the student can get discounts on tickets to school activities. Answer the questions below about discounts with a senior activity card. Write your answers on the lines. Show your work on a separate sheet of paper.

Senior Activity Card

Name: **Carl Benes**

Age: **17**

Student number: **628-97-1010**

Carl Benes

1. With a senior activity card, all football games are discounted 60%. If a ticket to a football game costs $3.50, how much is the ticket with the discount? ___$1.40___

2. Carl has a senior activity card. He went to 5 football games.

   a. How much do 5 tickets cost without the discount? _____

   b. How much did Carl pay for 5 tickets with the discount? _____

3. A ticket to the senior picnic costs $8.00. With the senior activity card, the discount is 40%. How much is a ticket with the discount? _____

4. Tickets to the prom cost $85.00 per couple. With the senior activity card, the discount is 15%. How much is a prom ticket with the discount? _____

5. Carl went to 4 school dances during the year. A ticket to a dance is $5.50. Seniors with the activity card get a 50% discount.

   a. How much are 4 dance tickets without the discount? _____

   b. How much did Carl pay for 4 tickets with the discount? _____

Have I Learned? (✓)

Work with a partner. Check what you have learned. Review what you need help with.

1. percent ☐
2. original price ☐
3. discount ☐
4. sale price ☐

CHAPTER REVIEW

Exercise 1

A. Write each decimal as a percent.

1. .25 _25%_   3. 2.00 _____   5. 1.25 _____

2. .3 _____   4. .07 _____

B. Write each percent as a decimal.

1. 36% _.36_   3. 150% _____   5. 100% _____

2. 2% _____   4. 20% _____

Exercise 2

A. Write each percent as a fraction.

1. 35% $\frac{7}{20}$ 3. 80% _____   5. 2% _____

2. 66% _____   4. 130% _____

B. Write each fraction as a percent.

1. $\frac{1}{2}$ _50%_ 2. $\frac{3}{4}$ _____   3. $\frac{7}{8}$ _____   4. $\frac{2}{5}$ _____   5. $\frac{5}{5}$ _____

Exercise 3

Solve the following problems using proportions or decimals.

1. What number is 5% of 20? _1_   4. 4 is what percent of 20? _____

2. What number is 10% of 50? _____   5. 10 is 50% of what number? _____

3. 6 is what percent of 10? _____

Exercise 4

Solve the following problems using proportions or decimals.

1. A football is on sale at 25% off (discount). The regular price is $30.00. What is the sale price? _$22.50_

2. Maxine's Shoe Store is having a sale. Everything is 20% off. Helen received a $4.00 discount on a pair of shoes. What was the original price? ($4 is 20% of how much?) _____

3. Tom bought a new bike on sale at a 30% discount. The original price was $340.00. What was the sale price? _____

4. Lydia's new watch was on sale at a 25% discount. Her discount was $16.50. What was the original price of the watch? _____

5. Anita received a 15% discount on a CD player. The discount was $18.00. What was the original price? _____

Operations with Integers

In this unit, you will learn . . .

- **positive and negative integers**

- **adding positive and negative integers on the number line**

- **absolute value**

- **adding positive and negative integers**

- **subtracting positive and negative integers**

- **multiplying positive and negative integers**

- **multiplying more than two integers**

- **dividing positive and negative integers**

CHAPTER 19 More Work with Integers

19-1 Positive and Negative Integers

In Chapter 8, we learned about positive and negative integers on the number line.

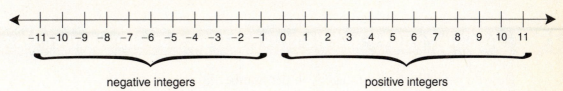

We write positive three as 3 or +3. It is not necessary to write the **positive sign** (+) in front of a positive integer.

Negative integers are less than zero. We write negative three as −3. It is necessary to write a **negative sign** (−) in front of a negative integer. It is also necessary to say *negative* when we read a negative integer.

Example:

We read: −2   +   −3

We say: | negative two | | plus | | negative three |

Example:

We read: 6   −   −4

We say: | six | | minus | | negative four |

On a separate sheet of paper, write the following problems using words. Then work with a partner. Practice saying the problems aloud.

1. −3 + −2 *negative three plus*
   negative two

2. 6 + 4

3. −2 − −3

4. 3 + −7

5. 3 − −7

6. 4 + −6

7. −1 − 0

8. −5 − − 26

9. 3 + −3

10. −2 + −7

19-2 Adding Positive and Negative Integers on the Number Line ..

How do we add positive integers on the number line?

Example:

We can add 4 + 3 on the number line.

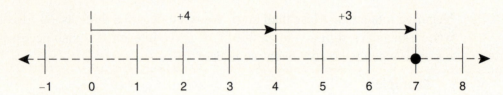

1. We begin at 0.

2. We go 4 points to the right. (+4)

3. Then we go 3 more points to the right. (+3)

4. The sum is +7, or 7. So, 4 + 3 = 7.

How do we add positive and negative integers on the number line?

Example:

We can add 3 + −1 on the number line.

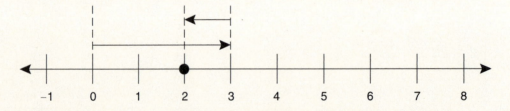

1. We begin at 0.

2. We go 3 points to the right. (+3)

3. Then we go 1 point to the left. (−1)

4. The sum is +2, or 2. So, 3 + −1 = 2.

On the number line, the direction to the right is positive and the direction to the left is negative.

Example:

We can add $-2 + 2$ on the number line.

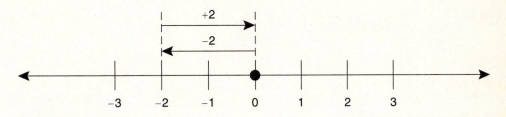

1. We begin at 0.

2. We go 2 points to the left. (-2)

3. Then we go 2 points to the right. $(+2)$

4. The sum is 0. So, $-2 + 2 = 0$

Exercise 2

Write a sum for each number line. Remember, always begin at 0.

1.

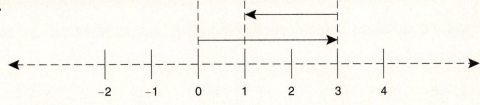

_3 + −2 = 1_

2.

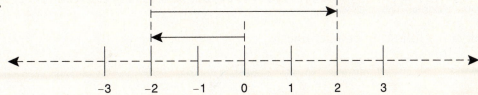

_____

3.

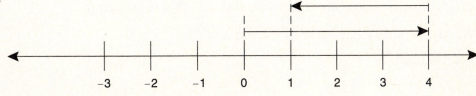

_____

4.

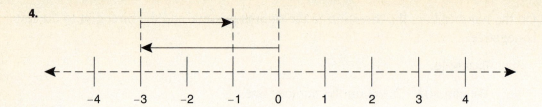

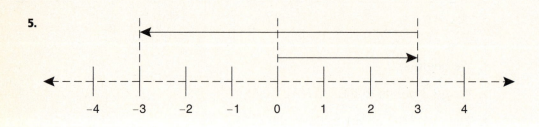

_____

5.

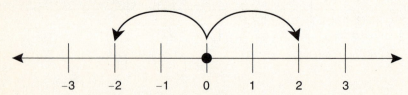

_____

Exercise 3

On a separate sheet of paper, draw a number line to show each sum.

1. $3 + -1 =$

2. $-3 + -3 =$

3. $4 + -1 =$

4. $-3 + 4 =$

5. $5 + -4 =$

6. $-4 + -5 =$

7. $4 + 0 =$

8. $-3 + 6 =$

9. $5 + -6 =$

10. $4 + -4 =$

19-3 Absolute Value

Look at the following number line.

-2 and 2 are both equal distances from 0. They are both 2 points from 0. Only their directions are different. (One is negative and the other is positive.)

We say, "The absolute value of -2 and 2 is 2."

The **absolute value** of an integer is its distance from zero. The symbol | | means *absolute value*.

Example:

What are the absolute values of −4 and 4?

Answer: Both −4 and 4 are 4 points from 0. So their absolute values are equal. The absolute value of both −4 and 4 is 4.

Examples:

$|-5| = ?$

Answer: 5

$|6| = ?$

Answer: 6

Exercise 4

Write the absolute values of the integers below.

1. $|-1| = $ _____1_____

2. $|13| = $ _____

3. $|-27| = $ _____

4. $|4| = $ _____

5. $|+7| = $ _____

6. $|-11| = $ _____

7. $|-21| = $ _____

8. $|15| = $ _____

9. $|-26| = $ _____

10. $|212| = $ _____

19-4 Adding Positive and Negative Integers

We use absolute values when we add positive and negative integers.

How do we add integers with **like signs** (the same signs)?

1. We add together the absolute values of each integer.

2. We use the common sign for the sum.

Example:

−4 + −2

Both integers are negative. The common sign is −. We add the absolute values.

|−4| = 4 |−2| = 2

4 + 2 = 6

We use the common sign.

−4 + −2 = −6

Exercise 5

Add the integers below. Write the sums on the lines.

1. −7 + −4 = _−11_

2. 11 + 2 = _____

3. −2 + −2 = _____

4. −1 +−5 = _____

5. +6 + 3 = _____

6. −5 + −5 = _____

7. −1 +−7 = _____

8. 11 + 0 = _____

9. −8 +−9 = _____

10. −15 +−15 = _____

11. −3 + −7 = _____

12. 14 + 23 = _____

13. −17 + −20 = _____

14. −35 +−42 = _____

15. −19 + −12 = _____

16. 34 + 29 = _____

17. −102 +−66 = _____

18. 78 + 56 = _____

19. −55 + −456 = _____

20. 55 + 456 = _____

How do we add integers with **unlike signs** (different signs)?

1. We find the absolute values of the integers. Then we subtract.

2. We use the sign of the integer with the greater absolute value for the sum.

Example:

−4 + 6

We find the absolute values.

|−4| = 4 |6| = 6

We subtract.

6 − 4 = 2

The integer with the greater absolute value is 6. It has a positive sign,

so the sum will be positive.

−4 + 6 = 2

Example:

$3 + -8$

We find the absolute values.

$|-3| = 3$ $|-8| = 8$

We subtract.

$8 - 3 = 5$

-8 is the integer with the greater absolute value. It has a negative sign, so the sum will be negative.

$3 + -8 = -5$

Exercise 6

Add the integers below. Write the sums on the lines.

1. $-3 + 2 =$ ___−1___

2. $-6 + 12 =$ _____

3. $5 + -5 =$ _____

4. $-4 + 9 =$ _____

5. $-5 + -7 =$ _____

6. $4 + 3 =$ _____

7. $-20 + 19 =$ _____

8. $-11 + 10 =$ _____

9. $-13 + 14 =$ _____

10. $15 + -27 =$ _____

11. $2 + -5 =$ _____

12. $-7 + 0 =$ _____

13. $7 + -1 =$ _____

14. $24 + -33 =$ _____

15. $-14 + -34 =$ _____

16. $11 + -3 =$ _____

17. $-11 + 3 =$ _____

18. $-19 + 27 =$ _____

19. $112 + -34 =$ _____

20. $35 + -36 =$ _____

21. $26 + -26 =$ _____

22. $-45 + 90 =$ _____

23. $457 + 84 =$ _____

24. $-34 + -12 =$ _____

25. $-857 + 346 =$ _____

19-5 Subtracting Positive and Negative Integers

We can subtract integers on a number line. Look at the following subtraction problem.

$3 - 1 = 2$

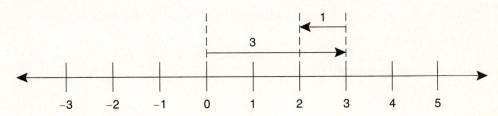

Now look at the following addition problem.

$3 + -1 = 2$

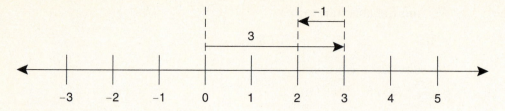

Both operations on the number line are the same. The results are equal.

Subtraction   **Addition**

$3 - 1 = 2$ $3 + -1 = 2$

We see that subtracting a positive integer is the same as adding a negative integer. Or, we can say that subtracting any integer is the same as adding its additive inverse. In the example above, 1 and -1 are additive inverses. Now look at two more examples.

$4 - 3 = 1$ $4 + -3 = 1$

Again, we see that subtracting an integer (3) is the same as adding its additive inverse (-3).

How do we subtract positive and negative integers?

1. We change the subtraction problem into an addition problem using the additive inverse of the subtrahend.

2. We add the integers using the rules for adding positive and negative integers.

Example:

We can change $10 - 3$ to an addition problem using the additive inverse.

$10 - 3 =$

The additive inverse of 3 is -3.

$10 + -3 = 7$

Example:

We can change $6 - -4$ to an addition problem using the additive inverse.

$6 - -4 =$

The additive inverse of -4 is 4.

$6 + +4 = 10$

How do we multiply integers with like signs?

1. We multiply the integers.

2. We use a positive sign for the product.

Exercise 9

Multiply the integers.

1. $-2 \cdot -4 = \underline{\quad 8 \quad}$

2. $-4 \cdot -5 = \underline{\qquad}$

3. $-6 \cdot 3 = \underline{\qquad}$

4. $9 \cdot -2 = \underline{\qquad}$

5. $-12 \cdot -3 = \underline{\qquad}$

6. $-34 \cdot -2 = \underline{\qquad}$

7. $45 \cdot -3 = \underline{\qquad}$

8. $11 \cdot -3 = \underline{\qquad}$

9. $-32 \cdot -8 = \underline{\qquad}$

10. $16 \cdot 3 = \underline{\qquad}$

11. $14 \cdot -56 = \underline{\qquad}$

12. $-33 \cdot -9 = \underline{\qquad}$

13. $56 \cdot -2 = \underline{\qquad}$

14. $18 \cdot 7 = \underline{\qquad}$

15. $-3 \cdot 67 = \underline{\qquad}$

16. $-56 \cdot -23 = \underline{\qquad}$

17. $-98 \cdot -5 = \underline{\qquad}$

18. $122 \cdot -6 = \underline{\qquad}$

19. $-34 \cdot -67 = \underline{\qquad}$

20. $45 \cdot 8 = \underline{\qquad}$

21. $-341 \cdot -9 = \underline{\qquad}$

22. $-87 \cdot -9 = \underline{\qquad}$

23. $756 \cdot -6 = \underline{\qquad}$

24. $-385 \cdot 0 = \underline{\qquad}$

25. $-66 \cdot -66 = \underline{\qquad}$

26. $-100 \cdot 45 = \underline{\qquad}$

27. $100 \cdot -54 = \underline{\qquad}$

28. $-26 \cdot -3 = \underline{\qquad}$

29. $-1,000 \cdot -33 = \underline{\qquad}$

30. $49 \cdot -11 = \underline{\qquad}$

19-7 Multiplying More Than Two Integers

Sometimes we need to multiply more than two integers.

Example:

$$-3 \cdot -2 \cdot -4$$

By the associative property, we can group.

$$\underbrace{-3 \cdot -2} \cdot -4$$

$$6 \cdot -4 = -24$$

Multiply the integers.

1. $-4 \cdot -3 \cdot 5 = \underline{\quad 60 \quad}$ **6.** $-1 \cdot 1 \cdot -1 = \underline{\quad\quad}$ **11.** $15 \cdot -2 \cdot -2 = \underline{\quad\quad}$

2. $3 \cdot -5 \cdot 9 = \underline{\quad\quad}$ **7.** $-9 \cdot 4 \cdot -4 = \underline{\quad\quad}$ **12.** $20 \cdot 3 \cdot -4 = \underline{\quad\quad}$

3. $7 \cdot -3 \cdot -2 = \underline{\quad\quad}$ **8.** $-2 \cdot 0 \cdot -2 = \underline{\quad\quad}$ **13.** $-35 \cdot -12 \cdot -5 = \underline{\quad\quad}$

4. $-7 \cdot -4 \cdot -5 = \underline{\quad\quad}$ **9.** $-8 \cdot 3 \cdot 4 = \underline{\quad\quad}$ **14.** $67 \cdot -2 \cdot -15 = \underline{\quad\quad}$

5. $3 \cdot 6 \cdot -4 = \underline{\quad\quad}$ **10.** $-12 \cdot 3 \cdot -4 = \underline{\quad\quad}$ **15.** $10 \cdot -10 \cdot -10 = \underline{\quad\quad}$

19-8 Dividing Positive and Negative Integers

We know that division and multiplication are inverse operations. Look at the following examples.

$$3 \cdot 8 = 24 \qquad 24 \div 8 = 3$$
$$3 \cdot -8 = -24 \qquad -24 \div -8 = 3$$
$$-3 \cdot -8 = 24 \qquad 24 \div -8 = -3$$

The rules for dividing positive and negative integers are the same as for multiplying positive and negative integers.

How do we divide positive and negative integers?

1. We divide the integers.

2. If the integers have like signs, the quotient is positive. If the integers have unlike signs, the quotient is negative.

Example:

$-15 \div -3 = ?$

The integers have like signs, so the quotient is positive.

$-15 \div -3 = 5$

$-12 \div 2 = ?$

The integers have unlike signs, so the quotient is negative.

$-12 \div 2 = -6$

Divide the following integers. Use a separate sheet of paper, if necessary.

1. $-10 \div 5 =$ ___−2___

2. $25 \div 5 =$ _____

3. $-35 \div -7 =$ _____

4. $-60 \div -2 =$ _____

5. $45 \div -9 =$ _____

6. $-33 \div 11 =$ _____

7. $-50 \div 25 =$ _____

8. $100 \div -10 =$ _____

9. $10 \div -1 =$ _____

10. $-124 \div -2 =$ _____

11. $345 \div -5 =$ _____

12. $-566 \div -2 =$ _____

13. $-450 \div 10 =$ _____

14. $200 \div 20 =$ _____

15. $675 \div -25 =$ _____

16. $904 \div -4 =$ _____

17. $-300 \div -15 =$ _____

18. $-870 \div 10 =$ _____

19. $925 \div -25 =$ _____

20. $108 \div -12 =$ _____

21. $-936 \div -4 =$ _____

22. $150 \div -15 =$ _____

23. $1,170 \div 15 =$ _____

24. $-1,035 \div -5 =$ _____

25. $3,267 \div -3 =$ _____

 Have I Learned? (✓)

Work with a partner. Check what you have learned. Review what you need help with.

1. positive integers ☐
2. negative integers ☐
3. positive sign ☐
4. negative sign ☐
5. absolute value ☐
6. like signs ☐
7. unlike signs ☐

Exercise 1

Add the following integers. Use a separate sheet of paper, if necessary.

1. $15 + -4 =$ _____11_____   **6.** $-18 + 18 =$ _____   **11.** $90 + -88 =$ _____

2. $-11 + -3 =$ _____   **7.** $-34 + 0 =$ _____   **12.** $-120 + -120 =$ _____

3. $-13 + 14 =$ _____   **8.** $15 + -35 =$ _____   **13.** $51 + -51 =$ _____

4. $5 + -5 =$ _____   **9.** $-23 + 12 =$ _____   **14.** $298 + -77 =$ _____

5. $-12 + -12 =$ _____   **10.** $-46 + 92 =$ _____   **15.** $-101 + -1 =$ _____

Exercise 2

Subtract the following integers. Use a separate sheet of paper, if necessary.

1. $32 - -12 =$ _____44_____   **6.** $-12 - -36 =$ _____   **11.** $355 - -223 =$ _____

2. $-23 - 45 =$ _____   **7.** $-83 - 22 =$ _____   **12.** $-66 - 12 =$ _____

3. $-99 - 67 =$ _____   **8.** $-35 - 77 =$ _____   **13.** $-315 - -203 =$ _____

4. $25 - 13 =$ _____   **9.** $81 - 81 =$ _____   **14.** $-64 - -2 =$ _____

5. $45 - 67 =$ _____   **10.** $122 - 45 =$ _____   **15.** $654 - -90 =$ _____

Exercise 3

Multiply the following integers. Use a separate sheet of paper, if necessary.

1. $-3 \cdot 12 =$ _____-36_____   **6.** $86 \cdot -13 =$ _____   **11.** $61 \cdot -7 =$ _____

2. $14 \cdot -5 =$ _____   **7.** $55 \cdot 19 =$ _____   **12.** $-900 \cdot -2 =$ _____

3. $-23 \cdot -8 =$ _____   **8.** $-322 \cdot -5 =$ _____   **13.** $-3 \cdot -2 \cdot 2 =$ _____

4. $87 \cdot -12 =$ _____   **9.** $746 \cdot -5 =$ _____   **14.** $8 \cdot 6 \cdot -1 =$ _____

5. $-44 \cdot -10 =$ _____   **10.** $-27 \cdot -7 =$ _____   **15.** $-4 \cdot -3 \cdot -5 =$ _____

Exercise 4

Divide the following integers. Use a separate sheet of paper, if necessary.

1. $90 \div -2 =$ _____-45_____   **5.** $75 \div -25 =$ _____   **8.** $-180 \div -90 =$ _____

2. $55 \div 11 =$ _____   **6.** $120 \div 60 =$ _____   **9.** $-184 \div 23 =$ _____

3. $-60 \div -3 =$ _____   **7.** $-39 \div 13 =$ _____   **10.** $-4,056 \div -52 =$ _____

4. $-121 \div -11 =$ _____

Introduction to Geometry and Measurement

In this unit, you will learn . . .

- points, lines, and planes
- angles
- triangles
- circles
- types of polygons
- congruent figures
- similar polygons
- proportions with similar polygons
- perimeter of a figure
- circumference of a circle
- area of a rectangle and square
- area of a triangle
- area of a parallelogram
- area of a circle

20-1 Points, Lines, and Planes

A **point** is an exact location in space. We name points by capital letters.

R
•

points *P*, *R*, and *S*

P
•

S
•

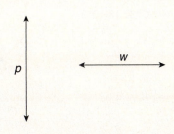

... number of points. It continues forever in two di... ...etters.

p

w

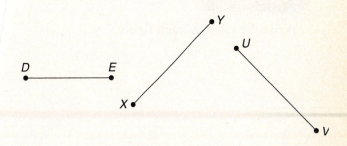

It has two endpoints. We name line segments by

D •——————• E

Y
X

U
V

A **ray** is part of a line. A ray has one endpoint and continues forever in one direction. When rays are single rays, we name them by their endpoints.

rays M, N, and O

When there are two or more rays with the same endpoint, we name them with lowercase letters.

rays a, b, and c

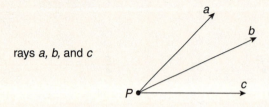

A **plane** is a flat surface formed by three points not in a straight line. We name planes by lowercase letters.

plane m

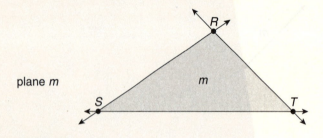

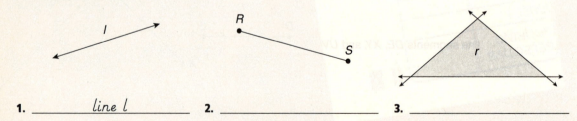

Exercise 1

Write the name of each figure.

1. _____line l_____   2. _____   3. _____

Q

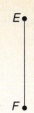

4. _____   **5.** _____   **6.** _____

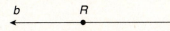

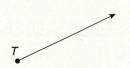

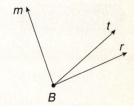

7. _____   **8.** _____   **9.** _____

10. Name all the line segments. (There are six altogether.)

_____

Exercise 2

On a separate sheet of paper, draw each of the following figures.

1. point *C*

2. line *c*

3. point *R*

4. line segment *BD*

5. plane *x*

6. line *r*

7. ray *Q*

8. plane *r*

9. point *D*

10. rays *e* and *f* with the same endpoint *O*

20-2   Intersecting and Parallel Lines   ··········

Intersecting lines cross at one point.

line *l* intersecting line *u* at *M*

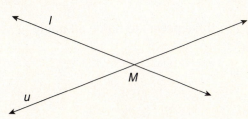

Parallel lines are the same distance apart and never intersect. The symbol // means *parallel*.

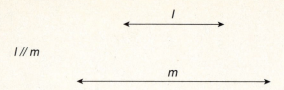

l // *m*

Exercise 3

On a separate sheet of paper, draw each of the following figures.

1. line *h* intersecting line *f* at *U*

2. line *d* // line *r*

3. line segment *UR*

4. plane *o*

5. lines *p*, *b*, and *c* intersecting at point *O*

6. line segments *FG* and *GP* on line *a*

7. rays *d* and *e* with same endpoint *P*

8. line *u* // line *i* // line *t*

9. lines *w*, *e*, *s*, and *f* intersecting at point *D*

10. line *u* // line *w* with line *m* intersecting both lines at *X* and *Y*

20-3 Angles

When two rays intersect at a point, they form an **angle**. We name angles by three points, or by one point at the **vertex**.

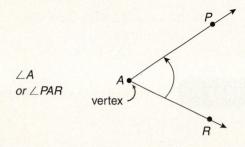

∠*A*
or ∠*PAR*

vertex

When we use three points to name an angle (∠*PAR*), the middle letter is always the vertex.

We use a protractor to measure angles. We measure angles in **degrees** (°).

∠*PQR* = 55° (fifty-five degrees)

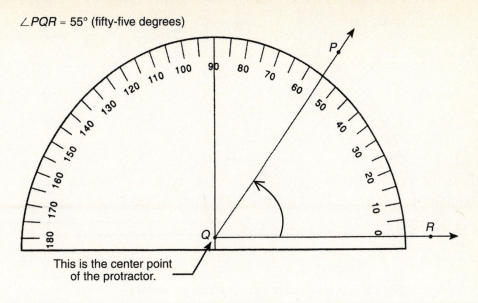

This is the center point
of the protractor.

Angles that measure 90° are called **right angles**.

∠*BEC* = 90°

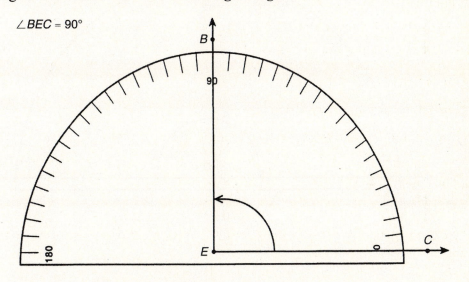

Angles that measure less than 90° are called **acute angles**.

∠*CRX* = 65°

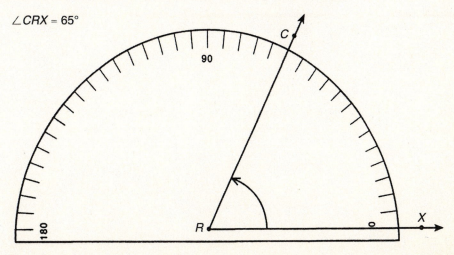

Angles that measure more than 90° are called **obtuse angles**.

∠*VFW* = 135°

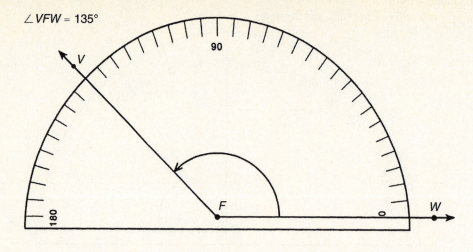

Angles that measure 180° are called **straight angles**.

∠*KDL* = 180°

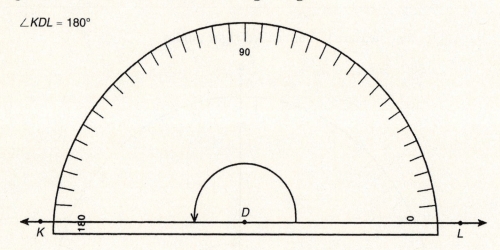

Look at the following angles.

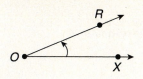
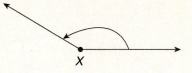
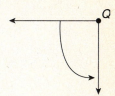

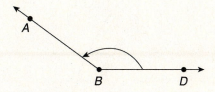

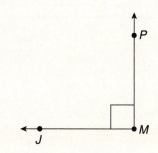
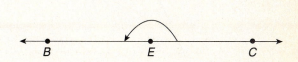

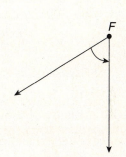

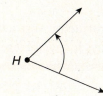

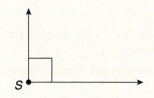
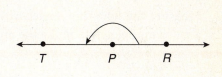

Find the following angles and write *right*, *acute*, *obtuse*, or *straight* for each one.

1. ∠ROX _____*acute*_____

2. ∠S _____

3. ∠BEC _____

4. ∠Q _____

5. ∠TPR _____

6. ∠ABD _____

7. ∠X _____

8. ∠H _____

9. ∠JMP _____

10. ∠F _____

To measure an angle, we place the center point of the protractor at the vertex of the angle, with one side of the angle through the 0° point.

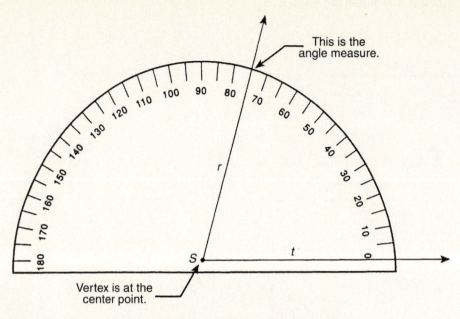

This is the
angle measure.

Vertex is at the
center point.

Ray *t* of ∠S is along the edge of the protractor, passing through 0°.

The angle measure of ∠S is where ray *r* passes through the scale.

∠S = 75°

Exercise 5

Measure the following angles with a protractor. Write the measures on the lines. (Hint: Use a ruler and pencil to make the angle rays longer before you measure.)

1. ∠G = _135°_

E

G   H

2. ∠Y = _____

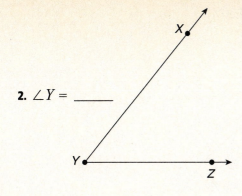

3. ∠B = _____

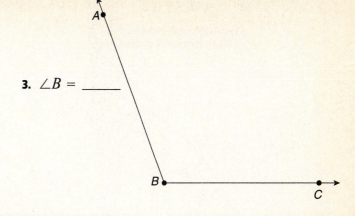

4. ∠Q = _____

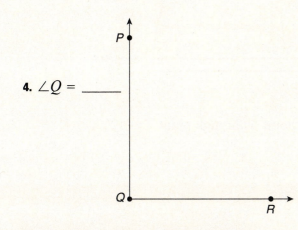

5. ∠T = _____

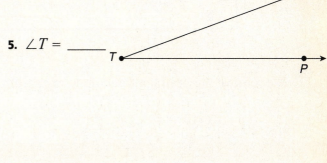

20-4 Drawing Angles

To draw ∠O of 120°, we first draw ray *r*.

Draw ray *r*.

We then place the protractor on ray *r* so that its endpoint is at the center point of the protractor and the ray goes through 0°.

We find 120° on the protractor. We mark a point X at 120°.

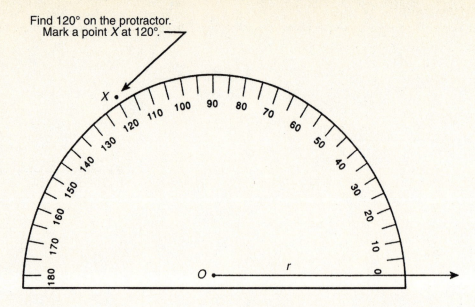

We remove the protractor and draw ray t from point O through point X at 120°.

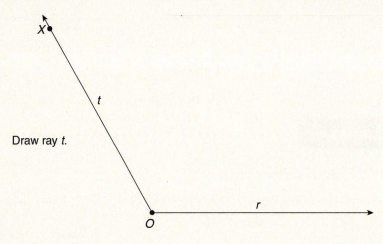

$\angle O = 120°$

Exercise 6

Use a protractor to draw the following angles on a separate sheet of paper.

1. $\angle BAT = 75°$
2. $\angle RUS = 90°$
3. $\angle COB = 135°$
4. $\angle XYZ = 18°$
5. $\angle ABC = 170°$

6. $\angle OAR = 100°$
7. $\angle EOP = 25°$
8. $\angle CAT = 60°$
9. $\angle TNX = 10°$
10. $\angle STP = 150°$

Measure the following angles with a protractor. For each angle, write the measure and *acute, obtuse, right,* or *straight.*

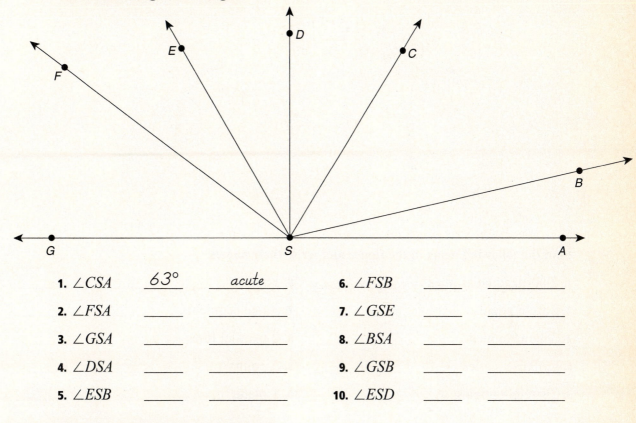

1. ∠CSA   *63°*   *acute*   6. ∠FSB   _____   _____

2. ∠FSA   _____   _____   7. ∠GSE   _____   _____

3. ∠GSA   _____   _____   8. ∠BSA   _____   _____

4. ∠DSA   _____   _____   9. ∠GSB   _____   _____

5. ∠ESB   _____   _____   10. ∠ESD   _____   _____

20-5 Perpendicular Lines

Perpendicular lines intersect and form right angles (90°). The symbol ⊥ means *perpendicular to.*

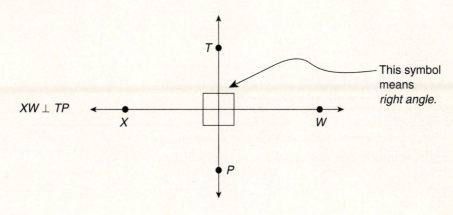

$XW \perp TP$

This symbol means *right angle.*

Look at the following figure.

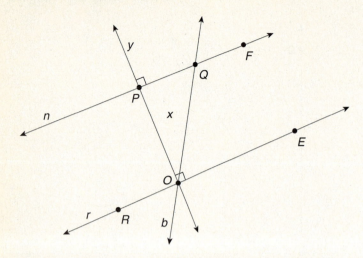

Find the following items in the figure and write their names.

1. 2 perpendicular lines _n and y_ OR _r and y_   **6.** 3 rays _____

2. 2 right angles _____   **7.** 3 line segments _____

3. 3 acute angles _____   **8.** 2 parallel lines _____

4. 2 obtuse angles _____   **9.** 3 points _____

5. 2 straight angles _____   **10.** 1 plane _____

20-6 Triangles

A **triangle** is a figure with three sides and three angles. We name triangles by the three points or angles.

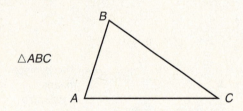

A **right triangle** has one right angle (right angle = 90°).

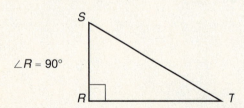

A **scalene triangle** has three sides with different lengths.

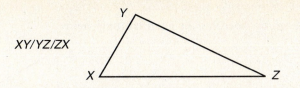

XY/YZ/ZX

An **isosceles triangle** has two equal sides.

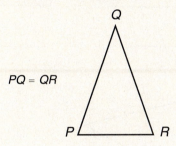

PQ = QR

An **equilateral triangle** has three equal sides.

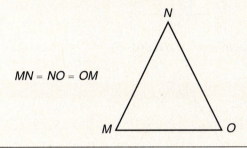

MN = NO = OM

An **obtuse triangle** has one obtuse angle (obtuse angle > 90°).

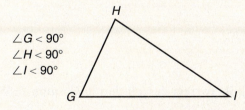

∠*E* > 90°

An **acute triangle** has three acute angles (acute angle < 90°).

∠*G* < 90°
∠*H* < 90°
∠*I* < 90°

If we add the measure of all three angles of any triangle, the sum always equals 180°.

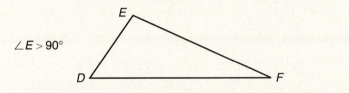

∠*A* + ∠*B* + ∠*C* = 180°   ∠*D* + ∠*E* + ∠*F* = 180°

Exercise 9

A. Write *obtuse, right, equilateral,* or *isosceles* for each triangle below.

1.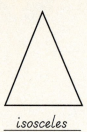

  <u>*isosceles*</u>

2.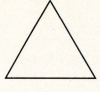

  _____

3.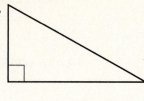

  _____

4.

  _____

5.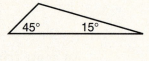

  _____

B. Write the measure of the third angle of each triangle.

1.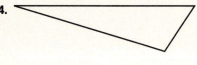

  <u>*100°*</u>

2.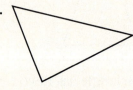

  _____

3.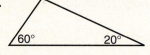

  _____

4.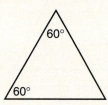

  _____

5.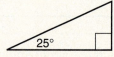

  _____

Exercise 10

Match each triangle in Column A with its correct description in Column B. Write the letter.

<u>**Column A**</u>   <u>**Column B**</u>

1. <u>*e*</u>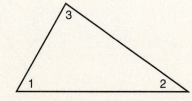

  a. $\angle 1 = 125°$
  $\angle 2 = 25°$
  $\angle 3 = 30°$

314

2. _____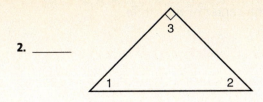

b. ∠1 = 75°
∠2 = 75°
∠3 = 30°

3. _____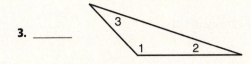

c. ∠1 = 30°
∠2 = 60°
∠3 = 90°

4. _____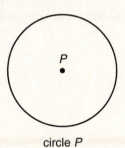

d. ∠1 = 45°
∠2 = 45°
∠3 = 90°

5. _____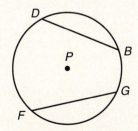

e. ∠1 = 60°
∠2 = 40°
∠3 = 80°

20-7 Circles

A **circle** is a closed plane figure in which all the points are the same distance from a point called the center point. We name a circle by its center point.

circle P

A **chord** is a line segment with endpoints on the circle.

DB and *FG* are chords.

A **diameter** is a chord that intersects the center of the circle.

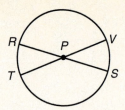

RS and TV are diameters. RS intersects TV at the center of circle P.

A **radius** is a line segment that is $\frac{1}{2}$ the diameter. It has endpoints on the center of the circle and on the circle. (The plural of *radius* is *radii*.)

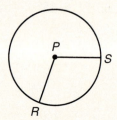

PR and PS are radii of circle P.

Exercise 11

A. Write *chord*, *diameter*, or *radius* for each line segment.

1.

___radius___

2.

_____

3.

_____

4.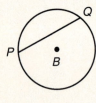

_____

5.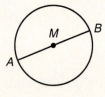

_____

B. Draw the following line segments for each circle.

1. chord *MN*

2. radius *ST*

3. diameter *PQ* with radii *PX* and *XQ*

4. chords *RS, MT,* and *CD*

5. radii *MR* and *MV*

20-8 Drawing Circles

We use a compass to draw circles. To draw a circle with a radius of 2 inches (a diameter of 4 inches), we first mark a center point. We will label this point *P*.

• *P*

We then place the point of the compass on point *P* and open the compass 2 inches.

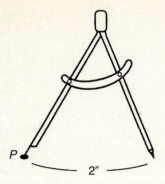

We turn the pencil end of the compass to the right or left, keeping the other point on *P*.

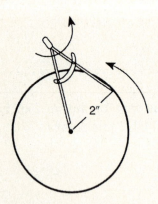

The result is a circle with radius of 2 inches (a diameter of 4 inches).

Exercise 12

On a separate sheet of paper, draw circles with each of the following dimensions.

1. a radius of 1 inch

2. a diameter of 4 inches

3. a radius of $1\frac{1}{2}$ inches

4. a diameter of 3 inches

5. a radius of $\frac{3}{4}$ inch

Have I Learned? (✓)

Work with a partner. Check what you have learned. Review what you need help with.

1. point ☐
2. line ☐
3. line segment ☐
4. ray ☐
5. plane ☐
   g lines ☐
   es ☐
   ☐
   ☐
   ☐
   ☐
   ☐
   gle ☐

15. straight angle ☐
16. perpendicular lines ☐
17. triangle ☐
18. right triangle ☐
19. scalene triangle ☐
20. isosceles triangle ☐
21. equilateral triangle ☐
22. obtuse triangle ☐
23. acute triangle ☐
24. circle ☐
25. chord ☐
26. diameter ☐
27. radius ☐
28. compass ☐

Exercise 1

Identify each of the following. Write your answers on the lines.

1. • _point_

6. _____

2. •————→ _____

7. _____

3. 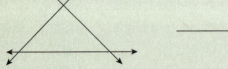 _____

8. _____

4. ←————→ _____

9. _____

5. •————• _____

10. _____

Exercise 2

Complete the sentences. Write *intersecting, perpendicular,* or *parallel.*

1. _Perpendicular_ lines form 90° angles.

4. The symbol // means _____ to.

2. _____ lines never cross.

5. The symbol ⊥ means _____ to.

3. _____ lines cross at one point.

Exercise 3

On a separate sheet of paper, write *straight, right, obtuse, acute, isosceles, equilateral,* or *scalene.*

1. _right_

2.

3.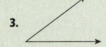

4.

5. An _____ triangle has two equal sides.

6. A _____ angle is equal to 90°.

7. An _____ triangle has three equal sides.

8. A _____ angle is equal to 180°.

9. A _____ triangle has one right angle.

10. A _____ triangle has three sides with different lengths.

CHAPTER 21 Polygons

21-1 Polygons

A **polygon** is a closed figure with three or more line segments. We name polygons by three or more points.

A triangle is a polygon with three sides.

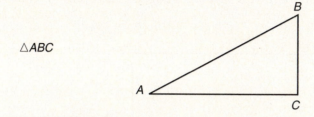

△ABC

A **quadrilateral** is a polygon with four sides.

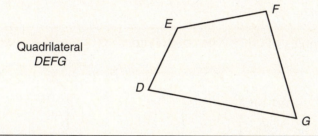

Quadrilateral
DEFG

A **parallelogram** is a quadrilateral with opposite sides that are parallel and equal in length.

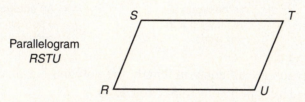

Parallelogram
RSTU

RS // UT and *ST // RU*
RS = UT and *ST = RU*

A **rhombus** is a parallelogram with four equal sides.

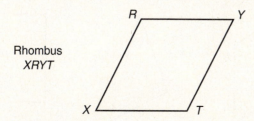

Rhombus
XRYT

XR // TY and *RY // XT*
XR = TY = RY = XT

A **square** is a rhombus with four right angles and four equal sides.

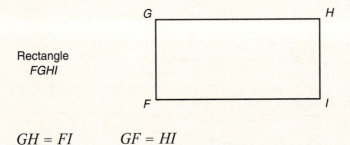

Square
STUV

$\angle S = \angle T = \angle U = \angle V = 90°$
ST // VU and *TU // SV*
ST = VU = TU = SV

A **rectangle** is a parallelogram with four right angles. The opposite sides are equal in length.

Rectangle
FGHI

$GH = FI$ $\qquad$ $GF = HI$

The following are examples of other types of polygons.

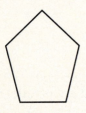 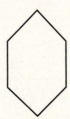 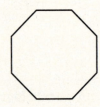

A **pentagon** is a polygon with five sides.

A **hexagon** is a polygon with six sides.

An **octagon** is a polygon with eight sides.

When the sides of a polygon are all equal in length, the polygon is called a regular polygon. We will study regular polygons in Section 21–4.

Exercise 1

Write the name of each of the following polygons.

1.  $\qquad$ 2. 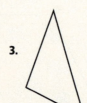 3. 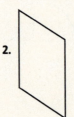 4.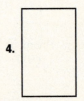

quadrilateral $\underline{\qquad}$ $\underline{\qquad}$ $\underline{\qquad}$

5.

_____

6.

_____

7.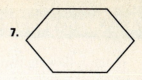

_____

8.

_____

9.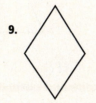

_____

10.

_____

21-2 Congruent Figures ....

Two line segments are congruent if they are equal in length. The symbol $\cong$ means *is congruent to*.

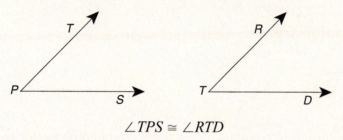

$$AB \cong CD$$

Two angles are congruent if they are equal in measure.

$$\angle TPS \cong \angle RTD$$

Two polygons are **congruent** if they have equal line segments and equal angles.

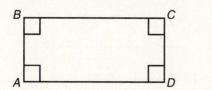

Since *ABCD* and *EFGH* are rectangles, all angles are equal to 90°.

AD = EH, BC = FG, AB = EF, CD = GH
ABCD $\cong$ EFGH

In the following two polygons, *ALDM* ≅ *PSTW*.

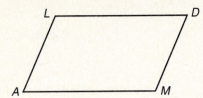 

If we pick up *PSTW* and put it on top of *ALDM*, the line segments and angles that touch together are corresponding line segments and corresponding angles.

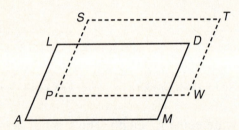

∠*A* corresponds to ∠*P*   *AL* corresponds to *PS*
∠*L* corresponds to ∠*S*   *LD* corresponds to *ST*
∠*D* corresponds to ∠*T*   *DM* corresponds to *TW*
∠*M* corresponds to ∠*W*   *AM* corresponds to *PW*

In congruent figures, the **corresponding parts** are congruent. In the two polygons above . . .

∠*A* = ∠*P*   *AL* = *PS*
∠*L* = ∠*S*   *LD* = *ST*
∠*D* = ∠*T*   *DM* = *TW*
∠*M* = ∠*W*   *AM* = *PW*

Exercise 2

A. In the following two congruent triangles, name the corresponding angles and the corresponding sides.

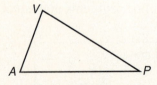 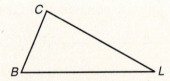

1. a. ∠*A* corresponds to ∠*B*   **d.** *AV* corresponds to _____

   b. ∠*V* corresponds to _____   **e.** *VP* corresponds to _____

   c. ∠*P* corresponds to _____   **f.** *AP* corresponds to _____

B. Name the equal angles and equal sides of the following pairs of congruent figures.

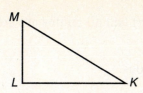 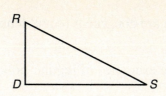 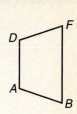 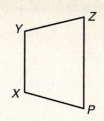

1. a. ∠L = ∠D   d. DR = _____   2. a. ∠Y = _____   e. YZ = _____

   b. ∠M = _____   e. RS = _____   b. ∠Z = _____   f. ZP = _____

   c. ∠K = _____   f. DS = _____   c. ∠P = _____   g. XP = _____

                                      d. ∠X = _____   h. XY = _____

C. Find and name the equal angles and equal sides of the following pairs of congruent figures. Write your answers on a separate sheet of paper.

1.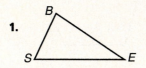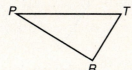

∠B = ∠R   SB = TR
∠S = ∠T   BE = RP
∠E = ∠P   SE = TP

2.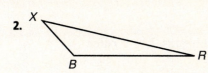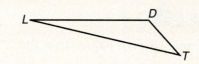

3.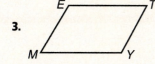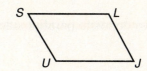

4.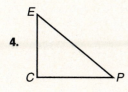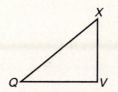

5.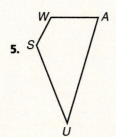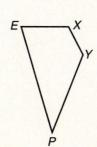

325

In a **regular polygon**, all sides are congruent (equal length) and all angles are congruent (equal measure).

The following polygons are examples of regular polygons.

square

hexagon

octagon

The following polygons are examples of **nonregular polygons**.

triangle

quadrilateral

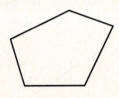

pentagon

Exercise 3

On a separate sheet of paper, draw the following polygons. Use a ruler.

1. a regular triangle

2. a nonregular hexagon

3. a quadrilateral with two opposite parallel sides

4. a rectangle

5. a quadrilateral with no opposite parallel sides

6. a nonregular octagon

7. two congruent quadrilaterals

8. a regular pentagon

9. a nonregular triangle

10. two congruent triangles

Two polygons are **similar** if their corresponding angles are equal and they have the same shape. The symbol ~ means *is similar to*.

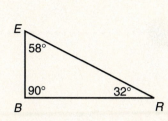
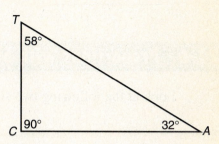

$$\angle B = \angle C$$
$$\angle E = \angle T$$
$$\angle R = \angle A$$
$$\triangle BER \sim \triangle CTA$$

The two triangles above have the same shape but different sizes.

Exercise 4

Look at the following pairs of polygons. Write *similar* or *not similar* for each pair.

1.

   not similar

2.

   _____

3.

   _____

4.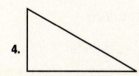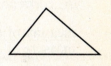

   _____

5.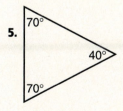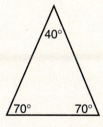

   _____

6.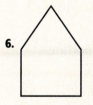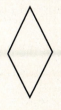

   _____

7.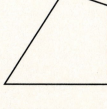

   _____

8.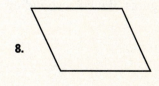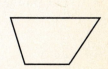

   _____

9.

10.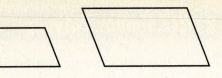

_____   _____

21-6 Proportions with Similar Polygons

Look at the following two similar triangles.

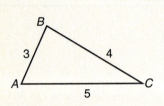 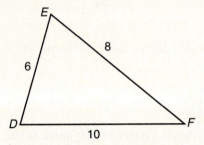

AB corresponds to DE. The measure of AB = 3 units, and the measure of DE = 6 units.

We can write a **proportion.**

$$\frac{\text{measure of } AB}{\text{measure of } DE} = \frac{3 \text{ units}}{6 \text{ units}} = \frac{1}{2}$$

BC corresponds to EF.

$$\frac{\text{measure of } BC}{\text{measure of } EF} = \frac{4 \text{ units}}{8 \text{ units}} = \frac{1}{2}$$

AC corresponds to DF.

$$\frac{\text{measure of } AC}{\text{measure of } DF} = \frac{5 \text{ units}}{10 \text{ units}} = \frac{1}{2}$$

Look at the three proportions.

$$\frac{AB}{DE} = \frac{1}{2} \qquad \frac{BC}{EF} = \frac{1}{2} \qquad \frac{AC}{DF} = \frac{1}{2}$$

$$\frac{AB}{DE} = \frac{BC}{EF} = \frac{AC}{DF}$$

In similar figures, the corresponding sides are proportional.

Example:

We can write three proportions for the following similar triangles.

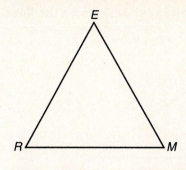

$$\frac{RM}{TX} = \frac{ER}{PT} \qquad \frac{EM}{PX} = \frac{RM}{TX} \qquad \frac{ER}{PT} = \frac{EM}{PX}$$

Example:

We can use proportions for the following similar triangles to find the measure of the side *PF*.

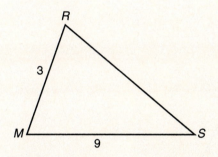

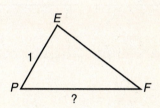

$$\frac{\text{measure of } MR}{\text{measure of } PE} = \frac{\text{measure of } MS}{\text{measure of } PF}$$

OR

$$\frac{3}{1} = \frac{9}{?}$$

We cross-multiply. $3 \times ? = 1 \times 9$

$3 \times ? = 9$

We use the inverse operation. $9 \div 3 = 3$

Answer: $PF = 3$

Use proportions to find the missing measure for one side in each pair of similar figures.
Show your work on a separate sheet of paper. Write your answers on the lines.

1.

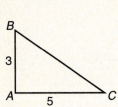

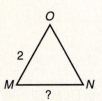

_10_

2.

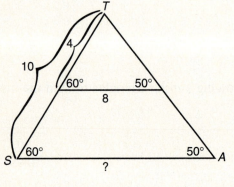

_____

3.

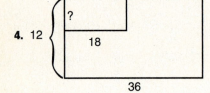

_____

4. 12

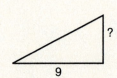

_____

5. 6.5

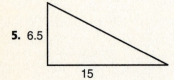

_____

Read each statement. Write *True* if the statement is correct. Write *False* if the statement is not correct.

1. A hexagon has six sides. _____*True*_____

2. A triangle is a polygon. _____

3. A scalene triangle is a regular polygon. _____

4. A quadrilateral has four sides and four angles. _____

5. A rectangle is a parallelogram. _____

6. A parallelogram is a rectangle. _____

7. All congruent figures are similar. _____

8. All similar figures are congruent. _____

9. A square is a rhombus. _____

10. A rhombus is a square. _____

11. A rhombus is a regular polygon. _____

12. Corresponding angles in two similar triangles are equal. _____

13. Corresponding sides in two similar triangles are equal. _____

14. There are 180° in a triangle. _____

15. There are more than 180° in a square. _____

Have I Learned? (✓)

Work with a partner. Check what you have learned. Review what you need help with.

1. polygon ☐
2. quadrilateral ☐
3. parallelogram ☐
4. rhombus ☐
5. square ☐
6. rectangle ☐
7. pentagon ☐
8. hexagon ☐

9. octagon ☐
10. congruent ☐
11. corresponding parts ☐
12. regular polygon ☐
13. nonregular polygon ☐
14. similar polygon ☐
15. proportion ☐

Exercise 1

Identify the figures. Write your answers on the lines.

1.   _quadrilateral_

2. 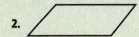 _____

3.   _____

4.  _____

5.   _____

6.   _____

7.   _____

8.   _____

The following triangles are congruent. Name the equal angles and sides.

9.

$\angle A = $ _____ $AB = $ _____

$\angle B = $ _____ $BC = $ _____

10.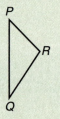

$\angle M = $ _____ $MN = $ _____

$\angle N = $ _____ $NO = $ _____

Exercise 2

Complete each sentence below with one of the words in the box.

corresponding	opposite	proportional	~~regular~~	similar

1. In a _____regular_____ polygon, all sides are equal.

2. In congruent figures, the _____ parts are equal.

3. _____ triangles have the same shape but different sizes.

4. The corresponding sides in similar triangles are _____.

5. In a parallelogram, the _____ sides are parallel.

CHAPTER 22 Measurements

22-1 Perimeter

The **perimeter** of a figure is the distance around the figure. If we measure distances in inches (") or feet ('), the perimeter of the rectangle below is 2" + 4" + 2" + 4" = 12".

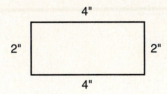

We call the distances **length** and **width**.

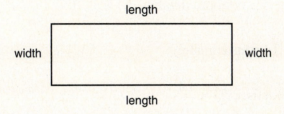

In the rectangle above, the length is the longer distance and the width is the shorter distance.

Exercise 1

Find the perimeter of each figure. Write it on the line.

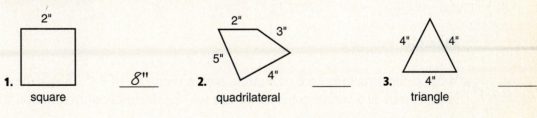

1. square — *8"*
2. quadrilateral — ____
3. triangle — ____

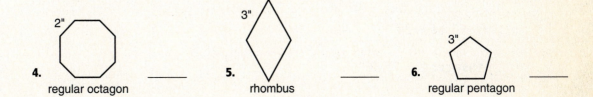

4. regular octagon — ____
5. rhombus — ____
6. regular pentagon — ____

333

7.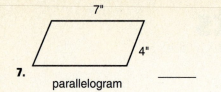
parallelogram _____

8.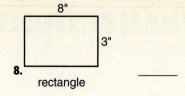
rectangle _____

9.
isosceles triangle _____

10.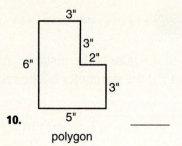
polygon _____

The distance around a circle is called the **circumference**. The ratio of circumference to diameter of all circles is exactly $\frac{22}{7}$, or approximately 3.14.

$$\frac{\text{circumference } (C)}{\text{diameter } (d)} = \frac{22}{7}, \text{ or } 3.14 \text{ approximately}$$

As a decimal, $\frac{C}{d} = 3.14$. As a fraction, $\frac{C}{d} = \frac{22}{7}$.

We call this ratio **pi**, and the symbol we use for pi is π.

$$\pi = \frac{C}{d} = 3.14, \text{ or } \frac{22}{7}$$

We use π in finding the circumference of a circle. Look at the formula for circumference below.

$C = \pi \times d$

Example:

What is the circumference of a circle with a diameter of 24"? Since the diameter is expressed as a whole number, we can use the decimal approximation for π.

$C = \pi \times d$

$C = 3.14 \times 24"$

Answer: $C = 75.36"$

Example:

What is the circumference of a circle with a radius of $\frac{2}{3}'$?

If the radius of the circle is $\frac{2}{3}'$, the diameter is $2 \times \frac{2}{3}'$, or $\frac{4}{3}'$.

$C = \pi \times d$

$C = \frac{22}{7} \times \frac{4}{3}'$

Answer: $C = \frac{88}{21}' = 4\frac{4}{21}'$

Exercise 2

Find the circumference of the following circles. Use $\pi = 3.14$ or $\frac{22}{7}$. Show your work on a separate sheet of paper. Write your answers on the lines.

1. 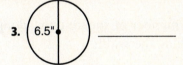 _12.56"_

2. 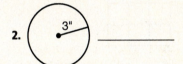 _____

3. 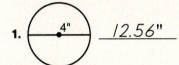 _____

4. 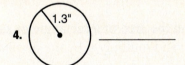 _____

5. 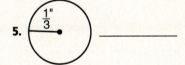 _____

6. 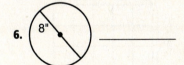 _____

7. 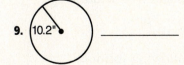 _____

8. 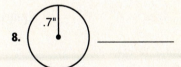 _____

9. 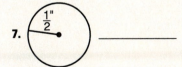 _____

10. 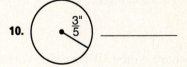 _____

• •

The **area** of a figure is the number of square units covering that figure. If we measure in inches, feet, or yards, the area will be in square inches, square feet, or square yards. In the rectangle below, there are 20 square units.

Area = 20 square units

In the square below, there are 9 square units.

Area = 9 square units

To find the area of a rectangle or square, we count the number of square units along the length and multiply it by the number of square units along the width.

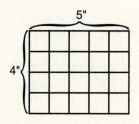

Area = 4" × 5" = 20 square inches

For rectangles, we use the following formula.

Area of a Rectangle: $A = l \times w$ (l = length and w = width)

In a square, since all four sides are equal, we use the following formula.

Area of a Square: $A = s \times s$, or s^2 (s = side of square)

Find the area of the shaded parts of each figure below. Write it on the line.

1.  2" × 2"   4 sq."

2.  5" × 3" _____

3.  4 yd × 4 yd _____

4. 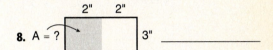 7.5" × 1.5" _____

5.  5.2" × 5.2" _____

6. 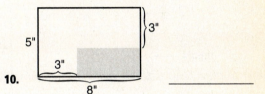 8" × 2" _____

7. 3" × 9" _____

8. A = ? 2" 2" 3" _____

9. 3" 1" 2" 5.5" _____

10. 5" 3" 3" 8" _____

22-4 Area of a Triangle

The triangle below is $\frac{1}{2}$ the area of the square.

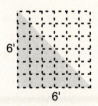

6'   6'

The area of the square = 6' × 6' = 36 square feet, so the area of the triangle is $\frac{1}{2}$ of 36, or 18 square feet.

337

Example:

We can find the area of the following triangle.

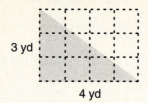

3 yd

4 yd

The area of the triangle is $\frac{1}{2}$ the area of the rectangle. Since the area of the rectangle is 3 yd × 4 yd = 12 square yards, the area of the triangle is $\frac{1}{2}$ of 12, or 6 square yards.

$$A = \frac{1}{2} \times (3 \text{ yd} \times 4 \text{ yd})$$

Answer: $A = \frac{1}{2} \times 12$ yd = 6 square yards

The following triangles are all $\frac{1}{2}$ the area of the rectangles or squares.

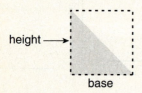

height

base

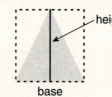

height

base

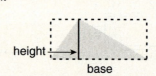

height

height

base

Each triangle has a **base** (length of rectangle) and a **height** (width of rectangle). Since the triangles are $\frac{1}{2}$ the area of the rectangles, we can find the areas of triangles by using the following formula.

Area of a Triangle: $A = \frac{1}{2} \times (l \times w)$, or $\frac{1}{2} \times (b \times h)$ (b = base and h = height)

The height of a triangle is the line segment drawn from one vertex of the triangle perpendicular to the opposite side of the triangle.

Exercise 4

Find the areas of the triangles below. Write them on the lines.

1. 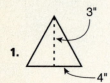 3"

4"

_____ 6 sq." _____

2. 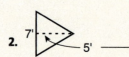 7' 5'

_____

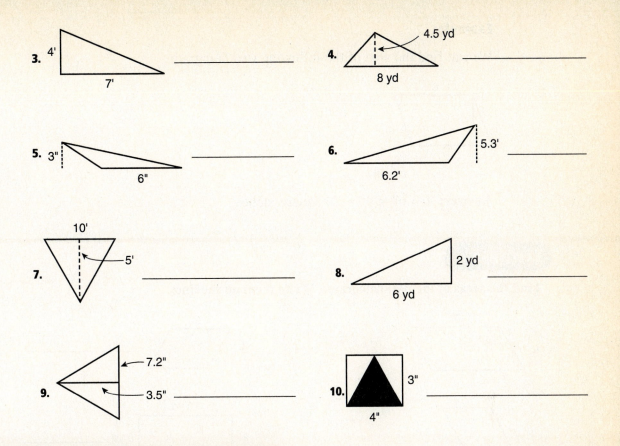

3. 4'   7'   _____

4. 4.5 yd   8 yd   _____

5. 3"   6"   _____

6. 5.3'   6.2'   _____

7. 10'   5'   _____

8. 2 yd   6 yd   _____

9. 7.2"   3.5"   _____

10. 3"   4"   _____

22-5 Area of a Parallelogram

Look at the area of a parallelogram.

If we move the shaded area (triangle) on the left and put it on the right side, we have a rectangle. Then the area of the parallelogram is equal to the area of the rectangle, or *length × width*.

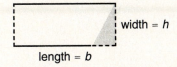

width = h

length = b

The width of the rectangle above is the same as the height of the parallelogram. The length of the rectangle above is equal to the base of the parallelogram. The height of a parallelogram is the line segment perpendicular to the base from the opposite side.

We use the following formula to find the area of a parallelogram.

Area of a Parallelogram: $A = b \times h$

Example:

We can find the area of the following parallelogram.

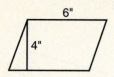

$$A = b \times h$$

Answer: $A = 6" \times 4" = 24$ square inches

Find the areas of the parallelograms. Write them on the lines.

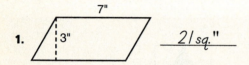

1. _21 sq."_

2. _____

3. _____

4. _____

5. _____

22-6 Area of a Circle

We can find the area of a circle by using the following formula.

Area of a Circle: $A = \pi \times r \times r = \pi r^2$ (r = radius)

Example:

We can find the area of a circle with a radius of 2".

$$A = \pi r^2$$

$$A = 3.14 \times 2" \times 2" = 12.56 \text{ square inches}$$

340

Example:

We can find the area of a circle with a radius of $\frac{1'}{5}$.

$A = \pi r^2$

$A = \frac{22}{7} \times \frac{1'}{5} \times \frac{1'}{5}$

$A = \frac{22}{7} \times \frac{1'}{5} \times \frac{1'}{5} = \frac{22}{175}$ square feet

Exercise 6

Find the areas of the circles. Show your work on a separate sheet of paper. Write your answers on the lines.

1. Circle P where the radius = 3" _____28.26 sq."_____

2. Circle R where the diameter = 4" _____

3. Circle A where the radius = 4' _____

4. Circle F where the radius = 6" _____

5. Circle C where the diameter = 10' _____

6. Circle O where the diameter = 6.8' _____

7. Circle D where the radius = 1.4" _____

8. Circle S where the diameter = $\frac{1'}{8}$ _____

9. Circle T where the radius = 6.3' _____

10. Circle H where the radius = 10" _____

Have I Learned? (✓)

Work with a partner. Check what you have learned. Review what you need help with.

1. perimeter ☐
2. length ☐
3. width ☐
4. circumference ☐
5. pi ☐
6. area ☐
7. base of a polygon ☐
8. height ☐

Exercise 1

Find the perimeters of the following figures. Write them on the lines.

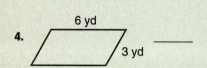

1. 4" / 4" / 4" _16"_

2. 3' / 3' / 3' _____

3. 2" / 3" / 4" / 5" _____

4. 6 yd / 3 yd _____

5. 8' / 6' / 3' / 5' _____

Exercise 2

Find the circumferences and areas of the following circles. Show your work on a separate sheet of paper. Write your answers on the lines.

1. Circle *D* where the diameter = 8"

C = _25.12"_ A = _50.24 sq._"

2. Circle *P* where the radius = 1/4"

C = _____ A = _____

3. Circle *H* where the diameter = 15 yd

C = _____ A = _____

4. Circle *M* where the radius = 4.5'

C = _____ A = _____

5. Circle *S* where the diameter = 11"

C = _____ A = _____

Exercise 3

Find the areas of the following figures. Write them on the lines.

1. 3" / square _9 sq."_

2. 4" / 6" _____

3. A = ? / 4" / 4" / 2" / 12" _____

4. 9' / 10' _____

5. 8 yd / 3 yd _____

Glossary

absolute value The distance an integer is from zero on the number line. For example, the absolute value of both 5 and –5 is 5. (p. 289)

acute angle An angle that measures less than 90°. (p. 305)

acute triangle A triangle with three acute angles. (p. 313)

addends Numbers added together to give a sum. For example, in 3 + 6 = 9, the addends are 3 and 6. (p. 39)

addition The operation of adding numbers together to result in a sum. For example, 3 + 6 = 9 is an addition problem. (p. 39)

Additive Identity Property of Addition The law of addition states that adding zero to any number does not affect the sum. For example, 7 + 0 = 7. (p. 42)

additive inverse A positive integer and its corresponding negative integer. For example, 7 and –7 are additive inverses. (p. 113)

angle Figure formed when two rays intersect at a point. For example, ∠PQR is formed by rays P and R. (p. 304)

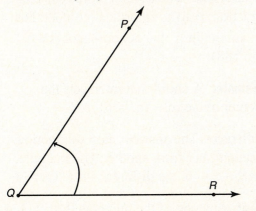

approximate To say *about how much* or *about how many*; also called *estimate*. (p. 32)

area The number of square units enclosed by a figure. (p. 336)

Associative Property of Addition The law of addition states that when we group three or more numbers in different ways the sum is not affected. For example, (5 + 6) + 3 = 5 + (6 + 3). (p. 41)

Associative Property of Multiplication The law of multiplication states that when we group three or more numbers in different ways the product is not affected. For example, $(2 \times 3) \times 5 = 2 \times (3 \times 5)$. (p. 69)

average The number found by adding a group of numbers and dividing by the number of addends; also called the *mean*. (p. 181)

B

base A number written with an exponent is called the base. In 10^3, the base is 10. In 5^2, the base is 5. (p. 123)

base of a polygon The side of a polygon to which the height is perpendicular. (p. 338)

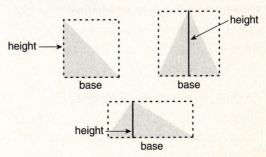

braces The symbols { }, which tell us to group numbers together. (p. 102)

brackets The symbols [ ], which tell us to group numbers together. (p. 102)

canceling A method of simplifying fractions before multiplying them. (p. 221)

Example: $\dfrac{\overset{1}{\cancel{2}}}{\underset{2}{\cancel{4}}} \times \dfrac{\overset{1}{\cancel{2}}}{\underset{3}{\cancel{6}}} = \dfrac{1}{6}$

cardinal number A number (*one, two, three, . . .*) used for counting and answering the question, "How many?" (p. 3)

chord A line segment with endpoints on a circle. (p. 315)

circle A closed plane figure in which all the points are the same distance from a point called the center point. (p. 315)

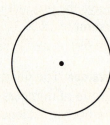

circumference The distance around a circle. (p. 334)

common denominator In adding or subtracting two or more fractions with different denominators, we need to use the denominator that can be divided evenly by those denominators. The lowest common denominator is the *smallest* denominator. (p. 236)

Commutative Property of Addition The law states that adding numbers in any order does not affect the sum. For example, $3 + 6 = 6 + 3$. (p. 41)

Commutative Property of Multiplication The law states that multiplying numbers in any order does not affect the product. For example, $3 \times 2 = 2 \times 3$. (p. 69)

composite number A whole number greater than 1 that is not prime and has more than two factors. (p. 120)

congruent figures Figures that are equal in size and shape. (p. 323)

corresponding parts In two or more similar or congruent figures, the parts (line segments and angles) that match. (p. 324).

cross-multiply To check if two fractions, or ratios, are proportional. (p. 258)

Example:

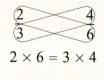

$$2 \times 6 = 3 \times 4$$

$$12 = 12$$

decimal numbers Numbers written with a decimal point and one or more digits to the right of the decimal point. For example, 3.45 is a decimal number. (p. 133)

decimal point A dot used to separate the ones place from the tenths place in a number. (p. 134)

decrease To become less in value. (p. 168)

degree A unit of measure for angles. The symbol is °. (p. 305)

denominator The bottom number in a fraction, read as an ordinal number. For example, in $\dfrac{3}{4}$, the denominator is 4. (p. 188)

diameter A chord that intersects the center of a circle. (p. 316)

difference The answer when subtracting one number from another. For example, in $9 - 3 = 6$, the difference is 6. (p. 51)

digit Any one of the numbers 0, 1, 2, 3, 4, 5, 6, 7, 8, and 9. (p. 3)

Distributive Property of Multiplication
Multiplying a sum by a number is
the same as multiplying each number
in the addition problem and then
adding the products. For example,
$3 \times (7 + 4) = (3 \times 7) + (3 \times 4)$. (p. 71)

divided by The symbol ÷ or $)\overline{}$. It tells
us to divide. (p. 87)

dividend The number that is divided
by another number. For example, in
$12 \div 3 = 4$, the dividend is 12. (p. 87)

division The operation of dividing
numbers to result in a quotient. For
example, $12 \div 3 = 4$ is a division
problem. (p. 87)

divisor The number used to divide
another number. For example, in
$12 \div 3 = 4$, the divisor is 3. (p. 87)

double Two together. (p. 21)

dozen Twelve of something. (p. 21)

equals The symbol =. It means *has the
same value as*. (p. 39)

equilateral triangle A triangle with three
equal sides. (p. 313)

equivalent decimals Decimals that have
the same, or equal, value. For example,
.5 has the same value as .50 (p. 137)

equivalent fractions Fractions that
have the same value, for example, $\frac{3}{4}$ and
$\frac{6}{8}$. (p. 200)

estimate To say *about how much*
or *about how many*; also called
approximate. (p. 32)

even integers Whole numbers that end
with a 0, 2, 4, 6, or 8, except 0. (p. 114)

expanded notation A way to write
a number that shows the place
value of each digit. For example,
327 written in expanded notation =
$(3 \times 100) + (2 \times 10) + (7 \times 1)$;
327 written in expanded notation
using base ten with exponents =
$(3 \times 10^2) + (2 \times 10^1) + (7 \times 10^0)$.
(p. 127)

exponent A number that tells how many
times the number, or base, is used as a
factor. For example, in 10^3, 10 is used as
a factor 3 times. (p. 123)

factors The numbers that are multiplied to
get a product. For example, in $3 \times 2 = 6$,
the factors are 3 and 2. (p. 67)

fraction A symbol, such as $\frac{1}{3}$ or $\frac{5}{2}$, used
to name a part of a whole, a part of a set,
a location on a number line, or a division
of whole numbers. (p. 187)

fractions equal to a whole Fractions
whose numerators are equal to their
denominators, for example, $\frac{3}{3}$ and $\frac{8}{8}$.
(p. 193)

fractions greater than a whole Fractions
whose numerators are greater than their
denominators, for example, $\frac{3}{1}$ and $\frac{8}{7}$;
also called *improper fractions*. (p. 193)

fractions less than a whole Fractions
whose numerators are less than their
denominators, for example, $\frac{1}{3}$ and $\frac{7}{8}$.
(p. 192)

greater than Symbolized by >; having a
larger value. For example, 7 is greater
than 6, or $7 > 6$. (p. 26)

greatest number The number with the largest value in a group of numbers; also called *largest number*. (p. 10)

half-dozen Six of something. (p. 21)

height The length of a segment from one vertex of a triangle or rectangle that is perpendicular to the base. (p. 338)

hexagon A polygon with six sides. (p. 322)

improper fractions Fractions whose numerators are greater than their denominators, for example, $\frac{3}{1}$ and $\frac{8}{7}$; also called *fractions greater than a whole*. (p. 193)

increase To become greater in value. (p. 168)

infinite Having no end. (p. 26)

integers Positive and negative whole numbers and zero. (p. 113)

intersecting lines Lines that cross at one point. (p. 303)

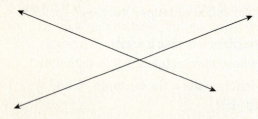

inverse operations Operations that are the opposite of each other. Subtraction and addition are inverse operations, so $6 + 3 = 9$ and $9 - 3 = 6$ are inverse operations. Multiplication and division are inverse operations, so $3 \times 2 = 6$ and $6 \div 2 = 3$ are inverse operations. (pp. 58, 96)

isosceles triangle A triangle with two equal sides. (p. 313)

largest number The number with the greatest value in a group of numbers; also called *greatest number*. (p. 10)

least number The number with the smallest value in a group of numbers; also called *smallest number*. (p. 10)

length The longer sides of a rectangle. (p. 333)

less than Having a smaller value. For example, 6 is less than 7. (p. 26)

like denominators Equal or same denominators. Fractions with like denominators, such as $\frac{3}{8}$ and $\frac{5}{8}$, are called *like fractions*. (p. 233)

like signs Common, or same, signs—positive or negative. For example, −6 and −3 have like signs. (p. 289)

line A set of an infinite number of points that goes on forever in two directions. (p. 301)

line segment Part of a line that has two endpoints. (p. 301)

lowest common denominator (LCD) See *common denominator*.

mean The number found by adding a group of numbers and dividing by the number of addends; also called the *average*. (p. 181)

minuend A number that another number is subtracted from. For example, in 9 − 3 = 6, the minuend is 9. (p. 51)

minus The symbol −. It tells us to subtract. (p. 51)

mixed number A whole number written together with a fraction, for example, $2\frac{1}{3}$. (p. 195)

multiple of ten The product of 10 with any other whole number. (p. 79)

multiplication The operation of multiplying numbers together to result in a product. For example, 3 × 2 = 6 is a multiplication problem. (p. 67)

Multiplicative Identity Property of Multiplication The law states that multiplying any number by 1 does not affect the product. For example, 7 × 1 = 7. (p. 70)

Multiplicative Property of Zero The law states that multiplying any number by 0 results in a product of 0. For example, 7 × 0 = 0. (p. 70)

nearest Closest. For example, 30 is the round number that is nearest to 28. (p. 28)

negative integers Integers that are less than zero (−1, −2, −3, . . .). (p. 113)

negative sign The symbol −. It tells us that an integer is negative (that is, less than zero) in value. (p. 285)

nonregular polygon A polygon with sides of unequal length and angles of unequal measure. (p. 326)

number line A line that shows numbers in order. (p. 26)

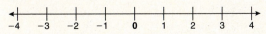

numerator The top number in a fraction, read as a cardinal number. For example, in $\frac{3}{4}$, the numerator is 3. (p. 188)

obtuse angle An angle that measures more than 90°. (p. 306)

obtuse triangle A triangle with one obtuse angle. (p. 313)

octagon A polygon with eight sides. (p. 322)

odd integers Whole numbers that end with a 1, 3, 5, 7, or 9. (p. 114)

ones place Position of a digit in a number. For example, in 3,924, the digit 4 is in the ones place. (p. 4)

order An arrangement of numbers from least to greatest or from greatest to least. (p. 13)

ordinal number A number that tells order (1st, 2nd, 3rd, . . .). (p. 13)

pair Two things of a kind (socks, shoes, . . .). (p. 21)

parallel lines Lines that are equal distance apart and never intersect. (p. 304)

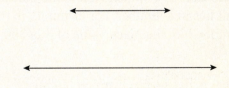

parallelogram A quadrilateral with opposite sides that are parallel and equal in length. (p. 321)

parentheses The symbols ( ). They group numbers together. (p. 41)

pentagon A polygon with five sides. (p. 322)

percent Percent means *part of a hundred*. It is also a ratio of parts to 100. The symbol for percent is %. (p. 265)

perimeter The distance around a figure. (p. 333)

perpendicular lines Two lines that intersect to form right angles. (p. 311)

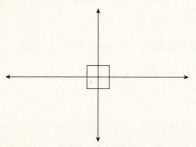

pi The ratio of the circumference of a circle to its diameter. It is exactly $\frac{22}{7}$, or approximately 3.14. Its symbol is π. (p. 334)

place value The value given to the place a digit has in a number. For example, in the number 345, the place value of 3 is 300. (p. 4)

plane A flat surface formed by three points not in a straight line. (p. 302)

plus The symbol +. It tells us to add. (p. 39)

point An exact location in space, often marked by a dot. (p. 301)

polygon A closed figure with three or more line segments. (p. 321)

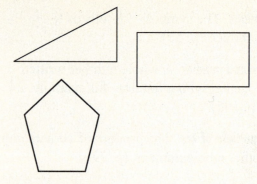

positive integers Integers zero and greater (0, 1, 2, 3, . . .). (p. 113)

positive sign The symbol +. It tells us that an integer is positive (that is, zero or greater) in value. (p. 285)

prime factors Factors that are prime numbers. For example, in $2 \times 3 = 6$, the numbers 2 and 3 are prime factors of 6. (p. 121)

prime number A whole number greater than 1 that has exactly two factors: 1 and itself. (p. 120)

product The answer when multiplying factors. For example, in $3 \times 2 = 6$, the product is 6. (p. 67)

proportion A statement that two ratios are equal. For example, $\frac{1}{2} = \frac{2}{4}$ is a proportion. (p. 258)

Q

quadrilateral A polygon with four sides. (p. 321)

quotient The answer when dividing one number into another. For example, in $12 \div 3 = 4$, the quotient is 4. (p. 87)

radius A line segment with endpoints on the center of a circle and on the circle. It is $\frac{1}{2}$ the diameter. (p. 316)

ratio A pair of numbers that shows a comparison of two amounts. A ratio is written as, for example, 2 to 3, 2:3, or $\frac{2}{3}$. (p. 255)

ray Part of a line that has one endpoint and goes on forever in only one direction. (p. 302)

reciprocal We can find the reciprocal of a fraction by writing the denominator as the numerator and the numerator as the denominator. If we multiply a fraction by its reciprocal, the product is always 1. For example, the reciprocal of $\frac{3}{4}$ is $\frac{4}{3}$, and $\frac{3}{4} \times \frac{4}{3} = 1$. (p. 224)

rectangle A parallelogram with four right angles and opposite sides that are equal in length. (p. 322)

regular polygon A polygon with all sides of equal length and all angles of equal measure. (p. 326)

remainder The number that is left over after dividing. (p. 92)

Example:

$$\begin{array}{r} 40\text{r.}3 \\ 5\overline{)203} \\ -20 \\ \hline 03 \\ -0 \\ \hline 3 \end{array}$$ The remainder is 3.

rhombus A parallelogram with four equal sides. (p. 321)

right angle An angle that measures 90°. (p. 305)

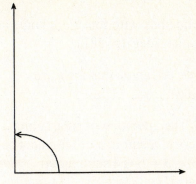

right triangle A triangle with one right angle. (p. 312)

round number A number ending in one or more zeros, such as 40, 350, and 5,000. (p. 25)

round off To change a number to a round number, for example, to change 389 to 400. (p. 26)

scalene triangle A triangle with three sides of different lengths. (p. 313)

similar polygons Two polygons that have the same shape and corresponding angles that are equal. (p. 327)

simplest form A fraction, for example, $\frac{1}{2}$, whose numerator and denominator cannot be divided evenly by a common number. (p. 212)

simplifying fractions Dividing a fraction by a fraction equal to 1. (p. 212)

Example: $\frac{2}{4} \div \frac{2}{2} = \frac{1}{2}$

single One of something. (p. 21)

smaller number The number with the lesser value in a group of two numbers. (p. 28)

smallest number The number with the least value in a group of numbers; also called *least number*. (p. 10)

square A rhombus with four right angles and four equal sides. (p. 322)

straight angle An angle that measures 180°. (p. 306)

subtraction The operation of subtracting two numbers to result in a difference. For example, 9 − 3 = 6 is a subtraction problem. (p. 51)

subtrahend A number that is subtracted from another number. For example, in 9 − 3 = 6, the subtrahend is 3. (p. 51)

sum The answer when adding two or more addends. For example, in 3 + 6 = 9, the sum is 9. (p. 39)

times The symbol ×. It tells us to multiply. (p. 67)

triangle A polygon with three sides and three angles. (p. 312)

twins A group of two of the same thing or kind. (p. 21)

unlike fractions Fractions with different denominators, such as $\frac{3}{8}$ and $\frac{2}{7}$. (p. 236)

unlike signs Different signs—positive or negative. For example, −6 and 3 (or +3) have unlike signs. (p. 290.)

vertex The point where two rays intersect to form an angle. (p. 304)

whole numbers The positive integers (0, 1, 2, 3, . . .). (p. 52)

width The shorter sides of a rectangle. (p. 333)

zero exponent A special exponent that makes all numbers equal to 1. For example, $100^0 = 1$, $3^0 = 1$. (p. 125)

Listening Scripts

Chapter 1

Listening, Page 7

Read each number aloud, slowly and clearly. Repeat once. Students will circle the letter next to the correct number.

1. two hundred ninety
2. fourteen
3. three hundred fifteen
4. nine hundred ninety
5. three thousand, one hundred fifty
6. four hundred twenty-six thousand, thirteen
7. six million, one hundred ninety thousand, two hundred sixty
8. five million, three hundred thousand
9. eight million, six thousand, ninety-five
10. six hundred thousand, nine

Chapter 2

Listening and Speaking, Page 16

Students will look at the program card on page 16 to answer the questions below. Read each question aloud, slowly and clearly. Repeat once. As students answer, correct their pronunciation of the numbers, as necessary.

1. Whose program card is this?
2. How many classes does Raúl have?
3. What period does Raúl have art?
4. On what floor does Raúl study history?
5. Who is Raúl's third period teacher?
6. What period does Raúl have algebra?
7. On what floor does Raúl study algebra?
8. On what day in October was Raúl born?
9. What grade is Raúl in?
10. What class does Raúl have fourth period?
11. In what year was Raúl born?
12. What period does Raúl have physical education?
13. What is the date on the program card?
14. In what room does Raúl study English?
15. Where does Ms. William teach art?

Chapter 3

Listening, Page 35

Read each question or statement aloud, slowly and clearly. Repeat once. Students will circle the letter next to the correct answer.

1. How many numbers are there on a number line?
2. When we estimate, we want to know _____.
3. A round number has one or more _____ at the end.
4. How many digits does the number 206 have?
5. Another word for *largest* is _____.
6. In the number 15, what is the place name of the digit 5?
7. Seventy-three dollars is _____ seventy dollars.
8. A number line has no beginning, and it has no _____.
9. *Two* is a cardinal number; *second* is an _____.
10. Cardinal numbers tell "how many"; ordinal numbers tell "_____."

Chapter 9

Listening, Page 126

Read each expression aloud, slowly and clearly. Repeat once. Students will circle the letter next to the correct expression.

1. four squared
2. Seventeen is less than thirty-two.
3. Sixteen is greater than twelve.
4. five times thirty
5. Eleven is equal to *m*.
6. Fourteen is less than *t*.
7. *x* squared plus y cubed
8. eight squared plus two cubed
9. *r* divided by s
10. three squared
11. ten to the fifth power minus one hundred squared
12. *b* to the fourth power
13. Negative six is greater than negative nine.
14. *m* cubed is greater than *m* squared.
15. Negative forty is less than negative fourteen.
16. six to the zero power
17. Three to the fourth power is equal to eighty-one.
18. ten to the sixth power
19. *x* squared is less than y cubed.
20. Ten to the third power is equal to one hundred.

Chapter 10

Listening, Page 140

Read each decimal aloud, slowly and clearly. Repeat once.
Students will circle the letter next to the correct decimal.

1. four and three tenths
2. seventy-four hundredths
3. one and ninety hundredths
4. six hundred thirteen thousandths
5. three and forty hundredths
6. one hundredth
7. seven and six thousandths
8. fifteen hundredths
9. forty-five and nine tenths
10. five hundred seven thousandths

Chapter 13

Listening, Page 198

Read each fraction aloud, slowly and clearly. Repeat once.
Students will circle the letter next to the correct fraction.

1. three fourths
2. two and a half
3. four thirds
4. seven tenths
5. five halves
6. four and two thirds
7. nine wholes
8. eleven sevenths
9. three and one fifth
10. four sixths